PRO FOOTBALL'S
100 GREATEST
PLAYERS

PRO FOOTBALL'S
100
GREATEST
PLAYERS

•

RATING THE STARS
OF PAST AND PRESENT

by
George Allen
with
Ben Olan

The Bobbs-Merrill Company, Inc.
Indianapolis/New York

Published by The Bobbs-Merrill Company, Inc.
Indianapolis/New York

Library of Congress Cataloging in Publication Data
Allen, George Herbert, 1922–
    Pro football's 100 greatest players.
    Includes index.
        1. Football players—United States—Biography.
2. National Football League. 3. Football—Records.
I. Olan, Ben. II. Title.
GV939.A1A43   796.332′092′2 [B]   82-4254
ISBN 0–672–52723–5   AACR2

Designed by Ken Diamond/Art Patrol
Manufactured in the United States of America
First Printing

TABLE OF CONTENTS

ACKNOWLEDGMENTS

George Allen and Ben Olan wish to thank the following for their assistance in the preparation of this book: Bill Libby, who leads the world in sports book authorships; Hal Bock of The Associated Press, Lou Sahadi and Eric Daum of *Pro Football Monthly,* Don Smith of the Pro Football Hall of Fame, Alan Ainspan of the National Football League, and Betsy Ballenger, a super editor for Bobbs-Merrill, who is partial to the Detroit Lions and New York Jets.

NOTE TO READERS

*George Allen's comments throughout
this book will be set off
by using this typeface.*

FOREWORD

When I was asked to pick the 100 greatest professional football players, it sounded like fun. I have been watching football for 50 years. I have been a big fan of this great game and its standout players. I was a player and I coached for 30 years, 21 of them in the National Football League. I have coached many players who were candidates for such a list.

A list like that is bound to be subjective. I suppose I am as qualified to make the selections and comment on the players of the past 50 years as others with my background. I knew going in there would be some difficult decisions to make. Others might agree with most of my selections, but some were likely to disagree on some players. There are bound to be arguments.

The book was conceived by and put together by Ben Olan. He invited me to make the selections and do the descriptions of the positions and the players who played these positions best, with the help of Bill Libby. They helped me in drawing up lists of candidates and their accomplishments, and Ben handled the biographical material which accompanies each selection.

We decided to pick the greatest players whose primes came from 1933 on. The reason for this is that professional football was a pretty loose affair prior to that year and the players of the earlier years could not be accurately judged against those who followed.

The National Football League, as we know it, really came into existence in 1933. That was the first year the league was set in divisions and a playoff for the championship was held.

Significant rule changes that made this the modern game we know started that year. The following year, incidentally, was the first one in which a forward pass could be thrown from anywhere behind the line of scrimmage.

The Bears, Packers, Giants, Cardinals (in Chicago), and Redskins (in Boston) were in the league in 1932. The Eagles and Steelers (then the Pirates) came in the next year, the Lions (from Portsmouth) the year after that. The Rams (then in Cleveland) entered in 1937.

It wasn't until 1940 that clipping penalties were cut from 25 to 15 yards. As late as 1946, substitutions were limited to three at a time. Free substitution started in 1949.

By sticking to players who were in their primes after the modern game evolved in 1933, we omitted some great players. But I would have no way of judging them and I doubt they can be compared logically to later players any more than the early NFL can be compared logically to the later NFL.

Among these are the following Hall of Famers:
quarterback Paddy Driscoll (1920–29), running back Red Grange (1926–34), running back Joe Guyon (1920–27), running back Johnny Blood (1925–39), running back Ernie Nevers (1926–31), running back Jim Thorpe (1920–28), end Red Badgro (1927–36), end Guy Chamberlain (1920–28), tackle Ed Healey (1920–27), tackle Pete Henry (1920–28), tackle Link Lyman (1922–34), tackle Cal Hubbard (1927–36), guard Walt Kiesling (1926–38), guard Mike Michalske (1926–37), and center George Trafton (1920–32).

I did get to see almost all of the outstanding players from 1933 on in person at one time or another and I have seen all of them on film. I also have discussed them with many professional football veterans, though in the end I relied on my own judgment.

I resolved to pick the 100 best players regardless of position and then assign them to the positions they played best and rank them within that position. Many played two positions almost equally, especially back in the two-way days of 60-minute players.

I gave weight to a player's versatility, but in the end he had to be one of the 10 or 15 or so best at doing what his primary position called for him to do. The requirements at different positions have changed over the years and I tried to take this into consideration. I did not try to have just so many offensive linemen, defensive linemen, and so forth.

I considered it important if a man was a 60-minute player, but that didn't give him much of an edge over a two-platoon player of recent years because, after all, he had no opportunity to play the entire game. Given the chance, I'm sure many could. But the game is faster today than it was yesterday.

Longevity is a key factor in my judgment. I think a player has to prove himself over a prolonged period of 8 to 10 years or more in pro ball to be qualified. If injuries cut short his career, that was simply unfortunate. Some of today's best players have proven themselves and some have not.

It is difficult to compare a player from the 1930s with one in the 1980s, but I did it as painstakingly as I could. I tried to consider each candidate objectively, whether or not I coached him.

I considered players from the old All-America Conference and the old American Football League equally with those from the National Football League. The AAC began in 1946, the AFL in 1960 and, in each case, they later merged with the NFL. Most of the greats from the AAC and the AFL proved themselves in the NFL, but a great player was a great player whether or not his league was equal to another.

I used the career statistics that were available at some positions as a yardstick, but I used my own judgment in the end.

I consider certain players to have been and to be winners now. They find ways to contribute to winning teams. This is probably the main characteristic I look for in a player, though I was not going to disregard those players who were stuck throughout their careers on losing teams.

Foreword

Performance is paramount, of course. Then, consistency. Durability. Leadership. The ability to make the big plays in the big games. The ability to dominate games and turn games around. I looked at these players from a coach's standpoint.

After coaching nine years of small-college football at Morningside, Iowa, and Whittier, California, I coached as an assistant one year with the Los Angeles Rams, in 1957, then eight years with the Chicago Bears, 1958– 65.

George Halas, a great coach, was the head coach of the Bears, but he gave me many important responsibilities. I drafted college players, made trades, and coached the defense. The greatest thrill of my career came in 1963, when we won the NFL title and the players awarded me the game ball. Essentially that gave me the prominence I needed to attract head-coaching offers.

I became head coach of the Rams in 1966 and remained five years, through 1970, though I was briefly fired, then rehired one year. I had a personality conflict with the owner, Dan Reeves, and it was another thrill when the players and press so strongly supported me that Reeves reversed his decision.

The Rams had had seven straight losing seasons, one year winning one game, another just two, when I took over. They were 4–10 the year before I took over, 8–6 the year I got the job. We never had a losing year, never lost more than four games in a year, and one year lost only one game.

We placed first in the Western Conference twice and were second two seasons. We did not win in the playoffs, but won two of those runner-up Playoff Bowls they played in those years.

Jack Kent Cooke, who had become my good friend in Los Angeles, hired me to coach the Washington Redskins in 1971 and I worked under E. Bennett Williams for seven years, through 1977.

I took over a team that had only one winning season in 15 years, that under Vince Lombardi one year before his death, and had won only one game a couple of seasons. I took them to a 9–4–1 record my first year there.

I had seven straight winning seasons in Washington. We won three divisional titles and went to the Super Bowl one year, though we did not win, losing, 14–7, to that unbeaten Miami team. Those were the happiest years of my life.

I quit because management withdrew an option I had been given to purchase part of the team and become part owner, and because my home was in Los Angeles, and Carroll Rosenbloom, the owner, convinced me to return to the Rams in 1978.

That was the saddest decision of my career. Many of the members of his official family campaigned against me and the authority I had been given. I was fired after losing two preseason games. I still have not gotten over the shock.

I am proud of my coaching record. I turned two longtime losers into winners the first season I took over. No other coach in the history of professional football coached as long as 12 seasons without a losing season. My teams won on the road almost as much as they won at home, a rare achievement. My teams beat the best. Only Don Shula's teams had an edge on mine, and that was only 4–5–1. I was 4–3 over Vince Lombardi's teams and 9–8 over Tom Landry's teams.

Until I signed with the Chicago team of the new United States League last June, I was out of coaching since the preseason of 1978. I believe the reason was because today's NFL owners hesitated to turn over the sort of authority to me that I believe a coach needs to be successful.

I've dreamed of being a clubowner ever since I came into pro football. I had a chance to own five percent at Washington, but the owners there pulled the rug out from under me. That five percent could turn out to be worth $2 million. Now, I own a part of a USFL team, and I am pleased about it.

I am confident the new league will succeed. We'll create our own stars. There are plenty of players around. When I was with Washington, we cut enough players to stock another franchise. Within three years, I think our teams will be competitive with any team in the NFL.

Still, part of my heart will always be in the NFL, and this book gave me the opportunity to examine the game there from a fresh perspective— selecting the 100 greatest players of the past 50 years. I hope my love of this great game and its outstanding players shows through in the following pages.

George Allen
1982.

PART I

THE
OFFENSE

CHAPTER 1

QUARTERBACKS

There is no doubt that quarterback is the single most important position on a professional football team. Whether or not he calls the signals, and he usually does, he is the leader. The others rally behind him. When I look for the great quarterbacks, I look for the outstanding leaders.

Actually, the first thing I think about as regards the great quarterbacks is their won-and-lost records and how many titles they won. You will find that most of the great quarterbacks took their teams to championships, or, at least, championship games. It is a tribute to their leadership as well as their abilities.

However, a few great quarterbacks have been locked into mediocre teams. Without talented support even a Sammy Baugh or a Sid Luckman, a Johnny Unitas or a Terry Bradshaw could not have carried their clubs to the top. So titles are not an absolute requirement in the record of an outstanding quarterback.

The different abilities a quarterback must have are very important, of course. There are few things more difficult to do in sports than to hit a target on the move far downfield, but there are a lot of different passes that are difficult to throw, and the more varied a passer's talents and touch the better an all-around quarterback he has been. And consistency is absolutely critical.

We think today primarily of T-formation quarterbacks because that's been the style for almost 40 years now, but I cannot exclude from consideration those old single-wing tailbacks who were primarily passers. Running ability is very important to a quarterback, though it has been possible for a few who were not mobile to achieve stardom.

It is important that a quarterback be able to use his blockers, avoid a rush, have the courage to stand up under a rush, and to wait if he has to until the last possible moment to throw the ball when a receiver comes open. He has to see receivers all over the field, to throw the ball away without an interception when he has to, and to take a tackle when he has to.

The great quarterbacks all have been very tough both physically and mentally, able to take punishment and keep playing well, and smart enough to know the best thing to do under different, often very difficult circumstances. The standout quarterbacks have been able to think very fast and very well. A lot of what they have had to do, they have had to improvise.

The great quarterbacks were at their best during the last few minutes of close games, on third downs, inside the 20, at the goal line. The standout passer is a lot like the outstanding hitter in baseball. Maybe another guy hits for a higher average, but the better batter hits with men on base and drives in runs. Maybe another guy drives in more runs, but the better hitter drives them in in close games, in the ninth inning, and in the big games. Maybe another quarterback completes more passes for more yards, but the better quarterback completes them when they count most heavily.

If some others were picking the ideal quarterback they'd probably go for a tall player who could see over the rushers, and a big guy who could stand up under tackles and take punishment and break tackles and run. But the fact is the outstanding quarterbacks have come in all sizes and I did not take their size into consideration, only what they were able to do. Some men simply make better use of their tools than others. Some learn from their experiences, others only get older.

The best quarterbacks have not made many mistakes. They have not fumbled the ball away a lot, which is important because they handle the ball on every offensive play. And they have not thrown a lot of interceptions. Some great quarterbacks have had so much confidence in their ability to throw the ball that they have had a tendency to try to throw it through difficult coverage, but few have thrown a lot of interceptions.

There have been exceptions. Joe Namath threw a lot of interceptions. It was his weakness and one reason he ranks as low on my list as he does. But he had his strengths, and they were sufficient to include him. Bobby Layne did not have the arm that others on my list had, but he made up for it in other ways, and he was one of the great leaders.

I have said leadership is the single most important quality a quarterback can have, and this often can be translated into titles won. Built into this is coolness under fire, performance under pressure, the ability to do more when it means the most—every quarterback I even considered had these. If a fellow couldn't consistently come through in the clutch, then I don't care about what wonderful things he could do at other times.

The more different things he did well, the higher I hold him, but the ability to get off his passes under rushes and the ability to throw all the different passes required of a quarterback are critical. Usually, over many seasons, these translate into statistics. The numbers tell me how high on the all-time list each ranks in passes completed, accuracy, yards per throw, total yards, touchdowns, interceptions, and so forth. I have weighed these things heavily. Longevity, durability, and career accomplishments are not to be regarded lightly, either.

I have considered several different factors and have made my judgments on balance.

So, here they are, the greatest quarterbacks as I have seen them.

1.
Sammy Baugh

Sammy Baugh's nickname was "Slingin'"—the perfect bit of alliteration for a quarterback. The irony, though, was that the nickname traced to Baugh's single season as a minor-league baseball player. He was an infielder with a shotgun for an arm and, when he switched from baseball to football, he became one of the finest passers in the history of the sport.

Like most quarterbacks of his time, Baugh started out as a tailback. A native of tiny Sweetwater, Texas, Baugh went to Texas Christian University, where Coach Dutch Meyer helped him learn football's developing weapon—the forward pass. In the hands of a player with the kind of arm Baugh possessed, it became a devastating technique for offense.

Baugh began his professional career as a tailback, used as a runner and blocking back. The pro game moved slowly to new offensive strategies and it wasn't until 1944—his eighth season—that Baugh became a quarterback as the Washington Redskins finally went to the newfangled T formation. Once he started slingin' the football, Baugh caught on quickly. He wound up his career with 21,886 yards gained via the aerial route.

The 6-2, 180-pound Texan's football production belied his rather slender physique. He was a triple-threat player. Besides being an outstanding passer, Baugh led the National Football League in punting for four years (he did not begin punting in the league until his third year) and posted a career average of 45.1 yards per kick—still an all-time NFL high. In 1943, when he split his time between offense and defense, Sammy paced the league by pulling down 11 interceptions.

Baugh led the NFL in passing six times, still a record, and completed 1,693 attempts for his career. His career completion percentage was an impressive 56.5 and, in 1945, he set the current league mark with a 70.33 completion percentage, connecting on 128 of 182 attempts.

In 16 NFL seasons, Baugh took his team to four championship games and two NFL crowns. He was chosen for the NFL's team of the decade for the 1940s and was named to the Pro Football Hall of Fame in 1963.

When I think of Sammy Baugh I think of a picture passer. I believe if you saw an old photo of Baugh in a football uniform and it didn't have his name under it and you didn't know who he was you'd know he was a great passer.

He was tall and thin but very wiry, and he had long arms and large hands and he threw the ball better than any passer I ever saw. He had a whiplike motion and he could throw soft and hard, short and long as well as anyone ever.

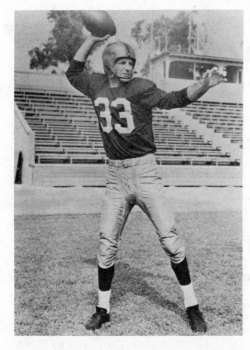

Sammy Baugh

He was more than just a passer. He could run a little. He was the greatest punter who ever lived. And he was one of the greatest defensive backs who ever lived. He completed passes against anyone, but few completed passes against him.

Originally a fine baseball prospect, he was an amazing all-around athlete and possibly the greatest all-around professional football player ever. For the first half of his career he was a single-wing tailback, then he converted successfully to being a T quarterback. There is absolutely no doubt in my mind that he has to be rated No. 1 among quarterbacks.

It was a couple of years after Sammy came into professional football that rules were put in to protect the quarterback—primarily because he was being given such punishment. Sammy took a beating, but he never faltered. He endured a long time as a player. He was the first player to make the pass as important as the run. With him, the pass no longer was surprise strategy but basic football.

They did not throw as much in his day as they do today, so he is not as high in total yardage as he would be had he played in recent years. But he threw more than others of his day and with as much accuracy as anyone has today. He was a great leader, a great passer, a great all-around athlete—the best I ever saw.

2.
Sid Luckman

Sid Luckman never wanted to be a pro football player, much less a T-formation quarterback. He grew up on the sidewalks of New York and played college football at Columbia University in the late 1930s. He was a tailback in a single-wing attack. Sid played for fun, never thinking about the possibility of being paid for what he was doing.

But the Chicago Bears had other ideas. They pictured Luckman as the type of player who could step in and operate the new T-formation attack toward which professional football was moving. Papa Bear George Halas, the head coach, had to convince Luckman first that playing pro football was a legitimate profession. And once he did that, Halas had to talk Luckman into a brand-new position—quarterback.

It was not a simple task. Luckman was stubborn, but Halas was more stubborn. He was determined to sign the young Ivy Leaguer and once he did in 1939, Halas was determined to make him into a T quarterback.

Luckman, a 6-foot, 195-pounder, tripped over his own feet on the first T play he ran. But eventually he got the knack of the position, and by 1943 he received the NFL's Most Valuable Player award. Two years later, in 1945, he tied Washington's Sammy Baugh for the passing championship.

Luckman set a record when he threw seven touchdown passes against the New York Giants on November 14, 1943. He passed for 433 yards in that game—the first NFL quarterback to top 400 yards in a single game.

For his career, Luckman completed 904 of 1,744 passes for 14,686 yards and 139 touchdowns. He was inducted into the Pro Football Hall of Fame in 1965. Not bad for a guy who never really wanted the job in the first place.

Sid Luckman also was a single-wing tailback originally, but he became the first T-formation quarterback in the National Football League when George Halas installed the system with the Bears. Halas had help from Clark Shaughnessy, who also introduced it to college football with his great Stanford teams of the 1940s.

Frankie Albert was the quarterback who developed the way to play the position at Stanford, and the little left-hander was the finest ball handler I ever saw at the position, back in the beginning when ball handling and confusing the defense were critical. But Albert, while later an excellent pro quarterback, wasn't quite a good enough thrower to make my list.

Luckman was a superb passer, very accurate and sure, especially with short passes. He was also an exceptional ball handler and he really modeled T quarterbacking for all the greats who followed him. He called his signals brilliantly and was a master tactician, maybe the smartest quarterback I ever watched work. He was the best ball-control quarterback ever. He wasn't a big guy and he didn't play as long as some others, but he was a commanding leader.

Sid Luckman (#42)

Sid is probably remembered best for the 1940 championship game in which he and the Bears crushed Baugh and the Redskins, 73–0, but that was just a matter of one of the greatest teams of all time having its greatest game of all time. He and the Bears had been beaten by Baugh and the Redskins, 7–3, only a few weeks earlier.

As with Baugh, the ball wasn't thrown nearly as much that many years ago, so Luckman isn't as high in total yardage as he might be, but he broke records for yardage in his years. Luckman played defense as well as offense. He was an all-around athlete. He was a coach on the field and coached the Bear quarterbacks for many years after he retired as a player.

3.
Johnny Unitas

Professional football teams use some of the most sophisticated scouting systems in sports. There are endless reports and computer printouts produced on even the most obscure player prospects. Nobody wants to bypass a potential star.

The scouting was less thorough in 1955, when Johnny Unitas graduated from the University of Louisville and was picked almost as an afterthought by the Pittsburgh Steelers on the ninth round of the draft. Ninth-round choices don't get top priority and Unitas was an early cut in the Steeler camp that season. He then signed to play for the semipro Bloomfield Rams on fields filled with rocks and shattered glass.

A year later, the Baltimore Colts decided to take a look at Unitas. They discovered the quintessential diamond in the rough.

Unitas, a 6-1, 195-pounder, played for 18 seasons, and when he retired in 1973, he took with him records for most pass attempts (5,186), most completions (2,830), most yards (40,239), most touchdown passes (290), most 300-yard games (26), and most consecutive games throwing touchdown passes (47). Several of the records subsequently fell to other passers, but that hardly diminishes Unitas' accomplishments. Johnny was named to the Pro Football Hall of Fame in 1979.

He led the Colts to one Super Bowl crown and three NFL championships. The most memorable was the 1958 title game in which the Colts beat the New York Giants, 23—17, in overtime in a game which seemed to lift pro football into the spotlight in American sports. Twice in that game Unitas took the Colts on brilliant 80-yard drives, the first one in the final two minutes of regulation time to gain the tying field goal, and the second in the overtime period producing the winning touchdown.

That championship game is often called the greatest pro football game ever played.

Johnny Unitas

Although I think Sammy Baugh and Sid Luckman are the best quarterbacks I ever saw, I believe Johnny Unitas is the greatest I ever coached against.

If I had to pick one player to build a team around in my time it would have been Johnny Unitas. Throughout almost my entire pro coaching career I had to go against Unitas and he was by far the most difficult man I ever tried to defense and probably the most valuable player of my time.

Boy, was he tough! That's what I think of first when I think of him. We tried to slow him down by beating on him until you'd think he couldn't get up, but he'd get up and beat the dickens out of you. They didn't protect the quarterbacks in the 1960s the way they do now, but he'd get up before the count of ten and knock you out.

Unitas was so smart he'd outsmart the best minds in the game. He'd fool you. He'd call the play you'd least expect in a given situation and make it work. He ran the two-minute drill better than any quarterback I ever saw. Roger Staubach was the only quarterback who came close. They could conserve the clock and cut your throat. Unitas was the best passer into the end zone I ever saw. It is difficult to throw effectively into the end zone, but he had the killer instinct.

Johnny moved around just enough to evade rushes. He was difficult to pin down. He wasn't too fast on his feet, but he was cool and courageous and he'd find space to throw, and he threw with an exceptionally fast motion just before taking a tackle. He was extremely smart and accurate with his throws. He and Staubach were the best screen passers I ever saw. A lot of good quarterbacks aren't good at this. It's tricky. You have to throw to the runner at just the right time and lead him just right.

Baugh and Luckman had the greatest teams of their times around them and brought out the best in them. Terry Bradshaw, the same. Unitas had an excellent team around him, too, but I believe he made it the best. The Baltimore Colts almost always were contenders when Unitas was at quarterback, mainly, I think, because Unitas was the quarterback.

4.
Terry Bradshaw

In 1970, the Pittsburgh Steelers, beginning their reconstruction following years of sad-sack football, made Terry Bradshaw a No. 1 college draft choice. He was labeled a can't-miss prospect but found himself in over his head in the NFL. The Louisiana Tech product led the league in being intercepted in his rookie year and, by 1974, he was nothing more than a bench warmer who, it seemed, would never deliver on his suspected potential. He simply seemed unable to solve the NFL's sophisticated defenses.

The Steelers were rotating Bradshaw with Terry Hanratty and Joe Gilliam at quarterback then, but when injuries sidelined the other two, Bradshaw was given the full-time assignment. This time he was ready to do justice to it.

When Pittsburgh reached the Super Bowl for the first time in 1975, Bradshaw was a first stringer because he had survived the rash of injuries. When they returned in 1976, he was there because he had earned the job and when Pittsburgh came back again in 1978 and 1979, Bradshaw was the star.

The 1979 Super Bowl was a pulsating shoot-out between Bradshaw and Roger Staubach of Dallas. The Steeler ace completed 17 of 30 passes for 318 yards and three TDs in that game, capturing the MVP award. A year later Bradshaw did it again in the Super Bowl, completing 14 of 21 passes for 309 yards and two more TDs. Once again he was named the game's MVP, but this time Terry wrote a unique piece of NFL history. He became the first player ever named MVP in the regular season and then repeating the honor in the Super Bowl game.

Terry owns career Super Bowl records for most touchdown passes (nine) and most passing yards (932), and is the only quarterback to have led his team to victory four times.

The 6-3, 215-pound Bradshaw was not quite as effective in 1980 and 1981 as he was during the 1970s, and the Steelers, too, were not nearly as successful during those two years. In 1981 he suffered a broken right hand in the club's fourteenth game and was sidelined for the remainder of the campaign.

Still, he finished his year's work with career aggregates of 1,893 pass completions in 3,653 attempts for a 51.8 completion percentage, 26,144 yards, and 193 touchdowns.

Terry Bradshaw is the modern mold for a quarterback. He's tall, powerfully built, and powerful. Like Unitas, you could beat Bradshaw half to death, but there'd still be enough life in him to kill you. Bradshaw just takes his licks and does his job, as tough and durable as a man can be.

He has had a great arm and great legs. He's been a better runner than most quarterbacks. And a stronger thrower. Whereas Unitas cut you up with the short passes and opened you up to a long bomb, Terry loosens you up for the short ones with the long ones. He's been the most accurate long thrower I've ever seen.

Bradshaw also has as strong an arm as I've seen in football. Now, a strong arm isn't enough. Dan Pastorini is as strong a passer as ever lived, but he's not as accurate as he might be. The same is true of Doug Williams. Bradshaw has accuracy as well as strength and he can throw the soft short one, too.

The knock on Bradshaw was that he wasn't supposed to be smart, but I'd guess he has a lot of what the big-city guys call "street smarts," and he sure has had an instinct for doing the right thing and throwing to the right

Terry Bradshaw (#12)

receiver on the football field. He plays smart, and that's all that matters to me.

He's had great receivers and an outstanding all-around team around him, but I'm not sure how many other quarterbacks could have taken Pittsburgh to four Super Bowl championships. That's an amazing record and I really respect it. He was just the right quarterback for the right team at the right time. He's been an inspirational leader and a super performer.

5.
Bart Starr

Bart Starr was the key performer when Vince Lombardi's Green Bay Packers achieved greatness in the 1960s. An unheralded seventeenth-round draft choice from the University of Alabama, Starr was the catalyst who led Green Bay to six division championships, five NFL crowns, and victories in the first two Super Bowl games.

In the eight-year period from 1960 to 1967, the Packers posted an 82–24–4 record, and most of the glory went to the glamor players—Paul Hornung, Jim Taylor, Ray Nitschke, and the charismatic coach—Vince Lombardi. But the man who made the machine move on the field was Starr, the soft-spoken quarterback.

Bart Starr

Starr was one of the most accurate passers ever to play in the NFL. For his career, he completed 57.4 percent of his 3,149 attempts, second best in history. In one stretch covering parts of the 1964 and 1965 seasons, Starr threw 294 passes without an interception, setting another league record. That is 86 passes better than the next-best mark for consecutive attempts without being picked off. His 1.2 interception percentage avoidance in 1966 is the second lowest ever recorded and he led the league in passing three times, winning the title in 1962, 1964, and 1966.

It was at the end of the 1966 season that Starr led Green Bay into the NFL's first Super Bowl. On the first Super Sunday, he was merely brilliant, completing 16 of 23 passes for 250 yards and two TDs. He was the first Super Bowl MVP, in a 35—10 Green Bay rout against Kansas City.

A year later, Starr had problems. Nagging injuries led to an uncharacteristic nine interceptions in the first two games of the 1967 season. But Green Bay battled back and the Packers returned to the Super Bowl. Again, the 6-1, 200-pound Starr rose to the occasion, hitting 13 of 24 passes for 202 yards, one TD, and an impressive 33—14 victory over Oakland. The MVP, once again, was the Green Bay quarterback.

For his career, Starr completed 1,808 of 3,149 passes for 24,718 yards and 152 touchdowns. Bart's selection to the Pro Football Hall of Fame was made in 1977.

Bart Starr was technically perfect as a quarterback. He executed plays with precision. He had the touch of a fine surgeon and he cut defenses apart. He seldom called his own signals, but I can't fault him for that. He was smart enough to do so superbly, and his audibles were almost always the right ones at the right times. He showed me a lot of fine leadership qualities.

Vince Lombardi preferred calling the plays from the sidelines, and Starr had the discipline to accept this and make the most of it. Green Bay had better running backs than, say, Unitas' Baltimore team, and the Packers used the running game to set up their passing game very effectively.

Once set up, Starr's passes were remarkably consistent and accurate. He was not the long passer Bradshaw has been, or even Unitas was. But Starr could throw the bomb effectively and he was the master of all the short passes from sideline to sideline and across the middle.

The only way we ever could hope to defense Unitas or Starr effectively was to mix up our defenses and show them a lot of different kinds of coverage because they executed the passing game so precisely you at least had to make them guess or gamble a little.

My teams did well against Green Bay over the years because we gave it the extra effort it needed. One time we defeated the Packers by intercepting Starr four times. That was very difficult to do. But he could come back the next game and beat you by passing perfectly.

Those Green Bay teams of the 1960s had as much talent and as good coaching as any I've ever seen, but I give Starr a lot of the credit for the NFL titles the Packers won. He was the perfect quarterback for that team.

Starr was as intelligent and disciplined a quarterback as professional football has had.

6.
Otto Graham

The year was 1941 and Paul Brown, who would go on to coaching greatness in the National Football League, was a young college coach at Ohio State. That season the Buckeyes were beaten in a Big Ten contest by Northwestern, and although Brown lost the game, he found a quarterback. The player who engineered the upset was Otto Graham. Brown never forgot the name.

Five years later, Cleveland was awarded a franchise in the fledgling All-America Conference and Brown was named the coach. The first player the coach picked for his team was the quarterback from Northwestern who had directed the upset of Ohio State. Brown had remembered.

Otto Graham was a consummate leader for 10 brilliant seasons, including six in the NFL. He led the Browns to conference championships every year of his career and seven league titles as well. Individually, Otto won two NFL passing crowns and holds the league record for the highest average gain for a career, 8.63 yards on 1,565 attempts.

Graham's performances resulted in some other outstanding career statistics. He completed 1,464 of 2,626 career attempts, throwing for 23,584 yards and 174 touchdowns. Graham said all of those impressive numbers did not come easily.

"I was born with good coordination, but I worked for everything else I got out of sports," the 6-1, 195-pounder said. "There is no shortcut to success. It takes practice. Too many kids like to think that because they have natural ability they're going to be stars. But it doesn't work that way unless they're willing to work hard to polish the skills God gave them."

After finishing his playing career, Graham remained in football as a coach, briefly with the Washington Redskins and, for many years, doubled as athletic director at the United States Coast Guard Academy. A member of both the College and Pro Football Halls of Fame (1965), he became an important spokesman for the American Cancer Society after being stricken by cancer of the colon.

Otto Graham

Otto Graham was much in the mold of Bart Starr. Paul Brown called the plays for the Cleveland Browns, and while Graham didn't like it, he had the discipline to accept it and make the most of it. He audibled brilliantly and he was in command of his club on the field.

Like Starr, Graham was surrounded by one of the truly great teams. His teams won a lot of titles and, after moving from the All-America Conference to the National Football League, they proved to the establishment they were for real. Otto was the perfect quarterback for the Browns, as Starr was for the Packers.

Like the Packers, the Browns had superb runners and used their running game to set up their passing game. When they got you set up, they picked you apart with passes. I think Starr might have been a little better short passer than Graham, but Otto was a bit better with the long pass.

Graham was a better all-around athlete than some of the other standout quarterbacks. He was a basketball star as well as a football star in college. He was a single-wing tailback at Northwestern when the Wildcats were a competitive team. He was a strong runner.

Graham didn't have to throw as much as some of the more recent quarterbacking stars, but he gained a lot of yardage with the throws he did make. He was accurate and intelligent with his passes and difficult to intercept. His ball-handling was good and he made very few mistakes.

7.
Roger Staubach

Roger Staubach was one of the greatest two-minute-drill quarterbacks in the history of professional football. He wasn't bad for the other 58 minutes of the game, either.

Staubach was brilliant at fighting the clock. He made every second count as the Dallas Cowboys moved downfield in the waning moments of a game, driving for important points. Fourteen times he sparked victories in the final two minutes of a game. There were nine other games in which the Cowboys trailed in the fourth quarter only to have Staubach bring them back to record triumphs.

He was the unquestioned star on the squad often referred to as "America's team," spending 11 years with the Cowboys. He completed 1,685 of 2,958 career attempts, a 57 percent accuracy figure, producing 22,700 yards and 153 touchdowns.

Staubach came out of the United States Naval Academy and won the Heisman Trophy as America's finest college football player in 1963. Because of his service obligation, he was largely ignored in the draft, chosen almost as an afterthought on the tenth round by Dallas. Staubach took the selection seriously, though, spending a two-week summer leave from the service in the Cowboy training camp one year and taking home a playbook to study.

When he joined Dallas in 1969, the 6-foot-3, 202-pounder spent two years sharing the quarterback job with Craig Morton. By 1971, however, it was all Staubach's and he led the Cowboys to the Super Bowl championship, a title his team repeated in 1977. He led the league in passing four times, including 1979, his final season. He had six 300-yard games and a club record of 99 consecutive passes without an interception in playoff games.

Roger Staubach was the best passer-runner I ever coached against. He was a better runner than Terry Bradshaw and Fran Tarkenton. Roger was a great passer, but when he saw the place to run, he could really run. He ran straight ahead to daylight.

When I was coaching the Redskins, our games with the Cowboys were the big games of the year for us. We beat them more than they beat us, but it was always tough. Tom Landry makes adjustments as a game goes along better than any coach in the game today. And Staubach was the best since Unitas at running the two-minute drill, conserving the clock, and moving the ball downfield to a score.

One time we led Dallas, 28–0, and wound up hanging on to win, 28–21. Another time we were tied and Staubach took an inside rush, slipped out of it to his left, found an open field, and ran 35 yards into the end zone to beat us. Another time we knocked him out and I thought he was through for the game. But he came back in a goal-line situation and dove over for the touchdown that beat us. Boy, he was a tough one!

Of course, our games were just a small part of his career. We had good defenses and tried very hard to contain him, but he just took many teams apart. Roger was a lot like Otto Graham or Bart Starr. Roger didn't like it, but he had the discipline to accept having the signals called for him. He just performed, audibled brilliantly and, when it was called for, he improvised brilliantly and still led the team.

The Cowboys have had a great organization and always are contenders for titles, but Staubach was the key player who led them to championships. They used a balanced attack, but he threw all the passes superbly. He was also the most difficult quarterback to intercept I ever coached against, and the best third-down quarterback I ever saw. At third and four or five, he came through consistently.

I think concussions eventually caused him to call it a career, but he stood up to punishment for a long time. Another great leader of recent years who came very close to making my list was Bob Griese, who was similar in style to Otto Graham and Bart Starr and didn't fall short by much.

Roger Staubach

Bobby Layne

8.
Bobby Layne

If one wants to know how tough Bobby Layne was, he might consider that Bobby was the last pro football player to insist on taking the field without benefit of a face mask. He also refused to wear rib pads or extra protection for his thighs, hips, or knees.

"I like freedom," he explained.

Layne spent his time in life's fast lane. He had a tough reputation and he made it stand up. "When Bobby said 'block,' you blocked," longtime teammate Yale Lary once said of Layne. "And when Bobby said 'drink,' you drank."

Another teammate, Doak Walker, said, "Bobby never lost a game in his life. Time just ran out on him."

That was the impression Layne delivered to his teammates. He had a cocky approach to the business of football and seemed convinced that sooner or later, one way or another, he could bring his team to victory. He was like the coach who would tell his team, "Keep it close until I think of something."

Layne, a 6-2, 190-pounder, came out of the University of Texas and played one year with the Chicago Bears and another with the New York Bulldogs before settling down with the Detroit Lions. He starred for them from 1950 to 1958, helping Detroit to consecutive NFL championships in 1952 and 1953. Each time the Layne-led Lions beat Otto Graham's Cleveland Browns in showdowns between two of the game's finest passers. Detroit won, 17—7, in '52 but needed a frantic 80-yard march in the final three minutes to score a 17—16 victory in '53. The man who pulled it off was Layne, completing four of six passes in the drive, including a 33-yarder to seldom-used Jim Doran for the winning TD.

The next year, the same teams met again and this time Cleveland won the championship, beating the Lions by a lopsided 56—10 count. Layne knew why. "We were pressing for three in a row, and everybody went to bed at 10 o'clock," he said.

So much for early curfews. They were rarely problems for Layne, who was the consummate leader on the field and off.

On the field, Bobby moved to Pittsburgh, where he ended his career in 1962. Overall, he completed 1,814 passes in 3,700 attempts for a 49.0 percentage. His final yardage total is 26,768, and he threw for 196 touchdowns. He became a member of the Hall of Fame in 1967.

Bobby Layne was as good a leader as I ever saw on the football field. He couldn't pass with any of the others I have on the list, but he got the ball to the receivers and he won big games. He took teams to titles almost by sheer force of will. He was mean and tough and he got on the guys, but he got more out of his teammates than almost anyone else could. He was always confident, even cocky, that he could get the job done, and his guys believed in him. His passes would wobble, but he found his receivers, especially under pressure. He was a great third-down quarterback, an excellent last-two-minutes quarterback, and a standout player under pressure.

Billy Kilmer, who took one of my Redskin clubs to the Super Bowl, reminded me a lot of Layne. Kilmer also had limited natural talent and didn't throw a pretty pass, but he was an inspirational leader who drove his teams to do more than they thought they could do.

I would like to have put Kilmer on my list because Billy did so much for me and I admired him so much, but I think physically Billy just couldn't do enough to rank with the greatest. Layne was just a little better, a little more able, and does belong with the best. But they were the same type. Some people thought I was crazy for playing Billy, but the bottom line was that we won with him.

Although I am a great believer in physical conditioning and in dedication to the game and admire the clean-cut family man, both Billy and Bobby were rarities in that they could stay out all night and still go as good as anyone on the football field the next day. They were fun-loving fellows but such intense competitors and determined winners that the straightest of coaches had to bend a little for them.

9.
Norm Van Brocklin

Norm Van Brocklin's career ended in 1960 after 12 seasons in the NFL, and the finish was entirely in character for the quarterback they called "the Dutchman." He led the Philadelphia Eagles to the NFL championship, beating Vince Lombardi's Green Bay Packers. Then he played in his eighth Pro Bowl game, throwing touchdown passes of 46, 43, and 36 yards and completing six consecutive passes in a two-minute drive near the end of the game. Then he retired.

Three times Van Brocklin won NFL passing titles and he averaged 8.16 yards per completion for his career, the third-best figure in history. In a game against the old New York Yankees on September 28, 1951, he passed for an all-time-record 554 yards. It remains the single most productive passing game enjoyed by any quarterback in NFL history. He was named to the Pro Football Hall of Fame in 1971.

Drafted No. 4 by the Rams in 1949, Van Brocklin passed up his final year of college eligibility at Oregon to turn pro. It was the start of a stormy career. When he joined Los Angeles, Van Brocklin found Bob Waterfield comfortably set as the quarterback. Van Brocklin sat for most of the season but played the final game and burned Washington for four TD passes in a 53–27 romp.

The next year, Van Brocklin and Waterfield alternated by quarters, an arrangement that didn't exactly satisfy the Dutchman. When he refused to carry out a play called from the bench in the final game of the 1951 season, he was replaced. Waterfield relieved, threw for five TDs and 256 yards and edged Van Brocklin for the passing crown.

But in the playoff game against Cleveland, Van Brocklin, after sitting for

50 minutes, entered the game with it tied at 17—17 and threw a 73-yard TD pass to Tom Fears to give LA the championship.

After Waterfield retired, Van Brocklin got stuck in another rotation role with Billy Wade, and although LA won another title that way in 1955, it hardly satisfied Van Brocklin. Finally, in 1958, he was traded to Philadelphia and he took the Eagles to their championship—without help from any other quarterback.

Van Brocklin, at 6-1 and 190 pounds, completed 1,553 career passes in 2,895 attempts for a 53.6 percentage. He compiled 23,611 yards and passed for 173 touchdowns.

Norm
Van Brocklin

No one ever played the game who was tougher than Norm Van Brocklin. He was dedicated to winning in a way that few have been and he snarled not only at opponents but also at teammates who made mistakes. He was not the best-loved guy who ever played football, but he got the best out of his teammates by driving them to do more. This attitude carried over to coaching, but he just missed being a great coach. He led by example on the field, and his push for perfection was a little too much as a head coach.

As far as rankings go, it was very tough to choose between Van Brocklin and Bob Waterfield, who at one time competed for the quarterback position in Los Angeles. No team ever had two such great quarterbacks at one time. And the Rams, who also had such all-time standout receivers as Elroy Hirsch and Tom Fears, rolled up spectacular scores, really leading the way to wide-open, high-scoring professional football. Waterfield was a better all-around athlete than Van Brocklin. But Van Brocklin was a little better passer. And he helped two different teams to NFL championships, which is a great accomplishment in my book.

Van Brocklin may have been the finest pure passer of more modern times, the best since Baugh. Van Brocklin may have been a better long passer than Baugh. Van Brocklin was one of the first outstanding long passers. He could throw a ball almost the length of the football field and hit a fast receiver in full stride right in the hands. He could throw bullets to the sidelines. He could throw right through defenses. He had strength, touch, and tremendous timing. He couldn't run a lick, and modern rushing defenses might have bothered him a bit, but he could overcome these obstacles with his arm.

Sonny Jurgensen was a lot like him on the field, a lot like Billy Kilmer off the field. But I got Jurgensen with the Redskins when he was near the end of his career. In his prime he never came up with a winner. But Sonny was a great thrower. John Brodie was another, one of the fine pure passers of all time. But John forced the ball a little too much and threw a few too many interceptions. And he never came up with a title. Y. A. Tittle came closer to titles and came very close to making this list. He was a fine quarterback and a standout passer. But at every position a few star players are bound just to miss out.

But there is no way anyone could leave off Norm Van Brocklin's name.

10.
Bob Waterfield

A rookie quarterback usually needs time to adjust to the rough-and-tumble world of professional football, and the last place one would expect to see a first-year passer after the season is in the NFL championship game.

Nobody told Bob Waterfield, though.

Waterfield joined the Cleveland Rams in 1945. The club was hardly a powerhouse but the addition of Waterfield made the Rams almost unbeatable. They posted a 9–1 record and then beat Washington and Sammy Baugh in the championship game, 15–14. Waterfield threw two touchdown passes, completing a dream rookie season during which he

Bob Waterfield

threw for 1,609 yards and 14 TDs. He also ran for five other TDs and was voted the league's Most Valuable Player award.

The next year, the Rams moved to Los Angeles, and Waterfield went on to win passing championships in 1946 and 1951. For eight NFL seasons he completed 813 passes for 11,849 yards and 98 touchdowns. He also averaged 42.4 yards for 315 career punts, scored 13 TDs running the ball, and scored 498 points on field goals and point-after-touchdown kicks. When he retired, his 573 points scored were third on the all-time list.

But that's not all. For his first four pro seasons, Waterfield, a 6-2, 200-pounder, also played defense and intercepted 20 enemy passes.

With Waterfield in the lineup, the Rams never finished below .500. They won three divisional titles, tied for another, and captured another NFL title in 1951.

Waterfield was a late bloomer. He was 19 when he enrolled at UCLA and did not play football until his sophomore year. The T formation was coming into vogue and Waterfield learned it well enough to earn college All-America honors in 1942. After military service, Waterfield was a third-round draft choice of the Rams in 1944. He played a final season at UCLA before turning pro for what then was an astounding $7,500 contract.

Bob Waterfield was one of the finest all-around athletes professional football has had. He was a lot like Sammy Baugh in this respect. He even reminded me of Baugh in that I think if you saw a picture of Waterfield you knew he was a passer. But he also was one of the best punters and place-kickers of all time, and an outstanding defensive back with superb timing and ability to intercept passes.

Norm Van Brocklin was a better pure passer, but Waterfield threw every kind of pass effectively. Where Van Brocklin was extremely temperamental and explosive, Waterfield was almost totally unemotional. I'm not sure Waterfield even talked to his wife, the beautiful movie star Jane Russell. But Bob was the type of quiet man who led by example, and although he wasn't the talkative type of inspirational leader, he inspired confidence in his leadership by being cool in the hottest of circumstances.

Waterfield led the Los Angeles Rams to title games and to titles. He had wonderful receivers and used them to their full potential. He was a good runner and used his running game superbly. He was one of the most intelligent quarterbacks I ever saw. He was a real student of the game and was impatient with players or writers who didn't really understand the fine points. Like Van Brocklin, Waterfield could have been a great coach, but whereas Van Brocklin failed because he was too emotional, Waterfield failed because he was too unemotional.

Waterfield's lack of emotion stood him in good stead on the field. He responded effectively to pressure. He could pick a defense apart after it had frustrated him for a while. I remember one game against Green Bay in which his Rams trailed, 28–6, at halftime and still trailed, 28–13, late in the game when he kicked a field goal and threw two touchdown passes to win, 30–28. Afterward he acted as if it were all in a day's work. He was a pure professional, a quiet killer who was outstanding from the first to the last day he stepped foot on a professional field.

11.
Arnie Herber

In pro football's pioneer era of the 1920s and 1930s, players were signed for all manner of reasons above and beyond their athletic ability. There was, for example, Arnie Herber, whose attraction to the Green Bay Packers included the fact that he happened to be a local boy who had starred as a triple-threat back at Green Bay's West High School. That was good enough for Curly Lambeau, boss of the Packers, who agreed to pay Herber $75 per game to play quarterback for Green Bay in 1930. That was fine with Herber, since it was a major improvement over his job as a locker-room handyman.

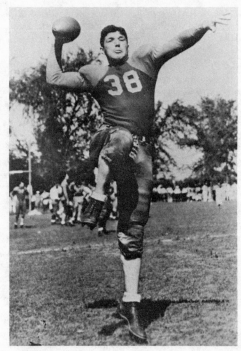

Arnie Herber

Herber proved pretty handy on the field, too. In his first pro game he threw a touchdown pass to Lavern Dilweg for a 7–0 Green Bay victory over the Chicago Cardinals. Green Bay won the NFL championship that year and again the next season, with Herber's passing leading the team. The NFL did not begin compiling individual statistics until 1932, so Herber's early accomplishments cannot be detailed. What is known is that he was the NFL's first official passing champion in 1932 when he completed 37 of 101 attempts for 639 yards and nine touchdowns. Typical of his perform- ance was a game against the Staten Island Stapletons in which he ran for touchdowns of 85 and 45 yards and completed 9 of 11 passes, 3 of them for TDs.

He won additional passing titles in 1934 and 1936 and combined with wide receiver Don Hutson to give Green Bay pro football's most deadly passing combination. Herber led the Packers to four championships.

Herber, a 6-1, 190-pounder, played for the Packers until 1940 and then retired. Four years later, the New York Giants, pressured by wartime man- power shortages, lured him back for two final seasons. His career ended for good in 1945 with 8,041 yards and 78 career touchdown passes— credentials which earned him admission to the Pro Football Hall of Fame in 1966.

I was only a boy when I first saw Arnie Herber play, but I never will forget the way he threw the long ball. He threw it with a tremendously high arc. Don Hutson would run downfield at great speed, outrunning the defenders, and Herber would arch this long pass downfield. It seemed to drop right out of the sky into Don's outstretched arms and he was on his way.

Herber revolutionized the game. He was the first outstanding long passer, way ahead of his time, and one of the finest long passers ever. The way they played the game in the 1930s —run, run, run—was perfect for Herber. The defenses would be bunched up close to the line and suddenly Hutson or one of the other receivers would break downfield and Herber would drop back and wait and then throw that incredible rainbow ball.

Herber was a single-wing tailback, but I have to assume he could have been an outstanding T-formation quarterback. He was an able athlete. He was an exceptional punter. He was a strong runner. He was a good defensive back. He was one of those fine all-around athletes who developed in an era when one man often carried a club. As I remember it, he threw all types of passes well. And he had that masterful touch with the long bomb long before it became commonplace.

Herber played in the NFL before it even had a championship game. He took his Packers to the top of the league twice before there was a championship game. And he won two championship games after the title game was started.

Cecil Isbell came along during Herber's last years and took the Packers to a couple of title games and one championship. Isbell was one of the finest early passers, but he played only five years and lacked the longevity to make my list. Ace Parker was another spectacular player and passer of the late 1930s and the 1940s. But Sammy Baugh, Sid Luckman, and Arnie Herber were the top passers of this revolutionary period.

12.
Fran Tarkenton

Fran Tarkenton played for 18 seasons as a pro, spending most of his time with the Minnesota Vikings. He established career records in most of the game's important quarterback categories—attempted passes (6,467), completions (3,686), yards gained (47,003), and touchdowns (342).

Until he came along in 1961, most quarterbacks were drop-back passers, careful to stay in the protective pocket formed by their blockers while a play developed. Tarkenton changed all that with his frantic scrambles, leading defensive linemen on a merry chase from one side of the field to the other.

The technique developed because of necessity. When Minnesota drafted the 6-foot, 190-pound Tarkenton out of the University of Georgia in 1961, the Vikings were a first-year expansion team and their passer protection wasn't always top quality. So Tarkenton ran with the football when he had to and, in doing that, he set still another record, gaining more yardage on the ground (3,674) than any other passer in NFL history. He also salvaged hundreds of busted plays, turning what looked like sure yardage losses into unexpected gains for his team.

In his rookie season, Tarkenton passed for 1,997 yards. For the next 15 years he annually soared past the 2,000-yard mark, establishing still another NFL record for consistent yardage production.

Tarkenton played for six seasons with Minnesota and then was traded to the New York Giants for four draft choices in 1967. Five years later the Vikings surrendered five players to get him back in another trade. He retired following the 1978 season after revolutionizing the position of quarterback and introducing a new option for passers. It was called "scrambling," and no one did it better.

When Fran Tarkenton and the Minnesota Vikings played their first game in the National Football League it was against the Chicago Bears when I was the defensive coach of that team. I will never forget it because Tarkenton took that expansion team to one of the most surprising upsets in professional football history. He scrambled around and ran the ball and threw it so well he kept the Bears in total confusion all afternoon, one of the most frustrating I've ever spent in football. I have had great respect for Fran ever since.

We shut him out later in the season, but it was on a muddy field that was so slippery he was unable to scramble effectively. I think the term "scrambling" was invented for him, or at least put into popular use with him.

He was not a strong passer, but one of those players like Bobby Layne who got the ball to the receiver somehow.

Tarkenton was a smart passer and a smart player. I don't think he liked it that he was best known for scrambling, but because of it he was extremely difficult to defense. He was one passer you tried to keep in the pocket instead of trying to chase him out of the pocket. And, because of his ability to keep his feet and evade tacklers while cutting back and forth, he really did wear down defenses by tiring out the defensive rushers who tried to catch him. They'd think they had him and he'd be gone.

Tarkenton didn't have a good defense behind him in his early years with the Vikings and Giants. And it's very hard for a quarterback to win consistently when he has a defense that seldom gives him the ball in good field position. Jim Hart of the Cardinals, one of the most underrated quarterbacks ever, has been a fine passer whose performances have been clouded by playing for teams with weak defenses. Tarkenton was on a loser a lot of his career, but when he returned to the Vikings they put

Fran Tarkenton

together the kind of defense that enabled him to be on a winner and reach the Super Bowl, though the title eluded him.

When he broke in, a lot of us didn't think the little guy could survive long, but he ended up enjoying one of the longest careers ever. He was tough and durable and through sheer longevity wound up with many of the major passing records.

13.
Ken Stabler

Ken Stabler finished the 1981 season, his twelfth as a pro, with 24,268 yards passing. On the record, he is the most accurate passer in NFL history, completing 60.3 percent of his career attempts, with 1,944 completions in 3,223 attempts. He has hit for 177 touchdown aerials.

Twice the leading passer in the American Football Conference, Stabler also owns the second highest single-season passing percentage. In 1976, when he led the Oakland Raiders to their first Super Bowl victory, Stabler completed 194 of 291 attempts for a 66.67 percentage. Only Sammy Baugh's 70.33 in 1945 was better over a season.

Drafted out of Alabama by the Raiders, Stabler spent his early days as a pro in a backup role before blossoming in 1973, when he won his first passing title. He led the Raiders into five straight AFC championship games from 1973 to 1977 and was selected the conference's Player of the Year in 1974 and 1976.

At Alabama, Stabler was one of the finest quarterbacks ever produced by Bear Bryant, who seemed to turn out great ones regularly. Bryant called him the best passer he ever coached. The Crimson Tide won the national championship in 1965, posting an 11−0 record with Stabler at quarterback.

Stabler, at 6-3 and 210 pounds, poses a particular problem for the defense because he is left-handed and so plays develop quite differently when he is at quarterback. It hardly interfered with Stabler's efficiency with Oakland and he flourished for a decade with the Raiders.

In 1980, Oakland dealt Stabler to Houston. In his first year with the Oilers he set club records for completions in a single season (293) and completion percentage (64.1). He dropped to a 57.9 completion average in 1981. He still owns several Raider passing records. Ken has been a three-time Pro Bowl selection and was picked for the NFL's team of the decade for the 1970s.

Ken Stabler

Ken Stabler has been a Bobby Layne with a strong southpaw throwing arm. Stabler has a strange throwing motion but can throw well on the run and get off a pass in the blink of an eye. In recent years he's lost a lot of his mobility, but in his prime he was as accurate a passer as anyone, especially good on short passes but explosive on long bombs too.

He may have been a bit hard to keep track of off the field, but he was an intense competitor on the field, dedicated to winning, very resourceful in the worst of circumstances, and an extremely inspirational leader. His teammates rallied around him. He ranked close to Johnny Unitas and Roger Staubach as a third-down passer and as a two-minute quarterback who seemed able to turn defeat into victory by sheer desire and determination.

Stabler took the Oakland Raiders to the top. They always seemed to have great defenses and great offensive lines but seldom had outstanding runners. Stabler used his runners effectively and helped make stars of his receivers. He's been an extremely tough, resilient, confident character who found ways to defeat his opponents.

We had standout quarterbacks in the 1970s and, while I have ranked a few ahead of him, I believe he could have played with anyone in any era.

14.
Joe Namath

Some quarterbacks perform significant functions for a single team. Joe Namath, however, assumed the rallying role for an entire league.

Namath was highly coveted when he came out of the University of Alabama in 1965. This was at the height of the battle for players between the established National Football League and the upstart American Football League. The bidding war for Namath became a showdown between the NFL St. Louis Cardinals and the AFL New York Jets. Sonny Werblin, owner of the Jets, saw in Namath the kind of charisma that his team and struggling league could rally around. Werblin signed the youngster to a three-year, $427,000 contract—huge, unheard-of figures in those days.

The contract made Namath an immediate celebrity and helped the AFL gain acceptance as a viable competitor for the NFL. Two years later the two leagues merged into one, and in 1969 Namath certified the AFL's arrival by directing the Jets to a 16–7 victory over the Baltimore Colts in the third Super Bowl game.

The Colts were 17-point favorites in that game but Namath stunned the football world by boldly guaranteeing a New York victory and then going out and delivering on his pledge.

That was Namath's style—swashbuckling, shoot from the hip. He was the prototype quarterback, playing his position with a swagger. And he had the arm to deliver on his cocksure attitude.

The 6-2, 200-pounder produced three straight 3,000-yard passing seasons, including 4,007 yards in 1967, becoming the first quarterback in his-

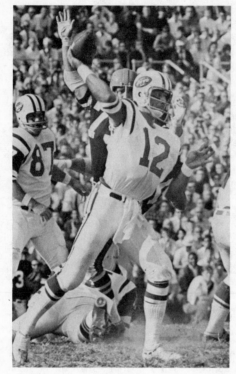

Joe Namath

tory to crack the 4,000-yard barrier. Others have done it since then, but none during the 14-game season in which he worked.

He had 21 games of more than 300 passing yards, third best in NFL history, and his 496-yard game against Baltimore on September 24, 1972 is the third-best single-game yardage production in history.

Injuries hampered Namath throughout his career, costing him large chunks of 3 of his 13 pro seasons, the last one with Los Angeles. He finished in 1977 with 1,886 career completions in 3,762 attempts, a 50.1 percentage, for 27,663 yards and 173 touchdowns.

Broadway Joe is a marginal selection. I gave it a lot of thought and decided he belonged among the greatest quarterbacks and 100 top professional players of modern times. He was, to some extent, a product of the New York media, who tried to make him the greatest ever. Maybe he would have been had he had better legs and a better supporting cast. But he was slowed by bad knees and played on a lot of losers. He may have tried to do it by himself too much. He forced a lot of passes and threw a lot of interceptions.

But Namath had one of the great throwing arms of all time and was one of the top pure passers ever. He played with exceptional courage on his bad knees and stood up to the roughest of rushes and passed superbly, with the quickest release I ever saw. And he became a winner. While maybe too much has been made of his predicting victory in the 1969 Super Bowl —what player worth his weight wouldn't expect to win? —Namath's performance in that contest was one of the classic performances of all time.

Players like Joe Namath do not come along very often. A Dan Fouts may endure to become one of the great ones, but only time will tell that. Somehow, Namath did play a surprisingly long time. He was not an all-around player, but he was an all-around passer, spectacular on every type of pass. He was a smart signal caller. He may have been a ladies' man off the field, but he was a man's man on the field. Most of his teammates loved him and followed his lead. A charismatic personality, he brought a lot of color and popularity to his sport, which is not bad.

CHAPTER 2

RECEIVERS

To me, the most important thing in judging a receiver is much the same as that in judging a quarterback. After all, they are a twosome, and have to work well together. A receiver is not nearly as responsible as a quarterback for leading a team to victory or defeat, or to titles. But the better a receiver has been able to come through in the clutch, in the big games, the higher my regard for him.

As with quarterbacks, and also running backs, we have many statistics to use as guides. Durability, consistency, and career performances are reflected in the number of passes caught, yardage gained, and touchdowns scored by the outstanding receivers who have played in professional football, and I have studied these. But other factors entered heavily in my final selections.

The most important factor in my mind in judging a receiver is his ability to make the difficult catch and the big catch—the third-down catch, the end-zone catch, the catch in a crowd when the quarterback has to gamble and force the ball, the catch when the game is on the line. Consistency, and especially consistency in the clutch, are critical factors. The best receivers keep drives alive and score touchdowns.

The standout receiver consistently runs his routes the way they were diagramed. He has to have the moves to get open, but he has to have the discipline to get where he is supposed to be when he is supposed to be there. Undisciplined receivers cause as many interceptions as undisciplined passers. On the other hand, the great receiver recognizes when he is covered or when the play is broken and has the resourcefulness to seek an open space where the passer can find him.

The great receiver may or may not have outstanding speed or size. That is what many look for in an ideal receiver, but I am not judging players on potential, but on performance. Most players waste most of their potential. The great receiver usually makes the most of what he has and the great ones have come in all sorts of sizes and speeds. All have had excellent moves. All have had good hands. All could make the spectacular catch of the poor pass.

It is important that they were able to concentrate on the catch and get the ball even when defenders were driving on them. It is important that they were able to hang onto the ball even when they knew they would be and often were hit hard a split second later. The great receivers are tough and durable. And they are at their best against the toughest defenders and defenses. They did the job even when double-teamed, and, sometimes, triple-teamed.

Receivers

The finest receivers were almost all able to run well with the ball after they caught it. Many ran as well as the best runners. This is the way the receivers accumulated yardage and broke loose for touchdowns. Many long passing gains are more run than just pass. Most of the great receivers could consistently catch and run the long ball for the scores that break up games, but a few were better short-yardage, first-down guys, and these were of value, too.

The best receivers did not make many mistakes. Everyone drops one here and there, but the most outstanding dropped fewer than others and seldom dropped an important one. Once they caught the ball, they did not drop it. They did not fumble often, even when hit hard, and no one gets hit harder than receivers in certain circumstances. A thing that may not often be noticed or taken into account is that the smart receiver knows when to bat the ball down to spoil an interception.

And while many may not make much of it, in my mind blocking is an important quality in a standout receiver. Many are frail and some coaches do not require a lot of blocking by them, but in my mind it is a wonderful asset if a receiver plays the entire game and sacrifices himself by acting as a decoy or by blocking when it will help the other receivers or the runners.

Blocking is required of tight ends and was critical in my evaluation of them. I have listed them separately at the end of my listing of the best receivers. Tight ends are primarily blockers and short-yardage receivers, and I think they have to be considered separately from the other receivers. But most of the same qualities that separate the finest receivers from the rest separate the greatest tight ends from the rest. While development of the tight-end position is a relatively recent one in football, certain players filled a similar role in years past, so there have been some strong candidates from the past.

I took into consideration that passers threw less in the early days, so a receiver caught less often. Another thing: New rules of the last couple of years free receivers from a lot of the punishment and interference they had to deal with in the past. Because of this it is easier for receivers to do outstanding jobs and harder for defensive backs to do their jobs, and I had to consider this.

You used to be able to use your hands in rushing the passer, but you can't do that much anymore. The defensive player no longer can slap the helmet of the receiver to knock him off stride. All contact between receiver and defender beyond five yards past the line of scrimmage has been eliminated. It is getting to be a lot easier to catch the ball and to catch the long ball. I hate to see long gains set up by incidental, perhaps uncertain, contact downfield. It happens too much to suit me.

Here, then, are those receivers I rank among the 100 finest professional football players I've ever seen.

1.
Don Hutson

Don Hutson was a unique performer whose awesome pass-catching abilities changed the face of pro football. Even now, 37 years after he retired, his name appears throughout the pass-receiving section of the NFL record book. And it figures to be there for a long time to come.

Hutson came out of the University of Alabama, joining the Green Bay Packers in 1935. He had only average size at 6-1 and 180 pounds, but he possessed lightning speed and was clocked at 9.5 seconds for the 100-yard dash. He also was an imaginative player and is credited with being the first receiver to run what we know today as pass patterns. In Hutson's day, ends lined up tight to the line, without the room to maneuver they enjoy today. So Hutson innovated. One time he reversed his direction on a pattern by grabbing the goalpost with his arm while in full stride.

Hutson's first reception as a pro was a 60-yard touchdown bomb and it set the pattern for his brilliant career. He is one of only three men in history to score more than 100 TDs, and his total of 105 include a record 99 through the air. That's 11 more than the next-best scoring total for a receiver.

Hutson led the NFL in scoring for a record five consecutive seasons from 1940 to 1944 and led the league in touchdowns eight times. No other player has led in TDs more than three times. He was the pass-receiving leader eight times, three more than anybody else has managed. There were a record five straight years as the receiving leader from 1941 to 1945.

Hutson's finest season was 1942, when he set a record by scoring 17 touchdowns. He caught 74 passes that season and became the first NFL receiver to top 1,000 yards, gaining 1,211. There were 14 catches in one game and 13 in another. Hutson accounted for 138 points that year, setting a record that stood for 18 years.

Hutson caught passes in 95 consecutive games, a feat that remained a record for three decades. He scored in 42 consecutive games, was a three-time MVP selection, and a charter member of the Pro Football Hall of Fame (1963).

Also for his career, Hutson caught 488 passes for 7,991 yards, a 16.4 average.

Americans are bigger and faster than they used to be. Athletes are larger, yet more agile. The breed is being improved. It is only reasonable that there have been more outstanding athletes in football in recent years than in earlier years. But a great athlete can come along at any time. And,

Don Hutson

although I did not see him play as often as I would have liked to, I don't think there is any doubt but that Don Hutson was the greatest receiver ever.

Hutson was the pioneer pass catcher. He blazed the trails over which others have followed. He had sprinter's speed, but also improvised moves and devised patterns that have been copied ever since. As much as Sammy Baugh did, Don Hutson turned modern football into as much a passing game as a running game. He was enormously intelligent, talented, and resourceful. And he was fortunate to have had a passer like Arnie Herber to team up with in those days.

When I think of Hutson I think of his fluidity. He just seemed to flow across a football field. He was slender and wore very few pads so as to be loose. His body was very limber and he had quick feet and sure hands. No defensive back of his day could keep up with him and if the ball was within his reach he caught it. And when he caught it he ran with it like a great runner.

Because he was so unique Don was double-teamed and triple-teamed, but he couldn't be contained then and I doubt that he could be contained if he were in his prime today. He was so special-looking in the things he did out on the field that I think you would not have to know much about football to have picked him out in the crowd. He was a great third-down and late-game pass receiver, dazzling in the end zone, at his best in the clutch.

He was good long and good short. Even though the modern passing game developed dramatically, it took years for others to surpass some records he set in the early days. He was a good all-around athlete. He was a superb place-kicker. Despite his lack of weight, he played a pretty good defensive end for some years and wound up a fine free safety, with, naturally, a nose for the ball.

2.
Lenny Moore

Lenny Moore came out of Penn State University as a lanky running back, and pro football scouts weren't sure his sparse frame could stand the punishment inflicted in the NFL. The Baltimore Colts gambled, making Moore their first-round choice in the 1956 draft. It was a selection they never regretted.

Moore proved to be a capable running back, gaining 5,174 yards in a dozen pro seasons. But it was at flanker back that his full pro potential was realized. He was an electrifying pass catcher, grabbing 363 aerials for 6,039 yards, an average of 16.6 yards per reception.

Combining with legendary quarterback, Johnny Unitas, Moore set an NFL record, scoring touchdowns in 18 consecutive games from 1963 to 1965. That's four more than anybody else ever managed.

The 6-1, 198-pound Moore scored 63 touchdowns on the ground and caught 48 passes for TDs. Add two more on kickoff returns and his career total of 113 visits to pay dirt is the second highest in history, trailing only Jim Brown's 126. Moore's most productive season was 1964, when he led the league with 20 touchdowns.

Lined up outside, Moore wrought havoc in defensive backfields as defenders tried to cover him. In his third season, 1958, the Colts won the NFL title, beating the New York Giants in the famous overtime game. Moore caught six passes for 101 yards in that contest. He was selected as an All-Pro for the first time that season, producing 1,633 combined yards, 938 of those on pass receptions. He also scored 14 TDs.

There were four more All-Pro selections and seven trips to the Pro Bowl for him.

Injuries slowed Moore in the early 1960s. There was a cracked kneecap that cost him four games in 1962 and an appendectomy at the start of the season and a head injury at the end of the year that sidelined him for seven games in 1963. But Moore bounced back to play four more years, leading the league in scoring in 1964 and continuing his march into the Pro Football Hall of Fame (1975).

Lenny Moore (#24)

With the exception of quarterbacks, Lenny Moore may have beaten my teams more than any other player I ever coached against. He was one of the most explosive players ever and almost impossible to contain for a full game. Others may have caught more passes, but no one caught more clutch passes. Lenny was a long-gain guy and extremely elusive in the end zone. He and Johnny Unitas were a wonderful touchdown combination.

Moore may have been the best combination receiver-runner pro football has had. Although frail-looking, he was tough and durable. He originally was a running back and an outstanding one. He gained almost as many yards as a running back as he did as a receiver, and his total yardage is among the highest ever. But he attained true greatness as a receiver, often, of course, running his catches brilliantly.

Moore was spectacular. Actually, he had kind of an effortless motion. He seemed to glide along, and often it looked like he wasn't moving too fast. Then, seemingly without effort, he'd shift gears and just pull away from the players covering him. He changed speeds as well as any player I've ever seen, and that made him very difficult to tackle. He ran with a wide base and high knee action and he broke a lot of tackles.

Lenny had marvelous moves, a feel for the open area, sure hands, and great concentration. He was always under control. He could make the most difficult catches imaginable, and when he caught the ball he really became dangerous.

3.
Elroy (Crazylegs) Hirsch

They called him "Crazylegs" because few players had ever displayed the kinds of moves Elroy Hirsch did when he caught the football. And Crazylegs Hirsch caught his share of footballs in 12 professional seasons.

After gaining All-America status playing at Wisconsin and Michigan, Hirsch joined the Chicago Rockets of the old All-America Conference in 1946. He chose the Rockets over the Los Angeles Rams because the Rockets were coached by Dick Hanley, for whom Hirsch had played while serving in the Marines. After three seasons in the AAC, Hirsch moved to the NFL with the Rams and established his Hall of Fame credentials, staying with them for nine brilliant seasons.

He established a record for receivers by catching scoring passes in 11 consecutive games in 1950–51 after becoming one of the first backs to make the transition to flanker. He scored 17 TDs in 1951, tying the record set by Don Hutson, and compiled a string of nine straight games in which he gained 100 or more yards receiving. For that season, Crazylegs grabbed 66 passes for 1,495 yards, an average of 22.7 per catch, all league-leading totals.

In nine seasons with the Rams, the 6-2, 190-pound Hirsch caught 343 passes for 6,299 yards and 53 TDs. Add to those totals 44 catches for 730 yards and seven TDs with the Rockets and his pro career statistics mushroom to 387 receptions for 7,029 yards and 60 TDs.

After retiring as a player in 1957, Hirsch became general manager of the Rams, succeeding Pete Rozelle, who left the job to become commissioner of the NFL. Later, Hirsch returned to Wisconsin, serving as director of athletics at the Big Ten school. He also had a brief fling in Hollywood, starring in three movies, including the title role in his biography. In 1969, he was selected as the flanker on the NFL's half-century team, a year after being inducted into the Pro Football Hall of Fame.

Elroy Hirsch was the greatest long-gain receiver who ever played the game. He had good height and long arms. He had great quickness, tremendous speed, great moves, and a knack for getting open deep. Once he caught the ball downfield, he was gone. His average of more than 18 yards a catch is among the highest ever. When he saw the end zone, he went for it with a true killer instinct.

Hirsch was a lot like Lenny Moore in that Hirsch was a converted halfback and one of the three or four greatest receiver-runners. But Elroy

Elroy "Crazylegs" Hirsch

ran very little from halfback in the NFL. He had been a fine halfback, but he suffered so many injuries, especially head injuries, that Clark Shaughnessy, then the coach of the Rams, put him outside as a receiver so Elroy didn't have to run through the line.

All during his career Hirsch came back from severe injuries, and it is remarkable he lasted as long as he did and accomplished as much as he did. I really admired his courage and competitive instinct. His love of football showed in the way he played the game. He was a very colorful performer. When you tried to tackle him, his legs were like limp spaghetti, and you couldn't get a hold on him.

As Don Hutson needed Arnie Herber, Elroy Hirsch and Tom Fears needed Norm Van Brocklin and Bob Waterfield to do what they did best. Seldom has one team combined such great passers and receivers, and the Rams of the late 1940s and early 1950s really opened up pro football, making the "long bomb" a standard part of offensive football for the first time.

As long as I live I will remember Crazylegs Hirsch in full flight speeding downfield, catching a pass over his shoulder without breaking stride, and speeding into the end zone. He was unsurpassed in big-play football.

4.
Charley Taylor

No man in the history of the NFL caught more passes in his career than the 649 gathered in by Charley Taylor over 13 seasons with the Washington Redskins. Not bad for a guy who came into the pros as a running back.

Taylor was an All-America ball carrier at Arizona State when the Redskins made him their No. 1 draft choice in 1964. He carried the ball for a couple of years but by 1966 he had become one of the league's best pass receivers. He led the NFL with 72 receptions for 1,119 yards that season and was permanently switched outside to the flanker position after that. He led the league again in 1967, catching 70 for 990 yards.

Taylor caught 50 or more passes in a season a record-tying seven times and gained 9,110 yards through the air. He holds 10 Redskin club records and was selected for the Pro Bowl eight times.

Overall, Taylor scored 90 touchdowns (sixth on the all-time list) and accounted for 10,833 total yards. As a pass catcher only, he scored 79 TDs.

The Redskins got the idea that Taylor's future might be as a flanker in his very first NFL season. He was picked as the rookie of the year when he set a record for a running back by catching 53 passes. The mark has been broken frequently since then, but when Taylor did it, it was a novelty to have a running back used as a receiver. He perfected the craft in a hurry and became a potent weapon in Washington's attack.

An injury sidelined the 6-3, 210-pound Taylor for the entire 1976 season, but he returned for one final fling in 1977 before retiring and moving into the front office as a personnel scout. He remains one of the most popular players in Washington Redskin history.

I have bent over backward not to be prejudiced in my selections, but a few players I coached clearly are among the 100 finest professional football players ever. Of course, others coached them, too. I don't take credit for their success. They, as much as anyone, made me successful. And Charley Taylor is one of them. He was clearly one of the best receivers ever.

Charley was another superb receiver-runner, who started out as a running back and became a standout receiver. He was one of the first running backs to be used regularly as a receiver and he was so good at it that he was converted into a full-time receiver.

Charley was a wonderful athlete. I don't think he was too fast. I never timed my receivers. Maybe they time kids in high school or college when they're trying to find the best position for them to play, but by the time they get to the pros they either can do the job or they can't. Charley could do a job—several jobs, in fact. He was a big, strong guy and easily could have been an outstanding tight end. He was a tremendous blocker. I can remember blocks when he destroyed opposing players. He was agile enough to be a great defensive back. I used to kid him that I was going to use him in my nickel defense.

Charley was very disciplined, had good moves, and ran perfect routes. He could catch the ball long or short. He could make the tough catch over the middle. He had sure hands and could catch the ball one-handed. The way they throw the ball around these days it won't last too long, but Taylor holds the record for the most catches ever. I was coaching him when he set the record and it was a thrill for me. I made him my captain because he had a tremendously positive attitude and great leadership qualities.

Since Charley some have developed who came very close to making my list. Fred Biletnikoff was small and slow but sure-handed, tremendous on the short throws, and a winner. Harold Jackson was small but fast and has made a lot of catches, many for long gains. Drew Pearson has been terrific, especially in the clutch. Harold Carmichael, a rare receiver at 6-8, has been incredibly consistent. Lynn Swann came closest of all to making my list. Fast, agile, acrobatic, and a tremendous pressure player, he had a lot to do with Pittsburgh's long stretch of success in the 1970s.

Unfortunately, they couldn't all make it.

Charley Taylor (#42)

5.
Raymond Berry

Pro scouts weren't too impressed with Raymond Berry's ability when he came out of Southern Methodist University. He was selected in the twentieth round of the 1955 NFL draft by the Baltimore Colts, picked almost as an afterthought. But Berry brought dedication to the NFL and, when he retired in 1967, he was the leading receiver in NFL history with 631 receptions for 9,275 yards and 68 touchdowns.

Berry, at 6-2 and 187 pounds, was a glutton for practice, working long and hard at perfecting the timing required for the sideline pass. He became an expert at the maneuver and in the memorable 1958 overtime championship game against the New York Giants, he caught 12 passes, setting a title-game record. Three of those catches—all against double coverage—came in the Colts' desperate march to the tying field goal. Berry caught two more in the overtime period before Baltimore scored the winning touchdown.

For three straight seasons, 1958—60, Berry led the NFL in receiving, catching 196 passes for 3,051 yards and 33 touchdowns over that stretch. The next season, 1961, he surrendered the league receiving championship but did set a single-season personal career high with 75 catches.

Berry said he had a repertoire of 88 maneuvers for getting around defenders and reaching the football, and he believed in practicing all 88 every week in practice. That's why he often was the last man to leave the field.

Berry played for 13 seasons and now stands third on the all-time receptions list, trailing only Charley Taylor (649) and Don Maynard (633). Berry shares the record of seven seasons with 50 or more receptions with Taylor, Lance Alworth, and Art Powell and is a member of the Pro Football Hall of Fame (1973).

When I think of Raymond Berry, I think of first downs. Raymond Berry was the finest first-down receiver in the history of football as I've known it. He did not have the speed to get loose and go long downfield. He did not run very well with the ball. But he had the moves to get open in a small area as has no other player I ever saw. And he could catch anything thrown anywhere near him.

Berry made incredible catches. He made catches in crowds—with defenders hanging all over him. And he almost never dropped a ball he got his hands on. He was a singles hitter, who moved men around on the bases. But his particular talent also made him exceptionally effective in the end zone, so he caught a lot of touchdown passes. You need this kind of short-gain receiver as much as you need the long-gain guy.

Raymond Berry—and everyone always called him Raymond, rather than Ray—beat me with Baltimore almost as much as Johnny Unitas did. They were a terrific combination and carried the Colts. They were an almost unbeatable ball-control combination. They practiced to perfection the short pass, especially the all-important sidelines pass that conserves time during the two-minute drill. I was told Berry used to ask Unitas to throw him bad passes so he could practice the difficult catch until Unitas protested that the practice was affecting his accuracy. I was also told Berry used to have his wife throw to him so he could practice away from the field. It didn't matter if she didn't throw well, because Berry could then practice catching those bad passes.

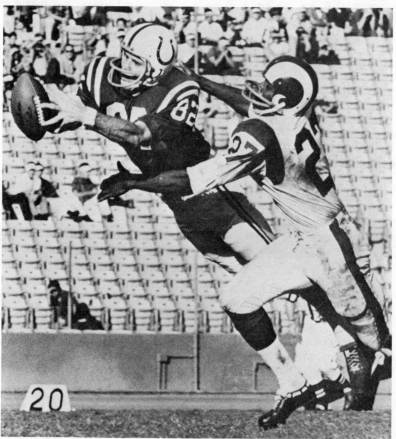

Raymond Berry (#82)

I coached Berry once in a Pro Bowl game and found him as disciplined a player as I ever knew. He took a projector and films to his room to study. He went to bed early so he got his rest. He stayed on the practice field longer than others. He took the Pro Bowl game as seriously as he would have a Super Bowl game. I never coached anyone who looked less like a football player. He wore contact lenses and couldn't even see very well. He didn't have very good physical tools. I guess he worked harder than others to make himself better than others. It doesn't matter how he got there, he got an important job done better than any player who ever played his position and he became one of the great ones.

Lionel Taylor, Billy Howton, and Boyd Dowler were among other receiving greats of the 1960s, but none of them accomplished what Raymond Berry did.

6.
Tom Fears

When Tom Fears was selected by the Los Angeles Rams in the eleventh round of the 1948 college draft, he was projected as a defensive specialist. He had gained that reputation at Santa Clara and UCLA and in his first pro game, he intercepted two passes. That's not a bad start, but the Rams decided to try him on offense and it was there that Fears established himself as a Hall of Fame receiver.

Fears went on to catch 51 passes for 698 yards that season, becoming the first rookie to lead the league in receiving. What's more, he won the title the next two years as well, soaring over 1,000 yards each time. He was the first player in history to win the receiving crown in each of his first three seasons.

That string reached its zenith in 1950, when Fears caught 84 passes, setting a record that lasted for a decade. Included was a record 18 receptions in a single game against Green Bay on December 3, 1950. Two weeks after that, Los Angeles defeated Chicago for the NFL's Western Division championship, 24–14, and Fears scored all of the Ram touchdowns on pass plays that covered 43, 68, and 27 yards. He set a divisional playoff record that day with seven catches for 198 yards. The next year, the Rams won their first NFL championship, beating Cleveland, 24–17, with Fears scoring the winning touchdown on a 73-yard pass play.

In nine seasons as a pro, all with the Rams, the 6-2, 215-pound Fears caught 400 passes for 5,397 yards and 38 TDs. He retired after the 1956 campaign and went into coaching, including a short stint as boss of the New Orleans Saints. He was named to the Pro Football Hall of Fame in 1970.

Tom Fears

Tom Fears was another great first-down receiver. Or third-down receiver. It depends on how you want to look at it. He was great in the clutch. He must have caught as many passes in the last five minutes of a game as any player ever. He was slower than his teammate Elroy Hirsch but a lot faster than Raymond Berry. Berry was the best at the short catch. Hirsch ran better. But Fears could get downfield and get open and catch the home-run balls that Bob Waterfield or Norm Van Brocklin threw for the Rams almost as well as Hirsch could.

When I think of Fears, I think of finesse. He made a science of developing and mastering pass routes. He was a pioneer from whom other receivers learned. He worked out his moves until he could not be well covered. You couldn't effectively double-team both him and Hirsch. Fears had sure hands and complete concentration. I used to tell my receivers to look at films of Fears and look at his eyes and see how he "looked" the ball into his hands. He set records for catches in one game and one season, and kept making an extraordinary number of pass receptions season after season. He was extremely consistent and durable.

Although he did not have sprinter's speed, he was fast for a man his size. He was a great blocker. He could have been a great tight end. But he was too valuable getting a step on the defender and going deep. Although he originally was a defensive back, not a running back, he was a strong runner and broke tackles. He caught a lot of short passes and ran well with them. And he performed superbly under pressure.

7.
Paul Warfield

Paul Warfield was a product of Ohio State and was the Cleveland Browns' No. 1 draft choice in 1964. His ability to make moves at top speed made him a devastating part of the Browns' air game and in his first five full seasons at Cleveland he never gained less than 700 yards through the air.

In 1970, the Browns decided to trade Warfield to Miami to get a first-round draft choice. There were five more brilliant seasons with the Dolphins, with Warfield's consistency producing more than 500 yards a year.

Then, in 1975, the 6-foot, 188-pound Warfield left Miami and joined star running backs Larry Csonka and Jim Kiick in a surprise move to the Memphis Southmen of the fledgling World Football League. The WFL was doomed to failure and after one year, Warfield returned to his NFL roots, signing as a free agent with the Browns for two final seasons.

Warfield's finest year was 1968, when he caught 50 passes for 1,067 yards and a league-leading 12 touchdowns. He also led the league with 11 TDs in 1971, and for his career he caught 85 scoring passes, tied with Lance Alworth for third best in NFL history, behind only Don Hutson's 99 and Don Maynard's 88. That total, of course, does not include the three TD passes Warfield caught in his one WFL season.

Paul Warfield

Warfield finished his NFL career with 427 catches for 8,565 yards. His 86 total TDs (he scored one on a recovered fumble) placed him tenth on the all-time list. And when Paul retired in 1977, he was fourth on the all-time yardage list behind Maynard, Raymond Berry, and Alworth. Warfield was selected for seven Pro Bowl games.

Paul Warfield was a receiver you had to double-team. This is as good a way to describe this type of receiver as any other—a double-team guy. You did it as much to discourage the passer from throwing to him as you did to contain him, because it was extraordinarily difficult to contain him. He didn't catch a lot of balls in a game, but he did a lot with the ones he caught. He was very explosive, and he was dangerous at all times.

That is reflected in his record. He played in the NFL 13 years and he's the only guy who ever averaged 20 or more yards a catch. Talk about your home-run hitters! Bobby Mitchell was a lot like him. But I think of Mitchell more as a running back. Also Tommy McDonald. Great home-run hitters. If it had been easy to find places for them on my final list I'd have done it. Some fine players had to be left off.

Bob Hayes was another explosive player, probably the fastest man ever to play football. He was a world-champion sprinter. Other world-class sprinters have tried to play football, usually as receivers, but couldn't make it. Hayes came the closest to making it as an all-timer. He was bigger and stronger than most great sprinters, he had good hands, and he developed as a very good receiver. But not truly great.

Warfield was great. He was outstanding with both Cleveland and Miami. With Washington, I had to coach against him in a Super Bowl game. We double-teamed and triple-teamed him. And we contained him. But at a cost. Containing him made it a close game for us against a superior team, but loosened our defense just enough for the Dolphins to defeat us.

He had sprinter's speed, good hands, super running ability. And boy, could he block! Some people may not remember that about him, but I do. The receivers who didn't block never got good grades from me. In my book, Warfield was strictly A-plus.

8.
Lance Alworth

They called him "Bambi" and somehow the nickname and the image of a young deer running free seemed to fit Lance Alworth perfectly. Attacking pro football secondaries as one of the game's greatest pass receivers, Alworth had the grace and speed one imagines in a fawn.

Alworth enjoyed 11 brilliant seasons, catching 542 passes for 10,266

Lance Alworth

yards. He averaged a shade under 19 yards per catch and scored 85 touchdowns, tied for third on the all-time list with Paul Warfield and trailing only Don Hutson (99) and Don Maynard (88).

Alworth's yardage total was second only to Maynard's 11,834. Alworth had 41 100-yard games, also second only to Maynard's 50. Alworth had five straight 100-yard receiving games in 1966 with San Diego—two short of the record—and eight 100-yard games in 1967—also two short of the record.

In 1965, the 6-foot, 184-pound Alworth gained 1,602 yards, the second-largest single-season production in history, trailing only the 1,746 by Charley Hennigan in 1961. And Alworth shares with Raymond Berry, Art Powell, and Charley Taylor the record for seven seasons with 50 or more receptions.

Alworth led the league in receptions three times, and his seven 1,000-yard seasons are still another record. He led the league in touchdowns three times and in 1963 scored TDs in nine consecutive games, just two short of the record shared by Elroy ("Crazylegs") Hirsch and Buddy Dial.

All of these accomplishments are impressive, of course, but the one Alworth probably cherishes most has nothing to do with cold, hard numbers. In 1978 he became the first original AFL player elected to the Pro Football Hall of Fame.

Alworth came out of Arkansas and signed with San Diego in 1962. He played nine years with the Chargers followed by two with Dallas.

Until the merger in 1966, the AFL was considered pro football's poor relation and its players, especially stars such as Alworth, bristled under the second-class-citizenship label. But there was no denial of his abilities, and official recognition came when he was named to the Hall in his first year of eligibility.

Lance Alworth was as fine a player to watch on the field as any I've ever seen. He was graceful, fast, and fluid. He was not big or strong, but he was extremely elusive. He got open, caught the ball, and went with it. A few others caught more balls, but few did as well with the ones they caught.

Lance was an American Football League player, largely responsible for San Diego's early success in that league. A lot of people put him and other AFL players down. It was a high-scoring league. There was more offense than defense. It was not nearly as good a league as the National Football League. There were not nearly as many good teams in the AFL as in the NFL. But the better teams in the AFL that came into the NFL did well there. And so did the better AFL players.

There were some standout players in the old AFL and they compare favorably with the great players of the NFL. Lance Alworth was one. Don Maynard was another. Lance Alworth and Don Maynard were the two greatest receivers produced in the AFL. Charley Hennigan and Art Powell were excellent receivers from the AFL who did not quite make my list. Mac Speedie and Dante Lavelli were fine receivers from the old All-America Conference who also did not quite make it. But they came close.

9.
Don Maynard

No player in the history of professional football gained more yards through the air than lanky Don Maynard. Maynard finished his career with 11,834 yards over 15 years. At the beginning there was one season with the New York Giants, another in Canada, and another at the end with the St. Louis Cardinals. But the bulk of Maynard's pro career was spent with the New York Jets. In fact, he was the first player signed by the franchise in 1960, when it was founded as the New York Titans.

Maynard was a product of Texas Western, where he was a raw-boned flanker. As an ex-Giant, he gave New York's new pro franchise an instant identity and he flourished in the pass-happy AFL. It was the start of a record-smashing career in New York for the rangy player, who wasn't the fastest man on the field but somehow managed to get free and catch passes.

Don Maynard

For his career, the 6-1, 185-pound Maynard caught 633 aerials—second on the all-time list to Charley Taylor's 649. Of his total, 627 of Maynard's catches came as a member of the Titans or Jets. He was one of the team's most popular players, especially after teaming with Joe Namath to give the Jets a devastating pass-catch combination.

Like running backs, receivers measure their games and seasons by yardage plateaus—100 yards for a game, 1,000 yards for a season. Maynard had a record 50 games in which he gained 100 yards or more. That's nine more than any other receiver in history. And Maynard had five 1,000-yard seasons, tying him with Art Powell for second place on the all-time list. Only Lance Alworth, with seven, had more.

Maynard caught 88 touchdown passes in his career, second only to Don Hutson's 99.

Despite all of his impressive statistics, Maynard never won an individual season receiving championship. It was one of the very few honors Don failed to achieve.

Don Maynard wasn't as impressive as some of the receivers on my list. He was not very big for a receiver. He was fast, but not as fast as some, I think. Others seemed to have better moves. But Don was cute. He got open, caught the ball, and sneaked away with it. I don't know how he did it, but he just kept getting open and catching pass after pass and piling up the yardage. He made the difficult catch, he caught the ball in a crowd, and he caught for touchdowns. He was consistent and he came through in the clutch.

Maynard may have been the most consistent of the modern receivers. He contributed a lot to Joe Namath's success. Coaches make mistakes on players. You try to make as few as possible. But it is possible for a player to be cut by one pro team and come back to become an immortal with another. Sometimes you look too much at a player's size and speed and things like that and think that he can't make it. I like to think I would not have cut Don Maynard because I try just to look at the job a player can do for me. Players like Don Maynard and Raymond Berry had determination and desire, and these attributes helped land them on the list of the great players.

10.
Bill Hewitt

Bill Hewitt was one of the best two-way players ever to perform in the NFL, a glue-fingered receiver on offense and a hard-charging end on defense. The remarkable part of his football accomplishments is that until his eighth season, when the league made it mandatory, he refused to wear a helmet. Hewitt felt it handicapped his play and, in the years when a helmet was not required, he lined up bareheaded.

On defense, Hewitt got such a quick jump off the ball that he often beat the play, making the tackle before it could develop. Opponents called him "the Offside Kid," but officials didn't call him for many infractions. He wasn't offside, he was just quick.

Hewitt played his college football at Michigan and, at 5-11 and 191 pounds, he was hardly an awesome-looking player. But he blossomed when he reached the Chicago Bears in 1932. He was named to the All-Pro team in three of his five seasons with the Bears beginning in 1933, when he helped Chicago win the NFL championship. In 1936 he played virtually 60 minutes a game because injuries had thinned the ranks of the club. After that season he decided to retire, but when Chicago traded his contract to Philadelphia, Eagles owner Bert Bell lured him back to the game. Again he was named to the All-Pro team, becoming the first player in history to win that honor with two different clubs. He spent three seasons with Philadelphia and one wrap-up year, in 1943, with the wartime combined Philadelphia-Pittsburgh franchise.

An innovative performer, Hewitt was famous for devising a forward-lateral play that helped the Bears beat the New York Giants, 23—21, in 1933 in the first NFL championship game. Chicago was trailing, 21—16, late in the game and had driven to New York's 36-yard line, mostly on plunges by Bronko Nagurski. On the next play, Nagurski started toward the Giant linemen again. This time, though, he stopped short and lobbed a pass to Hewitt, just beyond the New York defense. Hewitt gained 14 yards and then scooped the ball to Bill Karr, who went in for the winning touchdown.

The play, which Hewitt invented on the spur of the moment and which was later declared illegal as an offensive weapon in the NFL, became his trademark and was used for his mural when he was inducted into the Pro Football Hall of Fame in 1971.

As a receiver, Hewitt's career statistics include 101 receptions for 1,606 yards and 31 touchdowns.

Bill Hewitt

There have been as many standout players at the receiving position as at any. Accordingly, a lot of them had to be left off my list of great players. I've mentioned many. And many others played in the early years when so few teams passed a lot it was impossible for receivers to prove with statistics how good they were.

Among these were Red Badgro, Wayne Millner, Gaynell Tinsley, Jim Benton, and Ken Kavanaugh. I saw most of them in person, others on films. I have heard about them so much I feel like their greatness goes beyond dispute. But some came along too early for their real skills and there is no way I felt I could place them on my list.

However, one or two cannot be left off. One is Don Hutson, who was ahead of his time and the best of all time. Another is Bill Hewitt, who I feel has to be listed with the best. The real question with Hewitt is whether he should be listed with the best defensive ends or the best offensive ends. He belongs with the best of either list. I have put him on offense because he was so far ahead of his time there.

I saw Hewitt play and I never will forget it. He played that day without a helmet and with few if any pads. Others were wearing helmets and pads. It was a cold day and his face was reddened and scratched up. He wasn't too big, but he was tough. He'd drive right through blockers to get to the ball carrier, and he never seemed to miss a tackle. He'd dive into pileups and come up with the ball. He blocked for runners fiercely. And when the ball was thrown it was to him and he'd catch it and break tackles and run away from people. I was a young boy, but I could see he was among the best players I'd ever seen. And later, when I saw old films, I saw his greatness over and over again, unclear as those films were. His reputation backs up everything I saw.

THE
TIGHT ENDS

1.
Pete Pihos

One would expect a player honored with membership in the Pro Football Hall of Fame to have had his share of All-Pro team selections. That's normal. The unusual aspect of Pete Pihos' All-Pro career was that he was named to the team on both the offensive and defensive platoons.

Pihos was another classic two-way player, performing at tight end when Philadelphia was on the attack and at defensive end when opposing teams had the ball. It was a remarkable juggling of assignments and Pihos handled it with aplomb. There were times when he played the full 60 minutes of a game. In 1948 and 1949 he made All-Pro as a tight end, catching 46 passes for 766 yards the first year and 34 for 484 the next. But in 1952, the Eagles played him most often on defense. His reception total fell to 12 passes for 219 yards, but he was an All-Pro choice once more, this time on defense.

When Philadelphia switched Pihos back to offense the next year, he started a string of three straight pass-receiving titles, leading the league in his specialty in each of his last three pro seasons. He enjoyed his finest season in 1953, celebrating a full-time return to offense with 63 catches for 1,049 yards. He caught 60 for 872 in 1954 and 62 for 864 in 1955, his final season as a pro. In each year he again won All-Pro honors.

Pete Pihos

Drafted by the Eagles in 1945, the 6-1, 210-pound Pihos first completed his military service obligation and earned his degree at Indiana before turning pro in 1947.

In his nine years, Pihos caught 373 passes for 5,619 yards and 61 TDs. He played in each of the first six Pro Bowl games and at the end of the 1955 season, playing in his final professional game, he caught a 12-yard TD pass, helping the East stars beat the West, 31—30.

Pete Pihos was the first great tight end. He didn't go deep very often, but he made the short catch, especially over the middle, very well, and he was a brilliant, brutal blocker.

Pihos was a fine all-around athlete. He was one of the last to play both offense and defense. He was one of the last of the 60-minute players. He also was a very good running back and an effective fullback. But he was a standout offensive end with sure hands who made more catches than anyone else in his prime.

He was no giant, but he was big enough. He was no sprinter, but he was fast enough. He was extremely tough and durable and determined, and he seemed to me an exceptionally smart player. He was the kind of player coaches like me wanted to captain their clubs. He never gave an opponent anything. Everyone wants to win, but few will sacrifice everything to do it. I got the impression Pete would do almost anything to win, and I really respected him for that.

2.
Mike Ditka

When Mike Ditka came out of the University of Pittsburgh in 1961, he was a consensus All-American, the prototype of an NFL tight end. The Chicago Bears made him their first-round draft selection and he paid immediate dividends.

Very few rookies have enjoyed as brilliant a first season as Ditka did in 1961. He caught 56 passes for 1,076 yards and 12 touchdowns. It was the beginning of an outstanding 12-year professional career and, although Ditka had seasons in which he caught more passes, he never cracked the 1,000-yard barrier again. That's a plateau usually reserved for long-range receivers, not tight ends, who must combine blocking ability with their pass catching and thus concentrate on shorter-yardage plays.

For the next three seasons, Ditka was an All-Pro performer for the Bears. He was selected for five straight Pro Bowl games from 1962 through 1966. For his three All-Pro years, he totaled 192 catches, an average of 64 per year.

In 1967, the Bears dealt Ditka to Philadelphia in exchange for quarterback Jack Concannon, and after two seasons with the Eagles, the tight end moved on to Dallas, where he spent the final four seasons of his pro career.

The 6-3, 225-pound Ditka retired as a player following the 1972 season and went out in style. His final game was Super Bowl VI, in which the Cowboys defeated Miami, 24–3, and he scored the game's last touchdown on a seven-yard pass from Roger Staubach. It was the perfect ending to a standout professional career.

For his 12 years with the Bears, Eagles, and Cowboys, Ditka caught 427 passes and gained 5,812 yards, scoring 46 touchdowns. After retiring as a player, Ditka remained with Dallas, coaching special teams and tight ends for head coach Tom Landry before being named the Bears' head coach in January 1982. With Dallas he was credited with the development of three outstanding Cowboy receivers—Drew Pearson, Tony Hill, and Billy Joe Dupree. All of them, like Ditka, became Pro Bowl selections.

After they started to seek out a certain type of player to do a certain type of receiving job, catching the short third-down or first-down pass and blocking, the position became known as tight end. Mike Ditka was among the first outstanding players to be placed in that spot. In my mind he remains one of the two or three best ever to play it.

I was in charge of drafting for the Bears when I drafted him for the team. He hadn't caught a lot of passes in college, but I thought he might make a perfect tight end—and I was right. Almost from the start he was better than others at the position.

He was an excellent blocker; he seldom missed. He was an excellent receiver; he seldom missed. He was big and very strong and extremely difficult to bring down. He broke tackles and ran over people.

I remember one time Ditka made an unbelievable catch and run against Pittsburgh, breaking tackles for a touchdown that helped us toward the league championship we won that year, 1963.

After I left, the Bears traded him to Philadelphia, and then he was traded to Dallas. I had to coach against him quite a few years and he was always, even in his last years, someone you had to defense carefully and work on very hard or he would hurt you badly.

He was very good for many years, always consistent and competitive. He modeled the tight-end position, really, and it hasn't changed much. You just couldn't do much more with it than Ditka did.

Mike Ditka (#89)

3.
John Mackey

In 1970, the National Football League celebrated the fiftieth anniversary of pro football and decided to select an all-time team. The tight end was John Mackey, a bull of man who came off the campus of Syracuse University and emerged as a walking textbook on that position.

Mackey played for 10 seasons in the NFL, 1963–1972, nine of them with the Baltimore Colts and one final wrap-up year with San Diego. He caught 331 passes for 5,238 yards (a 15.8-yard average) and 39 touchdowns, impressive statistics. But figures can't measure the power Mackey packed once he grabbed the football and started downfield. After watching one of Mackey's typical bull-like gallops through an opponent's secondary, Colts' receiver coach Dick Bielski said, "The lucky ones fall off." The others simply got dragged along.

Mackey's career was shortened by knee surgery that robbed him of some of the churning power that had marked his performances. It was that power, the sure hands and superior blocking talent that made Mackey a five-time Pro Bowl game selection and a perennial All-Pro. He had perfect tight-end size—6-2, 224 pounds—and he knew how to use it.

Ironically, Mackey is remembered almost as well in NFL circles for his off-the-field accomplishments as he is for the catches he made and the touchdowns he scored. He was elected president of the fledgling NFL Players' Association in 1970 and it was his suit that destroyed the Rozelle Rule, a compensation clause that the players claimed was an unreasonable restraint of a player's right to bargain freely with another club for his services.

The court action challenged the NFL establishment, and Mackey's victory was a landmark in management-labor relations. The case formed the cornerstone for dealings between the league and the union for many years, and Mackey is still hailed by many of the current leaders of the Players' Association.

Next to Mike Ditka, John Mackey was the best of the tight ends of recent years and one of the finest all-around receivers of all time. He was the tall type of tight end they've come up with in recent years. I don't know where they find these big guys with great strength and good speed, but Mackey is the prototype. He could catch a six-yard pass and run 60 yards with it, just bowling over opponents. His average of almost 16 yards a catch is the highest for any tight end over any period of time. He was one of the great blockers, giving his team an extra tackle on running plays.

John Mackey

Great athletes are coming into the tight-end position. Jackie Smith and Dave Casper had the kind of careers that brought them very close to making my list. Given a longer career, Kellen Winslow could deserve a position on such a list. He is the ideal type of tight end and a gifted, gutsy performer. His performance in San Diego's playoff game against Miami in January 1982 was one of the most competitive and courageous I've ever seen.

John Mackey proved himself over ten years. He was competitive and courageous, intelligent and destructive, and it took the toughest type of linebacker or defensive back to try to defense him and keep him from breaking up a ball game. Despite his size, he was fast enough and nifty enough to have been an effective wide receiver, but he was, instead, an almost perfect tight end.

CHAPTER 3

RUNNING BACKS

Again, there are statistics to serve as a guide at a position —running back: years played, carries, yards per carry, yards gained, and so forth. These things matter. They are a measure of a man's performance and durability, his contributions to his teams. But other things matter, too.

The special thing I look for in a running back is his ability to gain ground without help —his ability to find holes, turn a loss into a gain, break tackles, pick up extra yardage after being hit. I want to see how well he does without blockers, then how well he uses blockers.

When I was first helping to coach the Chicago Bears, our critics said we lacked a good offensive line. Then we drafted Gale Sayers, and the critics coupled the improvement in our offensive line with Gale's success. But it was the same offensive line. And it wasn't playing any better. Gale made it look better.

Of course, all successful running backs benefit from good blocking. A characteristic of a great running back is his ability to pick a hole. O. J. Simpson began to break loose with Buffalo after the Bills got some blockers. But just as good blockers make backs look better, so do good backs make blockers look better. The really great backs do a lot on their own.

I also look for breakaway ability. You need the strong, determined, resourceful back who can get you the first down on the third-down, short-yardage situation. Some are better at it than others. But the back who can turn the short gain into the long gain frequently is a lot harder to find.

There are more backs able to break away in college ball by far than in the pro game. There were more in the pro game years ago than there are these days. Professional football provides the most sophisticated defenses, and they are getting more sophisticated every year. Pro teams provide the sort of pursuit and coverage that protect against the long gain and make it difficult to attain.

The guy who can go all the way several times a season is an enormously valuable running back.

I look for pass-catching ability in a running back. In modern football we have gone from three running backs and two receivers to two running backs and three receivers. But three receivers are not enough to deal wtih sophisticated pass defenses. You need five. You need to be able to use your running backs as receivers in various situations, men who can come out of the backfield to find the seams in zone defenses, to get into one-on-one situations with linebackers, to overburden an area of coverage, to take the short swing pass and be sprung into an open-field situation where they can use their running ability.

The great running back is a good receiver who adds depth and dimension to your passing attack.

The great running back does not fumble a lot. Turnovers turn football games around. Interceptions and fumbles end drives and give away good field position. The great football players do not make a lot of mistakes. The great passer does not throw a lot of interceptions, especially in pressure situations. The great runner does not fumble the ball away a lot, especially in pressure situations.

Some backs like to freewheel with the ball held in one hand, not tucked away. I say such a back has to sacrifice some of his freedom in order to protect the ball and his team's position. He has to tuck the ball away from the side of the pursuit. He has to tighten his grip on it when he is hit. A lot of this is coaching. I have turned fumblers into nonfumblers. I don't care how brilliant a runner is, if he tends to fumble, especially in pressure situations, I don't want him because I feel I can't count on him.

Then I look for blocking ability in a running back. I do not always see it. A few of the greatest running backs were not good blockers. If not, it is a minus. But if a runner is a blocker, is willing to sacrifice himself for others, is interested in playing the game even when he is not carrying the ball, is interested in playing the whole game, then it is a big plus.

Finally, I look for consistency and durability. You are going to give the ball to the great running back many times a game. He is a marked man and he is going to get hit and hit hard by many tacklers many times a game. If he's not tough and strong and determined he's not going to do the job for you he was meant to do. The really great running back has had really great durability.

There are several types of running backs. There are those who are basically short-yardage guys and blockers—the fullbacks. And there are the long-gain guys who carry the ball a lot and catch the ball a lot—the halfbacks.

But going back to the early days of professional football, there were the single-wing tailbacks, often triple-threat players who ran, threw, and kicked. Those whose great strength was passing I have included with the quarterbacks. Those whose great strength was running I included with the running backs.

The "skilled" positions are quarterback, running back, and receiver. But it takes great skill in my book to play other positions. Still, I think the most talented all-around athletes of all have been halfbacks, and it is not surprising to me to find that I wound up with more players at running back than at any other position on my list of the 100 best players.

1.
Jim Brown

For nine seasons in the NFL, Jim Brown established a standard for running-back excellence. Year in, year out, Brown was the picture of rushing consistency, a workhorse who churned out yardage at a record-shattering pace.

Brown was 6-2 and 232 pounds and was simply explosive when he took a hand-off and hit into the line.

Drafted by the Cleveland Browns out of Syracuse University in 1957, Brown never missed a game in his nine seasons as a pro. He rushed for over 100 yards 58 times, almost half of his pro starts. He won eight NFL rushing championships, missing only in 1962, when he fell just four yards short of the 1,000-yard plateau. In seven of his nine seasons, he rushed for more than 1,000 yards, with 1,863 yards in 1963, his top year. For his career, Brown rushed for an all-time record 12,312 yards, averaging 5.2 yards every time he carried the football. He was also frequently used as a receiver out of the backfield and caught 262 passes for 2,499 more yards. Between rushing, receiving, and punt and kickoff returns, Brown gained 15,459 yards for his fabulous career.

Brown never carried the ball less than 200 times in a season. He set a league record, scoring 126 career touchdowns, 106 of them rushing, and his 756 career points are an NFL record for nonkickers.

Brown was named to the Pro Bowl game for each of his nine seasons. He averaged 104 yards and 20 carries for each of his 118 regular-season games, and those statistics took him into the Pro Football Hall of Fame in 1971, six years after he retired.

When he left the game, the handsome, rugged Brown pursued a motion-picture career highlighted by a featured role in *The Dirty Dozen*. It was among only a scant few successes he enjoyed as an actor.

Jimmy Brown was not only the greatest running back of all time, but one of the four or five finest professional football players of all time. He was a very big, very fast guy who combined size and speed, strength and speed, power and elusiveness better than any other runner pro football has ever had. He was a fullback who played halfback, and no other runner was as equally well suited to either role.

Earl Campbell has been carrying the ball more often in the early years of his career than Brown did in his early years. Campbell could surpass Brown. But will he? Campbell is the closest thing to Brown to come along, the closest to a true combination fullback-halfback, and he's been doing a great job, but his coaches could break him down. In his best year so far he

Jim Brown

averaged what Brown averaged for his career, and Earl's 1981 season, only his fourth in the league, was his worst. Some may see him as a flagrant notable omission from my list, but he simply hasn't earned his place yet.

Brown proved durable and consistent over a prolonged period, gaining more yards than any other running back ever. When I tried to defense him, I tried to stop him before he got started. That's the way Sam Huff and the Giants stopped him in some of the big games of the 1950s—rushing and tackling him in the backfield whether he got the ball or not. But he was very difficult to stop, especially when he got up a head of steam. He was so big and strong, had such powerful legs and good balance that he broke more tackles than any player who ever played, and once he got loose he had the speed and moves to get away from you and break a long one.

Brown was the epitome of the back who could make yardage on his own, get the short yardage you needed, and often turn a short gain into a long one. Yet he used his blockers well, too. His one weakness was that he didn't block much. But then, he ran the ball so often, he shouldn't have had to block as much as other runners.

I used to be especially afraid of him on the screen pass, because he really could catch the ball and go with it.

He took terrible beatings but seldom was hurt. He used to act like he couldn't get up off the ground after a while, but he'd get up, and when they'd give him the ball he'd run with it as hard as ever. He was simply stronger and more determined than his opponents and wore them down. He had incredible endurance and consistency and sustained his endurance better than any other running back ever.

Off the field Jimmy was a controversial character, strong-willed and outspoken, who got into trouble from time to time. But I worked with him on telecasts in recent years and came to feel he was a good man and a good friend. I really like him as a person. As an athlete, I could not have admired anyone more.

2.
O.J. Simpson

In the early 1970s, the members of the offensive line of the Buffalo Bills began calling themselves "the Electric Company." Asked why they picked that nickname, guard Reggie McKenzie explained with perfect logic, "We turn on the Juice."

The Juice was O. J. Simpson, an enormously talented running back who, in 1973, enjoyed the finest season any running back has ever achieved. That year Simpson became the first and only man in NFL history to rush for more than 2,000 yards in a single season. He finished the year with 2,003, shattering the single-season record of 1,863 set by Jim Brown a decade before.

Simpson began the 1973 season by rushing for 250 yards against New England. The next time he saw the Patriots, it was in the next-to-last game of the season and he responded with a 219-yard effort. That pushed his season's total to 1,803—61 short of breaking Brown's mark with one game to go.

The Bills played the New York Jets in the final game of the season and the 6-2, 212-pound Simpson got his 61 yards early on a snowy, windblown day at Shea Stadium. Then he set out for a new target—the never-before-achieved 2,000-yard mark. Reaching that would require still another 200-yard game, and that's exactly what Simpson produced. When he reached 200 for the game and 2,003 for the season, he was carried off the field by his teammates, the culmination of a season-long odyssey that lifted Simpson into the NFL record book.

When O. J. appeared for the postgame press conference to discuss his achievement, he insisted on bringing the Bills' offensive line with him. The Electric Company shared the glory accomplished by their man, the Juice.

Simpson had six 200-yard games in his career, including a single-game record 273 in 1976—a mark later topped by Walter Payton's 275. Simpson also led the league four times in rushing. For his career, Simpson gained 11,236 yards rushing—the second-best total in NFL history, trailing only

Brown's 12,312. Simpson's average per rush was 4.7 yards and he scored 61 touchdowns rushing.

O. J. retired as a player after the 1979 season. He remained a familiar figure as a spokesman for Hertz Rent-a-Car on television and by his appearances in films made for TV and theater presentation.

O. J. Simpson (#32)

Some may rate O. J. Simpson ahead of Jimmy Brown, but I can't. O. J. broke Jimmy's record for ground gained in one year, but he couldn't break Jimmy's record for ground gained in a career, though O. J. played more years. O. J. was a workhorse, too, but he wasn't as durable as Jimmy. Eventually O. J. suffered injuries and broke down and he wasn't too effective his last few years.

However, Simpson achieved what he did with a lot less help than Brown had. Brown had some great blockers and all-around backfield support with the Cleveland Browns, while Simpson had little help in his early years with the Buffalo Bills and last years with the San Francisco 49ers.

O. J. was a world-class sprinter. He had pretty good weight for a fellow as fast as he was, but he had a thin build and it is amazing how durable he was. No one ever took a beating better. He was the best late-game running back I ever saw, even better than Brown. Simpson went well in all kinds of weather, all kinds of footing.

O. J. also picked a hole as well as anyone. If there wasn't one where there was supposed to be, he was very good at bouncing outside and finding somewhere to run. He wasn't locked into a play the way many backs are. And he was very good at catching the screen pass and moving through an open field. He wasn't a power back, but he could knife through a line for a few yards when you needed them and sometimes break into the open. He was the original "spaghetti legs." He'd be tackled, a leg would go limp, and the tackler would slip off. He didn't block much, but I'm not going to take a long negative look at such a positive guy.

O. J. Simpson has an engaging personality. He is, as he appears to be, a great guy. He has attracted as much attention off the field as on it and been a big plus for football. And on the field he was close to the best.

3.
Gale Sayers

Instinct.

Coaches can't teach that very special quality which separates ordinary running backs from great ones. One has to be born with it. Gale Sayers had that special gift of instinct. Before injuries shortened his career in 1971, Sayers had quickness and lightning speed that enabled him to break through the smallest hole in the line to turn ordinary plays into long gainers.

Sayers was stamped as something special in his first season in the NFL in 1965. Drafted by the Chicago Bears from the University of Kansas, Sayers responded with a brilliant rookie campaign. He ran for 867 yards on 166 carries, averaging 5.2 yards per attempt, returned 21 kickoffs for 660 yards (a 31.4 yards average), and ran back 16 punts for 238 more yards (a 14.9 yards average). He set a rookie record by scoring 22 touchdowns and tied another first-season NFL mark when he raced into the end zone six times in a single game, against San Francisco on December 12, 1965.

A possessor of quickness and balance, Sayers was the ideal kick-return man. During the 1967 season, he returned one punt and four kickoffs for Chicago TDs. When he retired after the 1971 season, he led active NFL players in punt returns and was second in kickoff returns.

For his career, the 6-foot, 200-pound Sayers twice cracked the 1,000-yard plateau, both times winning the league rushing crown, and set a half dozen NFL records and 16 Bears standards. He finished his career with 4,956 yards rushing, a 5.0 average, and gained another 1,307 yards on 112 pass receptions for a total of 6,263 yards. Add his punt- and kick-return yardage and the total reaches 9,435 yards. He was a five-time All-Pro selection, a Hall of Famer since 1977, and scored 56 touchdowns—39 of them rushing—in a career constructed almost totally around a single element.

Instinct!

If he had played longer, Gale Sayers might have been the best. He lasted only seven years, which could have made him a marginal candidate for my list. A knee injury ended what was becoming an incredible career. But as I see it, he lasted long enough and accomplished so much while he played that he belongs high on the list. Maybe I'm prejudiced, but it is impossible not to be prejudiced in favor of Gale Sayers if he played for you.

I was personnel director of the Bears as well as defensive coach in 1965 when I recommended we draft Sayers, who had been a successful runner at Kansas but was not a big-name All-American. He didn't have much help there and the films showed me he had moves few backs have had. We needed help at running back and linebacker. We had three first-round draft choices that year and we got Gale Sayers and Dick Butkus out of those three, so no one ever had a better draft.

We needed a running back to replace Willie Gallimore, who was on the verge of greatness when he was tragically killed in an automobile accident. Gale was so good as a rookie, as was Butkus, that I wrote the league office to suggest it would be a shame if either lost the Rookie of the Year award, so maybe they should have an award for offense and another for defense. That's when they started the two awards, and both Sayers and Butkus won them.

Gale Sayers (#40)

Sayers was the most exciting running back I ever saw, the best long-gain guy I ever saw. He is among the top two or three halfbacks of all time with an average of five yards a carry. He wasn't big, but he could run inside or outside. He was the quickest at hitting a hole. If there wasn't a hole, he was the best at finding a place to slide through. When he was going wide and found a crowd, he was the best at reversing his field and getting loose.

Sayers was left-handed and could run right as well as left. Some backs are much better to one side, usually the right. Gale had quick feet, dancing feet, and perfect balance. He was an instinctive runner who made up moves on the spot and was extraordinarily elusive. He was a will-o'-the-wisp.

He was one of the best I ever saw at returning kickoffs and punts. He caught and ran with passes brilliantly and even passed well. He was also an effective blocker.

There were some great runners in the 1960s. Dick Bass was an excellent halfback, more durable than Sayers and almost as elusive. Bass had 1,000-yard seasons with mediocre support and darn near made my list. Leroy Kelly was another very good one. But I think Sayers was superior. I wish he'd lasted longer. I'm grateful he lasted as long as he did.

4.
Bronko Nagurski

Bronko Nagurski was one of pro football's early legendary heroes, a power-packed all-but-unmovable man who seemed born to play football. He was among the game's greatest fullbacks, but in college, at the University of Minnesota, he was an All-America selection at tackle as well. In one game during his junior year in college, Nagurski broke three of his ribs playing fullback. It hardly slowed him. He simply shifted to tackle and played there in the next game.

That was Nagurski's style. He gave no quarter and asked none. He was a devastating blocker and it was Nagurski's bull-like thrusts into the line that helped Beattie Feathers rush for 1,004 yards in 1934—the first NFL runner to go over the 1,000-yard mark. The 6-2, 225-pound Nagurski gained a career-high 586 yards himself that year. He didn't need Feathers' blocking in front of him, though. People said Nagurski was so strong, he ran his own interference.

Nagurski was born in Rainy River, Ontario, Canada, and his Ukrainian immigrant parents named him Bronislau. An early teacher stumbled over that and called him Bronko instead, tagging him with a nickname that would last a lifetime. Somehow it sounded just right for Nagurski.

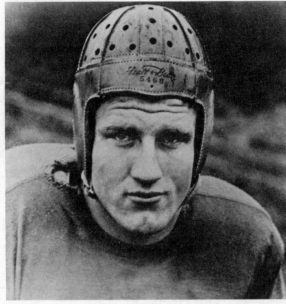

Bronko Nagurski

He joined the Chicago Bears in 1930 and quickly set a standard for power runners. But Nagurski could do other things, too. He was a quality linebacker when the occasion called for it. He could throw the football, too. In the first NFL title game ever played in 1933, Nagurski passed for two touchdowns in the Bears' 23—21 victory over the New York Giants.

Bronko left the sport in 1937. However, in 1943, with pro football's ranks depleted by World War II, he returned to the Bears for one season. He was at tackle at the start of the campaign but was placed in the backfield later on. He helped Chicago win the divisional title, and then the league champi- onship by defeating Washington.

Statistics were not kept in Nagurski's first two years in the NFL. How- ever, over the remainder of his nine seasons in the league, Bronko is cred- ited with having gained 2,778 yards rushing at an average of 4.4 yards a carry. He was a charter selection to the Pro Football Hall of Fame in 1963.

I have seen Nagurski only on film, but I don't think there's any doubt he belongs on a list of the ten best players of all time, much less the 100 best. The question about him is not whether he belongs, but where he belongs. When he was in college one year they only put ten men on the All-America team because he was honored at both tackle and fullback. He became an All-Pro at both linebacker and fullback. I think of him mostly as a fullback, so I list him with the running backs. He was the first great fullback in the NFL.

Bronko is one of several players whose career crossed over the deadline we have imposed on our selections. Clarke Hinkle and Dutch Clark are two other running backs in this category who are on the list. All had sufficiently long stretches of stardom from 1933 on to qualify. And all qualify clearly in every other respect.

Nagurski was a giant of his day. They say he was all muscle and bone. His reputation is that he was stronger and tougher than any other man ever to play the game. Veteran observers tell us he hurt the people he hit, whether they were trying to tackle him or he was tackling them. He sent people to the hospital with broken bones. Yet his reputation is that he was a clean player.

He did not have great speed. He was not a breakaway back. But he broke tackles with the sheer power of his legs. He carried people on his back. If you did not tackle him right, you didn't stop him. He was not a long-gain guy and so there were no long runs to improve his average, yet he averaged between four and five yards a carry for his career. He was supposed to be the most brutal of blockers. He didn't catch many passes, but he threw well.

He was, of course, a 60-minute man who played defense and offense throughout every game at a time it was mostly a ground game and very rugged. He lined up at times at tackle or end on defense, but he was used mainly at linebacker so he could move around, get to the ball carrier, and get into every pileup. He was tireless. And indestructible. He was a great athlete who dominated his games.

5.
Joe Perry

Joe Perry was nicknamed "The Jet" early in his pro football career by San Francisco quarterback Frankie Albert, who marveled at his teammate's quick-starting abilities. It was appropriate because Perry had the kind of speed that could break games wide open.

Perry came into pro football in 1948 after playing at Compton Junior College and in the Navy. In high school he was clocked in 9.7 seconds for the 100, sprinter speed that marked him as something special. But in his first high school football scrimmage, he broke an ankle. It was only a slight setback, though. When he got to Compton, Perry scored 22 touchdowns in one season, proving he was fully healed.

In the Navy he caught the eye of John Woudenberg, a tackle with the 49ers. San Francisco signed Joe the Jet for the 1948 season, launching a brilliant career that would lead Perry to the Pro Football Hall of Fame in 1969.

After playing two years in the old All-America Conference, Perry moved with San Francisco into the NFL in 1950. He instantly was recognized as one of the top runners in his new league. He became the first man in NFL history to rush for over 1,000 yards in two consecutive years. He had 1,018 yards in 1953 and improved that to 1,049 yards the next season. He gained 1,345 yards in his two seasons in the AAC and produced 8,378 for 14 NFL seasons. His 16-year career rushing total of 9,723 yards is fourth on the all-time list, trailing only Jim Brown, O. J. Simpson, and Franco Harris. Perry had a combined total of 71 touchdowns.

Perry, a 6-foot, 200-pounder, also was one of the first running backs to catch passes out of the backfield. He caught 260 passes for 2,021 yards and scored 513 points.

In 1961, San Francisco traded Perry to Baltimore. He spent two years with the Colts and then returned to the 49ers for his final season, 1963. It was hoped he could play in at least three games to qualify for an NFL pension. But Perry surprised everyone by playing in nine games instead.

I've said no one takes more punishment than a running back. Looking down my list of the greatest running backs I see they did not last as long as the greatest players at other positions. Nine of the 16 I have picked lasted less than 10 years. It's really quite striking. You simply cannot use this as an important measure of their greatness as you can with others.

Accordingly, it is especially impressive to me that Joe Perry endured 16 seasons of pro ball, more than any other runner on my list. Longevity by itself would not be enough, of course, but although he is not remembered as well as many others on the list, his credentials are really beyond dispute. That he sustained his excellence over so many years is a big plus.

Joe was really a tough guy. He was called "the Jet" because of his speed, but I think it was his quick start rather than his straightaway speed that stood him in good stead. He accelerated to speed faster than any running back I can remember. A hole didn't have to be open very long for Joe to move through it. He was a slashing type of runner with strong legs and good balance and was very hard to knock down. And he sustained his speed over the years better than most speed guys do.

Perry didn't carry the ball as much as Jimmy Brown or O. J. Simpson, but Perry was one of the few to average five yards a carry, which was a little more than O.J. did. Joe was a very fine pass receiver and dynamite on the screen pass. He was a very good blocker. And Joe had tremendous endurance. He was one of the most consistent and durable backs we have had.

▲Joe Perry (#34)　　　　　　　▼Jim Taylor (#31)

6.
Jim Taylor

Only once during his fabulous NFL career did Jim Brown fail to win the NFL rushing championship. That was in 1962, when the winner of the ground crown was Green Bay's great Jim Taylor, a hard-nosed fullback who was a throwback ball carrier.

Taylor came to the Packers from Louisiana State University in 1958, and when Green Bay became a dominant force in the NFL, Taylor was the club's most effective runner. He had five consecutive 1,000-yard seasons in an era when that plateau wasn't easily reached. Even Brown, the NFL's all-time rushing king, could not string five straight 1,000-yard years. In 1961, Taylor rushed for 1,307 yards, averaging 5.4 per carry. The next year he pushed his production to a league-leading 1,474 yards, again averaging 5.4 yards every time they handed him the football.

He teamed in the Green Bay backfield with Paul Hornung and often was the lead blocker in the famous Packer sweep, driving tacklers out of the way. Taylor's yardage was gained mostly on weak-side slants and, with Hornung working the outside, the Packers' ground game was diversified and tough.

In 1962, when he led the league's rushers, Taylor set a record by scoring 19 touchdowns. For his career, the tough fullback rushed for 83 touchdowns and caught passes for 10 more scores. Only three men—Jim Brown, Lenny Moore, and Don Hutson—hit the end zone more often.

Taylor, a 6-foot, 216-pounder, finished his career with 8,597 yards rushing, fifth on the all-time list and good enough for induction into the Pro Football Hall of Fame in 1976.

The best short-gain runner I've known in my coaching career in the NFL was Jim Taylor, who was very important to the tremendous success enjoyed by Vince Lombardi's Green Bay Packers. Taylor was almost never thrown for a loss, and if you needed a yard or two for a first down or a touchdown, Jim would get it. In that situation, he was the hardest to stop of any runner I've seen. And he usually got you more. He had little speed and seldom broke for a long gain, yet he averaged more than four yards a carry. Green Bay had a very diversified offense so Taylor didn't have to carry the ball as much as Jim Brown, but Taylor was a workhorse sort of guy.

He was a big back, a strong back, a tough guy, and as mean as any back I've seen. He ran with his elbows almost as much as his legs. He'd lower his shoulders and swing his forearm out in front of him and flail away with his elbows and hurt people as he ran through them. He couldn't run around people, but he could run over them. The Packers gave him good blocking, but Taylor was one of those players who could do a lot when he didn't have much help. Looking at his size, I see he wasn't as heavy as I remember him to be. He's listed as having played at 216. Maybe. He seemed bigger. He ran bigger.

I can remember having to coach against Green Bay three times a year—once in an exhibition game and twice in the regular season. You could do different things to defense a Bart Starr or a Paul Hornung, but there was no way to defense Jim Taylor. If you hit him with two guys, he carried them. He was the hardest man in the world to get down. He went down kicking and scratching. He wasn't much of a pass catcher, but he was a heck of a good blocker. And he'd be running and blocking as hard at the end of a game and the end of a season as at the beginning.

7.
Walter Payton

Season after season, Walter Payton grinds out the yardage for the Chicago Bears. After rushing for 679 yards in his rookie year of 1975, Payton ripped off an NFC record six straight 1,000-yard seasons through 1981 and stands fourth on the all-time list of NFL runners with 9,608. He will be the fourth man in history to crack the 10,000-yard plateau and he will do it faster than any of the first three—Jim Brown, O. J. Simpson, and Franco Harris.

Payton's best year was 1977, when he rushed for 1,852 yards, which was, at that time, the third-best single-season production in NFL history and is still the fourth best. Included in the total was a 275-yard single-game effort on Thanksgiving Day against the Minnesota Vikings, which set an NFL record.

The pro scouts knew Payton had the potential for greatness. At Jackson State he had scored 464 points to set an NCAA record. Included in the total were 66 touchdowns. He rushed for 3,563 yards in college, averaging 6.1 yards every time he carried the ball. He also punted and kicked field goals, and those credentials were enough to make him the fourth player chosen in the 1975 college draft and the first running back selected.

The 5-10, 202-pound Payton won five consecutive NFC rushing titles from 1976 to 1980 and developed into one of the league's most explosive runners. In 1977, he strung five straight 100-yard games together and soared over that plateau 10 times in 14 games.

Payton also is a dangerous receiver and he has caught more than 200 passes for almost 2,000 yards in his pro career. But pass patterns are strictly secondary for him. He has scored 71 TDs rushing and does enough damage just carrying the football, without having to worry about catching it.

Walter Payton is an excellent example of the kind of running back I most admire—the kind who can get you yardage on his own. He has had very little help on the Chicago Bears in recent years. They have been a bad team. They have been little help to him—no passing attack to take the heat off the running game, no fullback to take the heat off Payton, very little offensive blocking for him.

I hate to see what is happening to him. The 1981 season was very hard on him. Without help, he may be wearing out. Yet he still gained more than

1,000 yards for the sixth time. Only Jim Brown and Franco Harris have gained more than 1,000 yards seven times. In eight seasons, Payton has been incredibly consistent. His image is fading, but he has been one of the greats.

Payton succeeded Gale Sayers with the Bears. Walter doesn't have Gale's speed, but he has more strength. He doesn't run outside as well, but he runs better inside. He has good speed, good strength, and great balance. He hasn't had a lot of big holes to run through, but all he has to find is a sliver of daylight and he knifes through it.

In a relatively short time, Payton has moved up among the first four rushers of all time. He has run back kicks real well. He catches passes real well. He blocks well. He is a fine all-around athlete. With more help, he might have set more records. Without it, he is one of those who still succeeds. He has taken a terrible beating, and I only hope he can endure and excel for a few more seasons.

Walter Payton

8.
Steve Van Buren

Until he got to the NFL, Steve Van Buren was a well-kept secret. For his first two years at Louisiana State University, Van Buren's primary job was to block for backfield partner Alvin Dark, who would find his professional sports success years later in baseball instead of football. Even 832 yards rushing in his senior year failed to earn Van Buren All-America honors, and his availability in the draft was greeted with something of a shrug by most pro teams.

Philadelphia, however, had been tipped off by LSU Coach Bernie Moore and made Van Buren its No. 1 choice. The selection paid handsome dividends. Even though he underwent an appendectomy in his rookie season of 1944, he still was an all-NFL choice, rushing for 444 yards. A year later he was the league's leading rusher with 832 yards. In 1947 he became only the second man in NFL history to rush for more than 1,000 yards when he accumulated 1,008. It had been 13 years since Beattie Feathers accomplished 1,000 yards, and people were wondering if anybody would ever do it again.

Van Buren won two more rushing crowns, producing 945 yards in 1948 and 1,146 in 1949. That gave him three consecutive rushing crowns and four titles in a five-year span, and his total in 1949 set a single-season rushing record that lasted for almost a decade.

The 6-1, 200-pound Van Buren helped the Eagles to NFL championships in 1948 and 1949. He was an integral part of both title-game victories, scoring the game's only touchdown in a blizzard as Philadelphia beat the Chicago Cardinals, 7–0, in the 1948 game, and then setting a championship game record by rushing for 196 yards in a 14–0 Philadelphia victory over Los Angeles the next year.

Van Buren's accomplishments, which led to his induction in the Pro Football Hall of Fame in 1965, were even more amazing because he was essentially playing with only one arm. His left shoulder was lame and he always carried the football right-handed, unable to use the traditional straight-arm technique against tacklers.

Still, he gained a career 5,860 yards on the ground while scoring 69 touchdowns.

Steve Van Buren was a tough fellow. He had pretty good speed, but he didn't have a lot of moves. He kept his head down and didn't have much style. But he had good size and he was strong and he ran with tremendous determination. He lowered his head and he rammed right through the line and right through tacklers. It was very hard to bring him down. He played well with a lot of injuries. That's something I haven't mentioned from position to position because it applies to all positions, but the really great players played well despite injuries.

Offenses still weren't very sophisticated in the 1940s. Teams didn't move the ball a lot. One or two drives might decide a game. Scores were low. Individuals didn't pile up big statistics. But there were some outstanding backs. George McAfee and Bill Osmanski of the Bears were two of the greatest. McAfee was one of the most spectacular breakaway backs I've seen. Osmanski, who was called "Bullet Bill," also was a bull. Tony Canadeo of the Packers was a great little runner. Pat Harder of the Cardinals was a fine fullback and also an outstanding kicker. But Steve Van Buren was the best running back of his era.

Van Buren was a heavy-duty back. He got you the short yardage and from time to time went for long yardage. He could catch a ball and run well with it. He seldom was thrown for a loss. He seldom fumbled. He came up in the 60-minute days and early in his career played defense as well as offense, though I don't think of him as a great defensive player. I doubt that he ever made more than $15,000 a year. I suspect he played for half that early in his career. He played for the love of the game and his play showed it.

Steve Van Buren

9.
Clarke Hinkle

As pro football evolved from its early days to the modern game of today, it became a sport of specialists. Clarke Hinkle, one of the game's pioneer stars, was a specialist too—at just about every assignment that needs to be carried out on a football field.

Hinkle was a battering-ram fullback on offense and a skilled linebacker who delighted in bone-jarring tackles on defense. He also caught passes, threw them, punted, and place-kicked, possessing a multitude of skills that earned him admission to the Pro Football Hall of Fame in 1964.

Hinkle joined the Green Bay Packers in 1932, a product of Bucknell University. And in 10 years as a pro, he established himself as the complete football player who could perform a number of functions, all of them well.

Four times, Hinkle was an All-NFL selection. He led the league in scoring with 58 points in 1938 and was the field-goal leader in both 1940 and 1941.

Coming out of the backfield, Hinkle was a solid receiver, catching 49 career passes for 537 yards and nine TDs. He also was used on option pass plays and completed 24 attempts for 316 yards and two TDs. As a punter, he averaged 43.4 yards and he had 28 field goals and converted 31 of 33 extra-point attempts on placements.

Hinkle, a 5-11, 201-pounder, was a savage blocker on offense and a brutal tackler on defense, exulting in confrontations with the great ball carriers of his time.

When he retired in 1941, Hinkle had rushed for 3,860 yards from scrimmage, an NFL record at the time, and 32 touchdowns. The figure has been eclipsed often since then, but not by anyone who kicks, passes, catches, and plays defense too.

Clarke Hinkle played in the 1930s, when they really played for the love of it. He once said he didn't get $10,000 a season until his final year and he played for a fifth of that in his early seasons. Even in those days that wasn't much money. Back then they didn't have many pain-killers, either, and he played in pain, all busted up, many times. I never saw anyone play with more enthusiasm.

Clarke clearly loved contact. Bronko Nagurski may have been stronger, but no one ever was tougher than Hinkle. He weighed only a little more than 200 pounds, but he hit like a truck. When he ran the ball, he hit the tacklers instead of them hitting him.

He had some collisions with Nagurski that became famous all by themselves. The most famous was when Hinkle faked a punt, ran through the

Clarke
Hinkle

line, and ran right into Nagurski. Both went flying backward. Hinkle went down, Bronko was standing, but with a broken nose and split lip. The next time they met, Nagurski went for revenge. He collided with Clarke and knocked him flying. But Hinkle landed on his feet and went for a touchdown. Nagurski was knocked unconscious.

Curly Lambeau was a tough coach and his Green Bay Packers became one of the toughest teams of their time with a player like Hinkle in the lineup. Like Nagurski, Clarke played linebacker as well as fullback, played 60 minutes, and was a vicious tackler. Clarke also was a brutal blocker and one of the great punters of all time.

There were many great, tough running backs in the 1930s. Beattie Feathers was brilliant, but he didn't endure as well as some. Cliff Battles was brilliant. Tuffy Leemans also was a terrific back. Johnny Blood was excellent, too, but his best years came before our 1933 deadline.

10.
Hugh McElhenny

It didn't take long for Hugh McElhenny to establish himself as a very special running back after the San Francisco 49ers drafted him in 1952. The first time he touched the ball, he went 42 yards for a touchdown. McElhenny had the season's longest punt return—94 yards—and the longest run from scrimmage—89 yards. He averaged seven yards per carry and scored a rare awards double, selected as Rookie of the Year as well as Player of the Year.

McElhenny came to the 49ers from the University of Washington after prepping at Compton Junior College, which had produced his backfield partner at San Francisco, Joe Perry. Nicknamed "The King"—perhaps because he seemed like running back royalty—McElhenny had a unique style. He was a master of moves, often swerving from sideline to sideline, seeking the hole that would spring him for a big gain. His speed and balance made him a devastating open-field runner.

McElhenny moved into the pros with formidable college credentials. In three seasons at the University of Washington he set a Pacific Coast Conference record, rushing for 2,499 yards. He was a two-time All-America selection.

As a pro, McElhenny, a 6-1, 198-pounder, was a multifaceted player. He carried the football, caught passes, and returned punts and kickoffs. His combined yardage production was 11,369 yards and 60 touchdowns, but he posted those numbers in a variety of ways. In 13 seasons with San Francisco, Minnesota, the New York Giants, and Detroit, he rushed for 5,281 yards and scored 38 TDs on the ground. The remainder of his statistics were compiled catching passes (3,247 yards, 20 TDs) and returning punts and kickoffs (2,841 yards, 2 TDs). The Hall of Fame numbers are impressive, especially when it is considered that, when he was a boy, McElhenny severed all the tendons in his right foot in an accident and was bedridden for five months and on crutches for seven months after that. Doctors said he would never walk normally again. They should have seen him run later on, though.

I have said that Sammy Baugh was the picture passer. Well, Hugh McElhenny was the picture runner. He was the most beautiful back to watch, in my opinion. He was one of the most graceful players I've ever seen. They called him "The King" and he ran with a sort of majesty, erect, and fluid. He just seemed to glide through a broken field, slipping tackles here and there. He was a long-gain guy, at his best in a broken field. He was the best punt returner and kickoff returner I've seen.

The closest to him, the way I see it, was Tommy Harmon, who was sensational in an open field, but I best remember Tom from college ball; he was past his prime by the time he got to the pros. Glenn Davis was a great open-field runner, but he, too, did not play in his prime in the pros. Buddy Young was a spectacular breakaway back in a herky-jerky, jitterbug sort of way, but he did not last too long, either.

McElhenny lasted 13 years, which is among the most for running backs. With his style he was not hit as hard as often as some of the outstanding backs of his era, like John Henry Johnson and Alan Ameche. McElhenny used blockers better than any back I can remember. This is an art. A lot of backs waste their blockers. McElhenny glided behind them, often directed them, let them do a job for him, and made his move just as the block was made.

McElhenny was very fast, but he used his speed only as he needed it. He changed speeds effortlessly and changed directions at top speed. He ran with perfect balance, eyes scanning the field and seeing everything, and he kept tacklers uncertain. His moves pulled them out of balance. He was an intelligent runner and difficult to tackle cleanly. Because of his timing and broken-field ability, he was especially effective on screen passes. He never led the league in rushing, but he averaged close to five yards a carry and concluded his career with more than 5,000 yards rushing. He was special.

Hugh McElhenny (#39)

11.
Franco Harris

In 1981, Franco Harris became only the third man in pro football history to go past the 10,000-yard plateau in rushing. He finished with 987 for the season (only the third time in 10 pro seasons that he has fallen short of 1,000 yards), pushing his career total to 10,339. The only men with more rushing yards are Jim Brown (12,312) and O. J. Simpson (11,236).

Harris carried the football 242 times in 1981, increasing his career total for rushing attempts to a record 2,462. His eight touchdowns gave him 84 for his career, second on the all-time list only to Brown's 106 TDs rushing.

Although he has never won a season rushing title, Harris has been the picture of consistency coming out of the backfield for the Pittsburgh Steelers. His seven 1,000-yard seasons ties him with Brown in that category. From 1974 to 1979, Harris churned out 1,000 yards a year, setting a record for consecutive seasons over 1,000 yards rushing.

Harris played college football at Penn State and was one of the early building blocks in Coach Chuck Noll's rebuilding of the Pittsburgh franchise. Harris was drafted in the first round in 1972. Franco was the rookie of the year that season and was named to the Pro Bowl game for the first of nine consecutive times. That was the season Harris made the "immaculate reception," a dramatic catch of a deflected pass in the final seconds of the opening playoff game as the Steelers eliminated Oakland. It was the first of a string of remarkable playoff performances for Harris.

In the 17 postseason games he's played, Franco has been the leading rusher 13 times. He is pro football's all-time postseason leader in rushing yards (1,488), attempts (384), 100-yard games (five), and touchdowns (17). He owns Super Bowl records for career yards rushing (354), attempts (101), and TDs (four). He set a single-game Super Bowl rushing record when he ran for 158 yards against Minnesota in Super Bowl IX, and he was chosen the game's Most Valuable Player.

In addition, Harris is often used as a receiver coming out of the backfield and has 241 career catches for 1,757 yards.

At 6-2 and 225 pounds he has fullback size and halfback moves. The combination is devastating and helped make him a choice for a position on the NFL's team of the decade for the 1970s.

Perseverance made Franco Harris one of the best running backs and one of the 100 greatest professional football players. I know that through much of his career I could not have dreamed I'd put him on a list like this. He is certainly not a picture runner. He has few of the natural abilities of others on my list. But he has been a strong, determined, and hard-working player who has parlayed consistency over a 10-year career to become the third player to run for more than 10,000 yards. That cannot be ignored.

A talent like Tony Dorsett's is far more impressive. A few more seasons of excellence and Dorsett will deserve to be ranked with the greatest running backs. The same can be said for Earl Campbell. But Harris has truly proven himself. Beyond his staggering statistics, equally important to me is that he has been a superb pressure player, an indispensable part of Pittsburgh's fantastic four Super Bowl victories. While he has been surrounded by helpful players, he remains one of those runners I most admire who get you the yards when you need them, who get you extra yards, who do a lot on their own. In recent years, Larry Csonka was another on this level, but Franco outlasted him.

Harris has been an intelligent and inventive player. Most memorable was his catch and touchdown run with the deflected "Hail Mary" pass to defeat Oakland in the 1972 playoffs. He was the Most Valuable Player in one Super Bowl and I take note that he is the leading rusher in the history of the playoffs. It no doubt has helped that there are more playoff games by far than there used to be and Pittsburgh played more playoff games than most teams, but the accomplishment is still noteworthy.

Personally, I recall most vividly a Monday night TV game against Pittsburgh when we forced a fumble that was picked up by our Ron McDole and almost run into the end zone for a big touchdown. Inside the 10 he was tackled by a player who came across the field to pursue and get him. They stopped us and we lost the game. We, the Redskins, were the first team to win 10 Monday night TV games and this was the first we had lost. It hurt. I made a point of looking at the films to see who made the tackle and it was Franco.

He has been a great pass catcher, a great blocker, and a great runner; and he has had a knack of making the big play.

12.
Marion Motley

When Marion Motley was inducted into the Pro Football Hall of Fame at Canton, Ohio in 1968, it was a homecoming for him. The powerful fullback grew up in Canton and learned his early football at McKinley High School there.

Motley spent one year at South Carolina State and then transferred to the University of Nevada. He had played some football at the Great Lakes Naval Station earlier.

When Motley joined Cleveland in 1946, the team was playing in the All-America Conference. In four years in that league, Motley was the

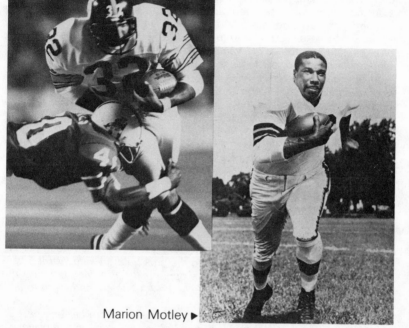

◀ Franco Harris (#32)

Marion Motley ▶

AAC's leading rusher, gaining 3,024 yards. He also scored 26 touchdowns and provided quarterback Otto Graham with excellent pass protection.

Cleveland moved into the NFL in 1950, and the league's rushing champion that season was Motley, who averaged 5.8 yards per carry and rushed for 810 yards. For four seasons in the NFL, Motley averaged 5.0 yards per carry, an impressive figure. But he did even better than that in the AAC, averaging 6.2 yards per carry for his career there and a remarkable 8.2 in his rookie season, when he gained 601 yards in just 73 attempts.

The 6-1, 238-pound Motley's finest game came on October 29, 1950, during the Browns' first year in the NFL. Cleveland played Pittsburgh that day and the big fullback carried the ball just 11 times but gained 188 yards. The average of 17.09 yards per attempt remains an NFL record for a single game by a running back.

For his NFL career, Motley gained 1,696 yards. That increased his pro production to 4,720 yards.

Early in his career, Motley was a standout linebacker and Cleveland often used him on their goal-line defense. It was on offense, however, that Motley found his way back home to Canton, Ohio.

No one ever ran over people like Marion Motley did. Maybe Bronko Nagurski or Clarke Hinkle, but I don't think so. Sometimes you see films of Motley knocking tacklers backward and you can't believe it. But I saw him do it in person and I believe it. He was not as quick as some other out-standing backs, but when he got up a head of steam, Motley was like a bowling ball scattering tacklers like tenpins. He was a big man with good speed when he gained momentum. He did not break off a long run very often, so his average of 5.7 yards a carry, best among the running backs who made my list or came close to it, is unbelievable.

Aside from his physical tools, Motley had a lot of character. He came from a small school without any press clippings. He'd played for Paul Brown at the Great Lakes Naval Training Station during World War II, when service bases had top teams. When Brown became coach of the Cleveland Browns of the new AAC in 1946, the year after the war ended, Motley asked for a tryout. After Brown brought in the great defensive lineman, Bill Willis, he invited Motley to provide a roommate for Willis. That was the year the color barrier was broken in professional football. There hadn't been any blacks since the early years of the game. The Rams brought in a couple in the NFL and the Browns brought in Willis and Motley in the AAC. Motley was an afterthought, but he turned out to be great, too. And I have to admire both of them for the racial taunts and rough play they endured in those first few years, while still playing superbly.

Many more blacks might have made my list if more had been playing first-class college ball and going on to the pros before World War II. I hate to think how many were denied the opportunity. But Motley made the most of his. Cleveland won every title in the AAC before coming in to take championships in the NFL.

Motley was in his middle 20s before he broke into pro ball and past 30 by the time he got to the NFL, but he was as important as any player on those great Cleveland teams. He was as good a short-gain guy as you could want. He had help, but he did a lot on his own and he gained the extra yards, the hard yards. He was effective with swing passes, was one of the best blocking backs ever, and one of the best punters ever. I can still remember his towering kicks. He also played defense. In short, he was a powerhouse.

13.
Earl (Dutch) Clark

Only three times in their history—1936, 1937, 1938—have the Detroit Lions led the NFL in rushing. The man who sparked that ground game was Earl (Dutch) Clark, a triple-threat tailback.

Earl (Dutch) Clark

Clark came out of tiny Colorado College—the only All-America ever produced by the school—and had the ability to score by running, passing, and kicking. He was an All-Pro choice in six of his seven seasons, spending the first two with the Portsmouth Spartans, forerunners of the Lions.

In 1932, the first year the NFL kept player statistics, the 6-foot, 185-pound Clark was the scoring champion, with 55 points accumulated on six TDs, three field goals, and 10 extra points. He also led the league in scoring in 1935 (55 points) and in 1936 (73 points). In 1936, the Lions' ground game produced 2,885 yards, an NFL record that lasted 36 years. Clark gained 628 of those yards, third best in the NFL that season. But he also led the Lions in passing, completing 53.5 percent of his attempts in a season when the overall league completion percentage was only 36.5.

His pro career was interrupted in 1933 when he took a year off, leaving Portsmouth to coach football at the Colorado School of Mines. When he returned to the NFL in 1934, Portsmouth's franchise had been moved to Detroit. Clark doubled as the Lions' coach in his last two seasons, 1937 and 1938, and finished his career with 2,772 yards rushing, a 4.6-yard average, and 27 touchdowns. He was a charter selection for membership in the Pro Football Hall of Fame (1963).

Before the T formation came in, backs weren't specialists and the best athlete on the team usually played tailback. He usually was the star runner, passer, and kicker on offense and he played defense, too. He played 60 minutes a game, or close to it. There has to be a place for the best of them because they were among the 100 best players of pro football. So I have put them where they fit best. Most were best at running the ball because there wasn't much passing in the early years.

Dutch Clark actually was a quarterback by his listed position because he called the signals—and no one ever called them more imaginatively—and the quarterback called the signals then. But he was a tailback in the things he did. He did everything. He was a great runner, shifty and elusive. He was an accurate passer, although he had such poor vision—just about legally blind, I've heard—that he couldn't see the whole field well and didn't always locate receivers to his left, his weakest side. Still, he was a real good defensive back and a terrific interceptor. He was a strong tackler. He was a good punter and a great dropkicker. He could drop-kick the ball through the goalposts from 40 to 45 yards. When they started to slim down the football and it became difficult to drop-kick it, he place-kicked effectively his final year as a pro.

Clark started as a pro in 1931. You could make more money at a regular job in those days, so there was little incentive to play a lot of years. It was a rugged game and injuries didn't get treated as well as they do now. An ankle injury ended Dutch's career.

A player of Clark's era of almost equal ability was Ken Strong. The old New York Giant was a great kicker and a fine runner. He could catch a pass well and throw one pretty well. He was a powerful fellow, a strong blocker and tackler, and flawless at fundamentals. He was the last player I cut from my list. That makes him the first after the 100 greatest players. There is nothing tougher for an old coach than making those last cuts. Choosing between a Ken Strong and a Dutch Clark or one of the other greats was difficult.

14.
Frank Gifford

When he came into the NFL in 1952, Frank Gifford was a gifted two-way performer who had honed all-star abilities in both the offensive and defensive backfields at the University of Southern California. The New York Giants were so impressed, they didn't bother picking out a specialty for the young man. They played him both ways, at a time when pro football was moving away from that type of iron-man regimen.

The coaches were wearing the 6-1, 195-pound Gifford out when the turning point of his career occurred in 1954. The Giants hired a new offensive coach named Vince Lombardi. He immediately claimed Gifford for his unit. The decision lengthened Frank's career and pointed him on a path that led to the Pro Football Hall of Fame (1977).

By 1956, Gifford had settled in as one of the NFL's finest halfbacks and he enjoyed a brilliant season, leading the Giants to the first of six division titles over the next eight years. In 1956 Gifford rushed for 819 yards, fifth best in the league, and caught 51 passes for 603 more yards, third best. He was named Player of the Year and it marked the beginning of a brilliant stretch for him. He doubled as the Giants' rushing and receiving leader for three more years.

Frank Gifford

Gifford's pro career seemed to have ended in 1960 when he suffered a head injury while being tackled. He sat out the 1961 season but then came back for three more years, switching positions from halfback to flanker. Over that period, he caught 110 passes for 1,184 yards and 17 touchdowns and pushed his career yardage to almost 10,000 yards. Included are 3,609 yards rushing, 5,434 yards on 367 pass receptions, and 710 yards on interception, kickoff, and punt returns. Gifford scored 78 TDs—34 of them rushing—and threw for 14 more.

Frank Gifford was one of the last of the 60-minute players, a great all-around athlete. He ran, he passed, he caught passes, he blocked. He was the best all-around running back of the 1950s. He was one of the best defensive backs in his early years as a pro. He was a fine pass defender and a sure tackler. He could kick effectively, but wasn't called on for that. He was asked to do everything else and he did everything well.

Gifford was the key Giant when they were one of the two or three best teams in the NFL for many years. His rushing statistics do not measure up to those of many who did not make my list, but his overall performances did. He played especially well under pressure. He was an intelligent, imaginative, resourceful player who came up with the big play game after game. He was consistent and dependable and he played 12 years. One year he even tried to play quarterback. He wasn't a pure passer, but I think if he'd played the position during his development days he'd have been a good quarterback.

There were others who ranked close to him. Charley Trippi, who started his career a few years before Gifford, was an outstanding all-around athlete. Ollie Matson, who was a contemporary of Gifford's, was a tremendous all-around athlete who came close to making my list. But there was something special about Gifford that gave him a little edge over the others. For one thing, he was a winner in a way that few others were.

15.
Bill Dudley

Leading the NFL in one individual statistics category is difficult, but in 1946, halfback Bill Dudley paced the league in three departments. And the remarkable part of the achievement was that one of them was on offense, another on defense, and the third on special teams.

Dudley won his second rushing title that season, gaining 604 yards to pace all NFL runners. And he also intercepted 10 passes on defense, leading the league in that department as well. His 27 punt returns for 385 yards ranked him No. 1 in that department, too.

A product of the University of Virginia, where he set a national college scoring record, Dudley was the first player selected in the NFL's 1942 draft. He paid immediate dividends for the Pittsburgh Steelers, leading the league in rushing with 696 yards.

Like so many players of his era, the 5-10, 176-pound Dudley had a variety of football talents and excelled in many different phases of the game. Besides being a quality running back, he often was used as a passer and a receiver, returned kicks, punted, and kicked field goals and extra points. He had a unique style in several of those specialties, throwing the ball sidearm on passes, and never using any approach steps on place-kicks. He would stand at the point where the ball was to be spotted and kicked from there

Bill Dudley

without any of the momentum most kickers need. He booted 33 field goals and 121 extra points after touchdowns that way.

Dudley's nine-year pro career was divided almost evenly among Pittsburgh, Detroit, and Washington, and was interrupted for a two-year service stint during World War II when he was a B-29 pilot. He sat out the 1952 season before returning for one final year with the Redskins.

For his career, his combined yardage production from rushing, receiving, and returns was 8,147 yards. His rushing total was 3,057 yards. He also had 23 career interceptions. Dudley was inducted into the Pro Football Hall of Fame in 1966.

No one ever did as many things as well on a football field as Bill Dudley and he was one of the most intelligent players I ever observed. Bill was the best runner in the league for a few years. He was one of the best pass catchers and passers. He was the best pass defender, a real ball hawk. And he was one of the best place-kickers and punters. He was a 60-minute man in the 1940s.

Dudley was small for football and his form was unorthodox. He had a funny way of running, a funny way of passing, even a funny way of kicking. But he figured out ways that worked for him, and no one worked harder on the field than he did. Still, I don't think it was work for him. You can tell when something is work for someone. You can tell when it's fun for them. Bill always looked like it was fun for him out there. He got beaten up regularly by bigger guys, but he went at every play with enthusiasm.

He played for three teams, but I think he was at his peak with Pittsburgh. The Steelers were coached at that time by one of the great coaches, Jock Sutherland. I've heard that Dudley and Sutherland did not get along. Dudley was a fun-loving fellow, and Sutherland was serious and glum. So Bill was going to give up the game after three seasons until another team, Detroit, obtained rights to him. And he wound up with Washington. Wherever he went, he was one of the best. A player like him comes along only every ten years or so. He came along just in time to be able to make the most of his many talents.

16.
Paul Hornung

No player in NFL history has ever produced more points in a single season that the 176 Paul Hornung scored for the Green Bay Packers in 1960. That was the second of three straight years in which Hornung led all NFL scorers. He produced 94 in 1959, and 146 in 1961 for his other two scoring titles.

Only Don Hutson and Gino Cappelletti, with five apiece, won more scoring championships than Hornung, the Golden Boy from Notre Dame who was one of the Packers' greatest running backs and an efficient place-kicker.

Hornung, a 6-2, 220-pounder, scored 15 touchdowns, kicked 15 field goals, and was a perfect 41 for 41 on extra points in his record-smashing 1960 season. In six seasons as the Packers' placement specialist, Hornung missed only four of 194 conversion-point attempts.

But Hornung was much more than just a kicker. He was a key runner for Green Bay as Vince Lombardi constructed a dynasty during the decade of the 1960s. Hornung rushed for 3,711 yards and scored 50 touchdowns on the ground in his career.

Twice Hornung enjoyed near-record games against the Baltimore Colts. On October 8, 1961, he scored four touchdowns and kicked a field goal and six extra points, accounting for 33 points against the Colts that day. That is the fourth-highest single-game scoring production in NFL history. Four years later, on December 12, 1965, Hornung had another big game against the Colts. He accounted for five touchdowns—three running and two on passes. Only three men—Ernie Nevers, Dub Jones, and Gale Sayers—have ever scored six TDs in one game.

Paul Hornung (#5)

Hornung was an All-America selection at Notre Dame, won the 1956 Heisman Trophy as the finest college football player in America, and was drafted on the first round by Green Bay. He was selected for two All-Pro teams and two Pro Bowl games but a shadow was cast over his career in 1963 when he was suspended for the season by Commissioner Pete Rozelle for betting on NFL games. He returned in 1964 and played three more seasons before retiring with a career total of 760 points, second highest in Green Bay history behind only the great pass receiver Don Hutson.

If I had my way players would devote every minute of every day to football. As a coach, I came as close to it as I could. The closer you come to it, the closer you come to making the most of yourself in football or any profession. But there is more to life than any one pursuit. We have to share life with others for it to be meaningful, and while I always felt my team was my family, I also found time to have a family away from the field—a great wife and great kids. I'm sure they felt I didn't find enough time for them, but they had to share me with football.

There have been many players who found a lot of time for other things in their lives besides football but who were so gifted they still attained greatness on the field. I had a couple, including Billy Kilmer. Another was

Joe Namath. Still another was Paul Hornung. Almost everyone knows about their exploits off the field. But the one thing they had in common, besides great natural ability, was that on the field they gave everything they had. Winning was as important to them as it was to me. Maybe they weren't as willing to sacrifice off the field for it as much as a fellow like me would like, but they made all the sacrifices on the field. They were fun-loving fellows, and even a straight fellow like me finds it hard not to love them.

Hornung may have been the most underrated player of his era. He was one of the outstanding pressure players of any year. He was a good running back who became a great running back when he got near the goal line. He was good at getting the hard yard and getting over the goal line. He was a great scorer, also because he was a superb place-kicker. Originally a quarterback, he was one of the best passers of any halfback ever. He was a fine pass catcher, especially effective on swing passes. He also blocked well. Sure, he was fun-loving, but he was also one of the greatest of the great Green Bay Packers.

CHAPTER 4

OFFENSIVE LINEMEN

Offensive linemen will attract less attention, get less glory, and probably make less money than, say, defensive linemen. Nowadays the names of offensive linemen come up primarily when they are called for holding and an official steps up in front of a television camera, signals the infraction, and calls out the player's number. As far as I know no official ever called the viewing public's attention to a good offensive block.

Thus the good offensive lineman has to play for the love of it as much as anything. He'll never be more than mediocre if he wishes he were playing in the defensive line. He has to have good size—height, width, and weight. They come bigger these days, but the bigger guys always have been the better offensive linemen. Some pulling guards, who run out in front of the runners, are smaller—and quicker—but size usually has come ahead of speed. Sheer bulk put between the tackler and the runner or passer will do a lot of the job for them. Strength is critical. Good balance is critical. Frankly, I look for big fannies in offensive linemen. The good ones usually have them. It indicates a solid base.

The great offensive linemen have had fast feet and fast hands to go with their good size. You have to be fast on your feet and have good footwork, and be agile and able to move well from side to side to stay between the tackler and the runner or passer. You need quickness rather than straight-away speed. You have to be able to use your hands well, legally and illegally. All offensive linemen hold. Some hold more than others, usually because they lack the skills to do the job otherwise. Some hold more cleverly than others. Holding penalties never helped a team.

All outstanding offensive linemen have had intelligence. They may not be well read, but they know the playbook. They may not go to foreign films, but they know how to read football films. The more sophisticated football has become, the more is asked of the offensive lineman. He has to be able to read constantly changing defenses and pick up the tips that tell him the other team is going to blitz, and so forth. He has to have a quick mind as well as quick hands and feet. He may not know the theory of relativity but he has to know the theories of football.

Big as they have been, the great offensive linemen have had a lot of finesse. To block effectively, whether slowing down the pass rusher or taking down the run tackler, he has to have outstanding technique, especially against outstanding defensive linemen. And this is the most important measuring stick of greatness—how one great lineman does against another. You also judge them by how they do late in games. In big games. Late in the season. In playoff and championship games. It is subjective. You have few statistics to guide you on offensive linemen. Even beyond that it probably is harder to judge them than players at any other position.

I've considered how many times particular offensive linemen have been picked to All-Pro and Pro Bowl teams. I want to know how high the better ones have been held by some experts. But this consideration is not conclusive, especially among offensive linemen. Sometimes it takes coaches who know the plays and assignments and study the films to determine how well an offensive lineman has done. Sometimes it takes a coach's eye. A lot is hidden from the eye in the pit. I know from experience that reputation often determines the All-Pro lineups. Once a fellow makes one, he's apt to make others. Since so few see so little of what is happening in the pit, players often are picked on their reputation.

The offensive line is, in some ways, the hardest of all positions to play, largely because the players here can use their hands the least.

It's tough in the pit. The good players have to play in pain. They get hurt a lot. They have to perform with injuries if the injuries will permit it. The great offensive linemen have been so tough they've seldom missed games and they've had long careers. Running backs are much more fragile. Offensive linemen have to be strong, tough, physically superior people.

One of the most important characteristics in an outstanding offensive lineman is poise. He has to have presence of mind and patience to outwit and outmaneuver big, strong, quick defensive linemen, many of whom are the meanest men in football, some of whom are the dirtiest players in the game. The great defensive lineman loves to hit people. Many of them like to hurt people. It takes poise for an offensive lineman to deal with these people effectively.

Originally in football run blocking was an offensive lineman's most important job. He had to open the holes in the line for the runner to go through. And he had to pull out in front of the runner and cut down the secondary people. As the passing game has become more important, pass blocking has become equally important. The offensive lineman has to keep rushers off the passer. In considering offensive linemen from different eras, I have tried to judge players on how well they did the jobs they had to do.

Today, I consider pass blocking the most important job an offensive lineman has to do because it's the hardest job to do. It is harder to stand up a good rusher and keep him away from the passer during the long seconds it may take for the passer to pick out a receiver and get off a pass than it is to move into a man and knock him erect or backward or off his feet. The latter takes size, strength, quickness, technique, too. Both jobs are difficult. And usually unappreciated.

Here, then, are the greatest offensive linemen, as I have seen them and as I now see them, among the 100 greatest professional football players.

1.
Jim Parker

Jim Parker played for 11 seasons with the Baltimore Colts starting in 1957 and became the first pure offensive lineman to be inducted into the Pro Football Hall of Fame. There had been players previously chosen for the football shrine who were two-way performers, including work on the offensive line. But Parker was the first to spend his career working exclusively at the task of clearing the way for the backfield stars who dominated pro football's psyche.

Drafted out of Ohio State, Parker established himself quickly as a premier blocker. The amazing part of his career is that he split his playing days between left tackle and left guard—positions with vastly different blocking responsibilities. Yet when he made the switch there was no change in his efficiency. For eight straight years, Parker was selected as an All-Pro. The first four of those selections came as a tackle and the last four as a guard. He also was named to the Pro Bowl team for each of those seasons and was selected to the NFL decade team for the 1950s.

At tackle, the 6-3, 273-pound Parker's responsibility was to block the defensive end. When he moved to guard, he drew bigger and stronger defensive tackles. It hardly mattered to him, though. His level of performance remained outstanding.

Parker was a late bloomer. A fourth-team All-State choice in high school, he was recruited by Woody Hayes at Ohio State and became a two-platoon star there, winning the Outland Trophy as the nation's best college lineman in 1956. Hayes thought the youngster's future was on defense and advised the Colts of that when they made Parker their No. 1 draft choice in 1957. But he settled in with the offensive unit instead.

In Baltimore's first exhibition game that year, the Colts threw 47 passes. Parker, a graduate of Ohio State's run-dominated offense, got a rush course in pass blocking and mastered the job in a hurry. He demonstrated how well for the next 11 seasons.

Jim Parker is one of those who rises above even the best. He is one of the greatest of the greats. I do not think there is much doubt that he was the outstanding offensive lineman of all time even though it may be, as I have suggested it is, more difficult to judge players at this position than at any other position.

He not only was one of the biggest men of his day, but probably the fastest big man. He was massive and powerful physically. There was no way you could run over him. Rushers could not knock him down. It was like trying to topple a building. Yet he had quick feet and quick hands and

Jim Parker (#77)

was an excellent technique man.

I think Parker was the best pass blocker ever. Yet he also was one of the best run blockers. In the line, he drove his opponents backwards, opening huge holes. Yet he also was capable of pulling out and throwing the block past the line of scrimmage that sprung the runners.

No matter how tough you played him, he never lost his poise. I used to put two rushers against him in one way or another to divide his attention or to have one try to distract him while the other slipped by, but he usually could deal with two men at one time. The other option was to ignore his side and try to get your rush from the other side. All by himself, he took away half your rush, which was a big bonus for Johnny Unitas. And you never tried to run through Parker's side unless you had at least two men trying to take him out. It would have been like trying to run through a wall.

There were some outstanding offensive linemen in Jim's time. But Parker was not only the best physically, but also the most skillful, not only of his era, but, I feel, of all time.

2.
Forrest Gregg

When Vince Lombardi reflected on his coaching career and the assembling of one of the NFL's most awesome dynasties at Green Bay during the 1960s, he said, "Forrest Gregg is the finest player I ever coached."

That was lavish praise coming from one of the game's coaching legends but it was deserved, because in 15 years of pro football, Gregg starred as an offensive lineman, first at tackle and then at guard. He spent 14 of those years with Green Bay and one season at Dallas, playing on three Super Bowl champion teams, two with the Packers and one with the Cowboys.

Gregg was a two-way tackle at Southern Methodist University and captain of the Mustangs in his senior year. Green Bay picked him on the second round of the 1956 NFL draft and he spent one season with the Packers before a 21-month military-service stint interrupted his football career. He returned to Green Bay in 1958 and, a year later, Lombardi arrived there and began rebuilding the franchise. Gregg was a major factor in the effort.

At first Gregg had ambitions to play on the defensive line, but the Packer coaches decided that at 6-4 and 250 pounds he was better suited to the offensive unit. He started at tackle and was named to the All-Pro team eight straight times, maintaining the string when he switched to guard in 1965. He was selected for the Pro Bowl game nine times.

Gregg tried for early retirement several times, but his talent wouldn't let him. In 1963 he accepted an assistant college coaching job at Tennessee but Lombardi got him to change his mind and talked him back to Green Bay. In 1969 and 1970 he started the season as a member of the Packer coaching staff but was pressed back into action both times. He retired again, but was lured back for one last season in 1971 by Dallas and turned up in the Super Bowl once more.

A member of the Pro Football Hall of Fame, Gregg was selected for the NFL team of the decade for the 1960s and has been a head coach at

Forrest Gregg (#75)

Cleveland and Cincinnati in the NFL. In January, 1982 he led the Bengals into Super Bowl XVI, where they were beaten, 26–21, by San Francisco.

Forrest Gregg was the anchor of the finest offensive line of all time, on one of the finest teams of all time, the Green Bay Packers of the 1960s. He was a tackle. Jerry Kramer, who was strongly considered for my list, was a guard. Jim Ringo, who made the list, was a center. But Gregg was the greatest player of them all.

He had size, strength, and speed—all the tools. He used his talent to the fullest. He had quick feet and hands and superior intelligence. He had the best footwork I've ever seen on an offensive lineman and the best techniques. They called him the best dancer since Fred Astaire. He did his little dance and turned people around. He never seemed to make a mistake. He seldom was beaten.

Gregg always was a leader. Twice, when I was coaching in Los Angeles and in Washington, I tried to get him to join my coaching staffs, but each time there was something in his way. I am not surprised at the recent success he has had in coaching. He did not make it in Cleveland, but it was a maturing process, and he has made it with the Bengals. He has turned a loser into a winner in Cincinnati. He did it in three years. A team does not get to the Super Bowl without superior coaching. Gregg was one of those players a coach knew would make a superior coach someday.

The Packers developed disciplined blocking and Gregg was their most disciplined blocker. He protected Bart Starr beautifully and opened holes for Paul Hornung and Jim Taylor. Gregg never seemed to tire, or, at least, he never gave in to it. He never gave in to injuries, either. My teams avoided him as much as possible. At other times I double-teamed him. But I don't think I ever saw him play anything other than an outstanding game.

3.
Mel Hein

For 15 years, Mel Hein was an iron man two-way player for the New York Giants, the keystone of the offensive line at center and a hard-hitting linebacker on defense.

He was durable and strong, a 60-minute player in the era of one-platoon football. Only once did he find it necessary to call a time-out because he was injured. That was in 1941, when he suffered a broken nose, necessitating some quick repair work.

Hein played college football at Washington State, performing at center, guard, and tackle. Various All-America teams selected him at each of those positions and he helped his college team to the Pacific Coast Conference championship and a Rose Bowl berth in 1930.

In those days there was no draft to deliver college players automatically into the pro ranks. So Hein took it upon himself to write letters to three NFL clubs, asking for a job. The Giants made the best offer—$150 per game—and that's how this West Coast star turned up in New York in 1931.

Mel Hein

Hein, at 6-2 and 225 pounds, won a job in training camp, capturing a spot on the 25-man roster the pros had then. He was a center in the regular-season opener and performed there until 1945. He was an All-Pro choice for eight straight years, from 1933 to 1940. In 1938 he earned the Joe Carr Trophy, awarded at that time to the league's Most Valuable Player. He is the only interior lineman to have been honored with that award.

Hein was the Giants' captain for 10 years, and during that time the team won seven Eastern Division and two NFL titles.

After his playing career ended, Hein remained in football first as a coach, spending 15 years at USC, and later as a supervisor of officials for the American Football League.

Mel Hein was the prototype center. He developed the techniques of snapping the ball and blocking that have been passed on from center to center ever since. Center is the most difficult position to play on the offensive line. The center must snap the ball properly before he can make his move. This gives everyone else the jump on him. This was especially true years ago on the head-down, long snap to the tailback. It is still true today on the snap to the quarterback in the shotgun formation and on place-kicks and punts. Some of today's centers are so unsure on longer snaps that specialists are brought in to snap on place-kicks and punts.

Today's centers in the T formation can hold their heads up during the snap, as yesterday's could not. Yesterday's centers had to have their heads down, eyes targeting the receiver. Yesterday's centers had to be judged in large part on their ability to make the long snap perfectly. Hein seldom missed in 15 years. He was so quick on his feet, he got into blocking position fast enough on the snap to take his man out.

Hein was an extremely intelligent player. He was a fairly big man for his day, though not as big as some of the defensive players he opposed. He had quickness for his size and developed and mastered techniques his contemporaries did not have. He was strong, tough, and as durable as any player who ever played. He was a 60-minute man who played linebacker on defense, was a terrific tackler, and was deadly on pass defense. Hein never missed a game in his long career of 15 years. He was simply outstanding.

4.
Clyde (Bulldog) Turner

Possessor of one of pro football's most colorful nicknames, Clyde (Bulldog) Turner achieved stardom for 13 seasons in the NFL with the Chicago Bears. In the era of the two-way players, he was an excellent center and a skilled linebacker.

Turner came out of tiny Hardin-Simmons College and was the subject of a tug-of-war between the Bears and Detroit Lions. In fact, the Lions were fined $5,000—an enormous sum in those days—for tampering with the youngster before Chicago selected him in the 1940 draft.

By 1941, Turner was an All-Pro, ending Mel Hein's steak of eight straight selections as the All-NFL center. In all, Turner was honored six times as the All-Pro center. But he was no slouch on defense, and in 1942 he led the NFL with eight interceptions from his linebacker position. At 6-2 and 235 pounds he was big and fast. In fact, in one 1944 game when the Bears' backfield was thinned by injuries, he played there and responded with a 48-yard touchdown run.

In 1947, Turner enjoyed what must have been the highlight of his career. Playing on defense against Washington, he intercepted a pass by Sammy Baugh at his four-yard line. Turner took off up the sideline, sidestepping one tackle attempt after another. The last defender was Baugh, who was brushed aside at the 12-yard line, and Turner then barged into the end zone, completing a 96-yard touchdown run—the third longest in league history at the time.

Turner's first NFL interception also was achieved against Washington. He returned that one 24 yards for a TD, part of the Chicago rampage that became a historic 73–0 victory in the 1940 championship game. He made three other interceptions in title games later on.

A member of the Pro Football Hall of Fame, Turner was selected as the center on the All-NFL team for the decade of the 1940s.

Admitting he studied and copied Mel Hein, Bulldog Turner was the next great center to come into the NFL and become almost the equal of Hein. Turner also was a linebacker on defense. While both were at their best on offense, Hein was slightly superior to Turner on offense, Turner slightly superior to Hein on defense. Both were 60-minute players and incredibly durable. Turner lasted 13 seasons in the NFL.

Turner was a T center, so he did not have the snapping problems presented to Hein. Turner was bigger and stronger, yet quick as a cat and, if the fellows who lined up over him had the jump on him, he was moving before they got to him and drove them right back with devastating force. He may have been the best at getting away with holding I ever saw, and he pass-blocked effectively. He used to say no one ever got the better of him until late in his career, when he came up against the brilliant Bill Willis

Clyde (Bulldog) Turner

of Cleveland, who is on my defensive-line list and from what I saw of Willis, Bulldog was telling the truth.

Turner played with reckless abandon. He didn't just tackle people, he destroyed them. Despite his size, he was so quick he may have been the best linebacker against the pass I ever saw. For all of his abandon, he was smart, he seemed to know where the pass was going, and he picked off passes right and left. And when he picked off a pass, he ran with it like a running back. What a fullback he'd have made! If he'd played running back, he might have been one of the best. If I hadn't put him among the greatest offensive linemen, I'd have had to list him among the greatest linebackers.

Alex Wojciechowicz was another outstanding center of the 1940s who came very close to making my list. Frank Gatski was another outstanding center of the 1940s who deserved consideration. But Bulldog Turner's right to make the list is beyond doubt in my mind.

5.
Danny Fortmann

Scouting strategy and drafting techniques were much less scientific in pro football's early days than they are in the computerized world that the NFL occupies now. For the NFL's first player draft in 1936, the nine member clubs went about the job of dividing up the prospects in a most unscientific manner compared to today's standards. Chicago's George Halas had the last choice and picked Danny Fortmann, a guard from Colgate, simply, he said, because he liked his name.

That reasoning would never do nowadays but it paid off for Halas because Fortmann became a Hall of Famer and was named to the NFL's decade team for the 1930s.

Fortmann succeeded despite rather ordinary size. At 6-0 and 207 pounds he hardly looked like a "Monster of the Midway"—the nickname the Bear teams carried. He was a Phi Beta Kappa premed student at Colgate and was just 19 years old when Halas drafted him. But Fortmann responded to the challenge of playing in the NFL by developing into one of the game's great two-way players.

From 1938 to 1943 he was an All-Pro selection for six straight years, and he accomplished that while playing both offense and defense. Sometimes he lined up alongside Chicago's No. 1 pick in that 1936 draft, tackle Joe Stydahar from West Virginia. Both wound up in the Hall of Fame.

Fortmann was a member of the Bears' team that scored the most lopsided victory in NFL championship game history, Chicago's 73—0 destruction of Washington in the 1940 title game. He often joked that he made the key play in that game by winning the coin toss, providing the Bears with the ball from the start to ignite the massacre.

Offensive Linemen

While with the Bears, Fortmann pursued his medical school studies and eventually graduated as a full-fledged physician. He retired as a player in 1943 after eight years of pro football but returned to the game later as team physician for the Los Angeles Rams.

Danny Fortmann

Danny Fortmann may have been the greatest offensive guard ever to play the game. He was what we used to call a "watch-charm guard," smaller than the players around him but quicker, big enough, tough enough, and so good on techniques that he outmaneuvered just about every player he opposed.

Fortmann was a key performer on those great George Halas Chicago Bear teams of the late 1930s and early 1940s, which I rate with the Paul Brown Cleveland Browns of the late 1940s and early 1950s, the Vince Lombardi Green Bay Packers of the 1960s, and the Chuck Noll Pittsburgh Steelers of the 1970s as among the four or five greatest teams of all time in professional football.

Of those old Bears, center Bulldog Turner and guard Fortmann made my list on the offensive line and tackle Joe Stydahar made it on the defensive line. Guard George Musso, who was picked for the Hall of Fame early this year, and tackle Lee Artoe were given serious consideration for the offensive and defensive line lists, respectively. George Connor, who played later for the Bears, was one of the finest offensive linemen of all time and also was one of the finest defensive linemen, but I placed him among the linebackers, where he was one of the best ever.

Those were remarkably talented teams and these truly great players were 60-minute men, just about equally good on offense and defense.

Fortmann was just a tremendous talent who made the most of every tool he had, and he was the inspirational leader of that team. There are a lot of different blocks and he could make them all, but I think he was at his best pulling out of the line quickly, beating the running back into the secondary, and cutting down a defender.

6.
Jim Tyrer

If one could place an order for the ideal offensive tackle, the product would look something like Jim Tyrer, a 6-6, 275-pound giant possessed with size, speed, and quickness. For 13 years, from 1961 to 1973, he performed in the line of the AFL franchise that began as the Dallas Texans and later became the Kansas City Chiefs.

Tyrer set a club record playing in 180 consecutive games over that stretch. He was picked for nine All-Pro teams and nine Pro Bowl games and was a solid choice for one of the tackle spots on the all-time AFL squad.

Jim Tyrer

An All-American at Ohio State, Tyrer was coveted by the NFL Cleveland Browns as well as the Dallas franchise in the AFL. Tyrer saw a better opportunity playing in the new league and became one of the AFL's major early victories in the war for quality players. He was installed as a starter almost immediately and his devastating lead blocks opened huge holes for running backs Abner Haynes and Mike Garrett.

Tyrer played in the first Super Bowl game when the Chiefs lost to Green Bay and also was in Super Bowl IV, when Kansas City beat Minnesota. He also played in three divisional or conference championship games with the Chiefs.

At the end of his career, Tyrer left Kansas City for one wrap-up season with the Washington Redskins in 1974. But he is remembered as a Chief and as one of the team's best performers during the period when Kansas City was among the AFL's strongest franchises.

Tyrer's postfootball life turned tragic. Several business ventures failed and he shocked the pro football world in 1980 when, overcome by despair, he shot and killed his wife and then committed suicide.

Jim Tyrer was out of the mold of Jim Parker, actually a little taller and heavier, a massive man, yet quick on his feet and with his hands. He had a thick upper body but slender legs. He was so large and so strong he literally intimidated opponents. As a pass blocker it was almost impossible to get around him. As a run blocker you couldn't go through him and it was difficult to get around him. But I think he was at his best as one of the great pass blockers.

Tyrer and Ed Budde were a terrific twosome on those great Hank Stram Kansas City teams of the old American Football League, which did so well when they came into the NFL. Tyrer and Ron Mix were the All-Star offensive tackles eight or nine straight seasons in the AFL, and although they proved themselves in the late stages of their career in the NFL I think they were underrated by NFL diehards.

I had Tyrer with Washington in the late stages of his 13-year pro career. I'd grab these great players even when they only had a year or two left in them, when others thought they were washed up, because I always figured I could get one more good year out of them and that was always enough for me. You play one game at a time, one year at a time.

I remember we were leading the Giants by three points in a game we had to win to stay in contention in our division. We had a third down and needed a first down to protect our lead late in the game. We ran behind Tyrer and gained the first down. On his side, the Giants' defense seemed to collapse. When we studied the films later, we saw that he so submarined their line he caused it to collapse. It was an unbelievable play for one man to make. It was the sort of big play in a big game an offensive lineman can make. I said to our other coaches, "I haven't had many blocks like that in my coaching career."

7.
Ron Mix

In the days when the expansion American Football League was challenging the established National Football League, the AFL groped madly for an identity. One of the men who provided it was Ron Mix, who became one of the new league's premier offensive tackles.

Mix was an enigma. He preferred baseball over football in high school and college. But he performed considerably better on the gridiron than he did on the diamond, so that was the direction his athletic career took.

He started out as a receiver, but a vision problem interfered with his progress so he moved to tackle.

His 6-4 frame was more suited to his original position and he had to work hard at building his body up to offensive-line dimensions, often eating five or six meals a day to work himself up from his off-season 220 pounds to his playing weight of 250.

The AFL acquired Mix in a spirited bidding competition. He was a first-round pick in the 1960 NFL draft, selected by the Baltimore Colts. The fledgling AFL was just getting started and Mix's rights were obtained by the Boston franchise, which traded them to Los Angeles. The new league made a substantial contract offer—a $5,000 signing bonus and a two-year, no-cut $12,000 annual salary. The Colts countered with a less impressive $1,000 signing bonus and an $8,500 no-guarantee contract. What's more, Baltimore wouldn't budge. So Mix signed with the AFL.

After one year in Los Angeles, the Chargers moved to San Diego and Mix quickly became one of the league's top stars. His speed and strength coming off the ball made him a superlative offensive lineman. He played 10 years for the Chargers and one year for Oakland in 1971 before retiring.

He was an All-Pro choice for his first nine years, played in eight All-Star or Pro Bowl games, and participated in five of the first six AFL championship games. He was a unanimous selection for the all-time AFL team chosen in 1969 and is a member of the Pro Football Hall of Fame.

Ron Mix was the other great tackle in the American Football League who proved himself in the National League. He was not as tall or as heavy as Jim Tyrer, but Ron Mix was quicker and faster. Tyrer was more frightening and destructive, but Mix was a better technician and almost equally effective.

Mix and Tyrer were the all-time All-AFL offensive tackles. Billy Shaw and Ed Budde were the all-time All-AFL offensive guards. Shaw was strong, fast, and smart and was one of the last players I left off this list. Jim Otto was the all-time all-AFL offensive center and he can be found a bit lower on the list. Some of the greatest players who ever played were in the AFL and while they are in a minority among my 100 I have no prejudices against them.

I am just glad Mix didn't team up with Jim Parker with Baltimore, which drafted Ron, but he went to the AFL instead, where he became the leader of those fine Charger teams. Frankly, he didn't seem to me to play with the sort of enthusiasm that showed me he loved playing, but he was scientific in his approach and physically able to contain his opponents.

Where even many good offensive linemen take a step back and brace themselves to take the charge of the pass rushers, Mix took a step forward and took the rushers on aggressively. He was a superb pass blocker and an equally good run blocker. He was fast enough to pull out and block downfield for the runner. Mix almost never held. He didn't have to. He never rattled. He was a smart and poised professional.

Ron Mix (#74)

8.
Roosevelt Brown

Three decades ago, the NFL's college draft was an exercise in endurance, continuing as long as teams came up with names of players. In 1953 the exercise had dragged into its twenty-seventh round when the New York Giants, seeking new names, drafted an obscure offensive tackle from

Morgan State. And that's how Roosevelt Brown started on the road to the Pro Football Hall of Fame.

Brown was the Giants' starting offensive right tackle for 13 years. For eight straight seasons, from 1956 to 1963, he was a virtually unanimous All-Pro selection. He was chosen for 10 Pro Bowl squads and set the standard of play for his position. When he was elected to the Pro Football Hall of Fame in 1975, he became only the second player named strictly on the basis of his offensive line play, following Jim Parker. That's how good Brown was.

The Giants selected Brown with a minimum of information. He had been chosen to the Black All-America team by the *Pittsburgh Courier*, a weekly newspaper. That was good enough for New York to take a chance on him.

When he got to training camp, Brown had to be coached on the most basic elements of his game, such as the proper three-point stance for an offensive lineman. But his size—he was 6-3 and 255 pounds, with a 29-inch waist—made him attractive to the head coach, Steve Owen. On Brown's first day in camp he was turned over to Arnie Weinmeister, an All-Pro defensive lineman, for a scrimmage. Weinmeister worked the rookie over but when he had finished, Brown still had enough strength for a couple of laps around the field. His enthusiasm impressed Owen, and within a couple of weeks Brown had won a starting job.

Brown was a vital cog in the Giants' most successful era. During the middle 10 years of his career the club logged an 86–35–5 record, capturing six conference crowns and one NFL title. That twenty-seventh-round draft choice from Morgan State played a major part in the success.

Roosevelt Brown was a little like Jim Tyrer. Brown wasn't as big, but he was big enough. He was tall and had wide shoulders and good upper-body development, but narrow hips and legs. He was very fast. He had terrific quickness and excellent straightaway speed. He was one of the best in the pit, but at his best pulling out and blocking downfield. He was spectacular and attracted attention in a way that offensive linemen usually do not. Some think he was overrated, but I don't. He made All-Pro year after year and deserved it. He was an important part of those great Giants teams of the 1950s.

There were a great many outstanding offensive linemen in the 1950s I couldn't find room for on my list. Bob St. Clair was a redwood tree of a man who just took people out of the play for the 49ers. He was very underrated in his day, seldom if ever making All-Pro, but he came very close to making my list. Mike McCormack was big and efficient and also came very close. He, Lou Groza, Lou Rymkus, Gene Hickerson, John Wooten, and Frank Gatski were wonderfully effective blockers for Paul Brown's great Cleveland Browns teams and any of them could have been picked. Groza did make the 100 as a place-kicker with an assist from his all-around ability.

But Roosevelt Brown was special. I've said Jim Parker was the fastest big man ever on the offensive line, but Brown was faster. The thing is,

Parker was much bigger. We're talking about 275 pounds compared to 255. Where do you draw the line? Parker seemed like a charging rhino, Brown like a romping giraffe. Brown was extraordinarily consistent from game to game and endured for 13 seasons. He played best in the big games. He was an exceptional player.

Roosevelt Brown

9.
Jim Ringo

The action in football starts with the center and his snap of the ball. And in Green Bay, the Packer dynasty orchestrated by Vince Lombardi also started with the center, an iron-man anchor named Jim Ringo.

Ringo was the first Packer player in the decade of the 1960s to reach All-Pro excellence, and Lombardi built his team around the solid center from Syracuse University. Ringo spent 11 seasons in Green Bay, from 1953 to 1963, and was a seven-time All-Pro selection. He finished his career with four seasons in Philadelphia and was named to 10 Pro Bowl games in 15 NFL years.

When he reported to his first pro training camp in 1953, the 6-1 Ringo weighed only 211 pounds, smallish by NFL dimensions even then. He never weighed more than 235 during his playing career, yet he still flourished. His quickness made up for the lack of size and Ringo often opened the gaping holes that led running backs Jim Taylor and Paul Hornung to substantial gains.

Ringo played despite many illnesses and injuries. In his first All-Pro season, 1957, he was a victim of mononucleosis and spent five weeks hospitalized from Monday through Friday, released for the weekend to play, and then returning to the hospital the following Monday. He followed the same Monday-to-Friday hospital routine for six weeks during the 1962 season because of a staph infection. But on Sunday there he was, over the ball, set to snap it.

Jim Ringo

Injuries cost him the final seven games of his rookie season, but he then started 182 regular-season contests in a row, a total which represented an NFL record at the time of his retirement in 1967.

Ringo's long-term pro career almost never got started. Two weeks into his first Packer training camp, he went home to Easton, Pennsylvania, convinced that he was not big enough for the NFL. However, his father and wife convinced him to give it one more try. He was named to the All-NFL team for the decade of the 1960s and is a member of the Pro Football Hall of Fame.

Jim Ringo was small as NFL linemen go, but as tough as any. He was the center when Green Bay started building great offensive lines in the 1960s.

Ringo was a sure snapper and equally efficient at pass blocking or run blocking. He had good strength and used his size well. He was fast on his feet and used his hands to good advantage. He took good position and always was in balance. He was a very smart player and made very few mistakes.

Ringo was the best center of the 1960s, although Mick Tingelhoff of Minnesota, who succeeded him as the All-Pro center, also was outstanding. After Green Bay traded Ringo to Philadelphia, he played very well for the Eagles for some time. You just can't write off players like him.

The center is an underrated player in pro football, even among other offensive linemen. He is not going to attract the attention a guard or a tackle will because he is not able to be active all over the field. But smart coaches build offensive lines around them, and Vince Lombardi built his early around Ringo. No team has succeeded without an excellent center.

Jim Ringo personified excellence. Everything he was asked to do, he did well. He was a great part of a great team.

10.
Jim Otto

Jim Otto's pro football career had a somewhat hesitant start. In fact, it was so hesitant that it almost never got started.

Otto had been a center-linebacker at the University of Miami and was good enough to set a school record for tackles made during a career. But at 205 pounds he seemed too light for the rugged game of pro football. So when he came out of college in 1960 he passed through the NFL draft without so much as a nod of acknowledgment. That left only the new AFL which, at the time, was hardly the picture of stability.

The new league's Minneapolis franchise decided to risk a twenty-fifth-round draft pick on Otto. After setting out to join the team, there was a slight detour because the franchise was abruptly transferred from Minnesota to Oakland before its first season.

But Otto was determined to play pro football and so he joined the Raiders—something of a long shot as they took their first tentative steps in the sport. But there was nothing tentative about the way Otto settled in at center. For 15 years he started every regular-season game for Oakland at that position, setting a standard of performance that earned him election to the Pro Football Hall of Fame in 1980. He was the first Raider and only the third AFL player to gain that honor.

The 6-2 Otto blossomed to center size at 255 pounds and was an All-Pro selection for 13 straight years. No other man ever was chosen to the position during the years the AFL was in existence. He played in each of the AFL's nine All-Star games and in the first three AFC-NFC Pro Bowls, and he was a unanimous choice for the all-time AFL team.

Otto played a total of 308 games for the Raiders, including 210 straight regular-season contests. He was a tower of strength on the offensive line, a sure-handed ball snapper and a strong blocker who regularly cleared running lanes up the middle of the field. He called the offensive line's blocking signals and was a dependable pivot who rarely made mistakes.

His string of games played developed in spite of many disabling injuries that might have sidelined other players. But Otto was determined to play every game and that's what he did.

Jim Otto was another top center of the 1960s and 1970s, in both the AFL and the NFL. He was a lot like Jim Ringo. Originally Otto was small but tough. But he built himself up to 255 and wound up a large man.

A guy like Otto just gives and gives and gives. He anchors an offensive line, and the stability he gives to a team is critical to its success. He is just always there, doing his job. When you do it as well as Otto did it, his stature rises and rises in my estimation. And I'm sure his coaches appreciated it.

Al Davis and John Madden put together one of the outstanding offensive lines of all time at Oakland in the 1970s. Center Otto, guard Gene Upshaw, and tackle Art Shell were three of the greatest blockers ever. They provided Ken Stabler with superb protection and opened huge holes that made ordinary runners extraordinarily successful. Otto and Upshaw made my list of 100; Shell narrowly missed.

Jim Langer of Miami and Mike Webster of Pittsburgh were two other excellent centers of the 1970s. Webster is still going strong. But Otto was outstanding. He combined size, strength, and speed. He made perfect snaps and was a master of various blocks. He was an extremely disciplined player, a true pro.

Jim Otto

11.
Gene Upshaw

Gene Upshaw, who has anchored the offensive line of the Oakland Raiders since 1967, was the Raiders' No. 1 draft choice out of Texas A&I in 1967 and became a starter immediately. He helped Oakland to the Super Bowl that year and began a string of 207 consecutive games played which ended early in the 1981 season. Oakland's visit to the playoffs in Upshaw's rookie year started another string of 24 postseason games for the 6-5, 255-pound guard. No AFC player has been in more playoff games.

If his preseason and postseason games are included, Upshaw's starting streak reaches an iron-man total of 307 games, no small accomplishment for an offensive lineman, who has to carry a punishing workload.

Upshaw is the only Raider player to have appeared in all three of the team's Super Bowl games. Those three contests run almost the full range of his career. The first, in 1967, came when he was a rookie, still learning his craft. The second, in 1976, came with him at the top of his game, an awesome blocker who cleared defenders like a plow working its way through a snowdrift. The third, in 1980, came with him as a grizzled veteran, a master of his job.

He quickly assumed a position of leadership with the Raiders and has been the club's offensive captain for the past eight years. He also has been president of the NFL Players' Association and winner in 1980 of the Association's Byron White Humanitarian Award, given to the player who best serves his team, community, and country.

A four-time All-Pro selection, Upshaw has played in the Pro Bowl five times. In 1975 he was selected to the all-time pro team for players from the state of Texas. He is a native of Robstown.

Gene Upshaw and Art Shell dominated the 1977 Super Bowl as no other offensive linemen I've seen dominate a championship game. They just blasted big holes in the Minnesota defense and let a lot of Oakland Raider runners look like Jim Brown and O. J. Simpson. It was the best blocking I've seen in a title game and the sort of big-game performance that makes a man stand out in my mind.

Upshaw had size, speed, and durability. When you have a guy like him always there for you, you have stability and consistency built into your team. Gene was maybe the best blast blocker ever. He could drive men back two feet to create a huge hole for runners. The 1981 season was his fifteenth in pro football.

There are many other standout offensive-line candidates from the 1970s who didn't make my list of 100. At his best no one was better than big Bob Brown, who could take the best opponents apart, but he had to be inspired

Gene Upshaw (#63)

and he was inconsistent, often ordinary in ordinary games. Dan Dierdorf of St. Louis and Rayfield Wright of Dallas were remarkably good in their primes. Bob Kuechenberg and Larry Little of Miami were marvelous blockers on those marvelous Don Shula Miami teams of the early 1970s.

I suppose I'll take some heat because John Hannah of New England did not make my list. In 1981 a Sports Illustrated writer did a cover story on John, calling him the greatest offensive lineman of all time. It is amazing how much importance is given to the opinion of one writer for one important publication. He was backed by some other experts. Sure, Hannah has been outstanding. But in my mind he has not yet attained the heights of others or as yet accomplished enough.

Gene Upshaw has performed superbly in one key game after another. He has seemed to me to be as intelligent a player as I've seen and I understand him to be an unusually intelligent individual off the field, too.

12.
Ron Yary

When the Minnesota Vikings traded Fran Tarkenton to the New York Giants in 1967, they received four draft choices in exchange for the quarterback. One of those picks turned out to be the first selection in the 1968 NFL draft, and with it Minnesota chose tackle Ron Yary from the University of Southern California. That made Yary unique. He was the first offensive lineman ever selected as the draft's No. 1 pick.

Yary came with first-rate credentials. He had been a two-time All-America choice at USC, where he led the blocking for O. J. Simpson. In 1967 he won the Outland Trophy as the nation's top college lineman.

He quickly became the bulwark of the Vikings' offensive line, and from 1969 to 1980 he never missed a regular-season game. Yary was chosen for seven Pro Bowl games and was named to the All-Pro team six times.

At 6-6 and 255 pounds he has been the prototype for an offensive tackle, big and strong as well as quick on his feet. At the height of his career Yary was all but unbeatable. He was a big help to Tarkenton, who was reacquired by the Vikings in 1972.

Critics claimed that Ron also is expert at illegally holding opponents, but there is no denying his legitimate ability. He has played the position with textbook precision and he hasn't attracted many penalty flags from officials.

Yary was a fixture on four Viking NFC champion teams, anchoring the offensive line. His job was made even more difficult by Tarkenton's scrambling tendencies. One can't find blocking techniques for that style of play in any pro playbook, but Yary still flourished and, for a time, he was a perennial All-Pro choice at his position.

His accomplishments made the first Tarkenton trade pay off for the Vikings. Used properly, draft choices can be terrific commodities, especially if there are offensive tackles like Yary out there waiting to be chosen.

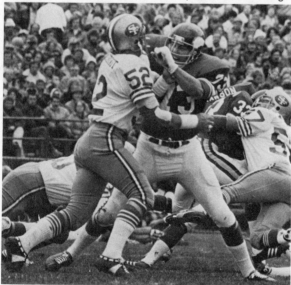

Ron Yary (#73)

Ron Yary has been a tower of strength for many outstanding Bud Grant Minnesota Viking teams. High, wide, and heavy, Yary has been an immovable obstacle for pass rushers, moving defensive ends and tackles around almost at will.

I think he has held more than most of the great ones, but with his fast hands he's gotten away with it most of the time. He's had determination, tenacity, staying power. He's never given up and sometimes it seems you never get past him.

At his best as a pass blocker, he also has been a good run blocker and, despite his size, he could get downfield and block well in a broken field, too, in his prime. He helped make Fran Tarkenton a standout and has made some runners look good as well.

Yary is one of numerous players out of the University of Southern California. Many have been outstanding offensive linemen. Marvin Powell, one of the best ones now, is another. Still another is Anthony Muñoz, a massive youngster who in his second season in 1981 helped Cincinnati get to the Super Bowl. He looks like an immortal in the making. But looking like one and becoming one are two different things.

Ron Yary finished his fourteenth season in the NFL in 1981. He took God-given size and abilities and built himself up into a massively effective football player. He took native intelligence and outsmarted opponents. He has overcome injuries of all kinds and has played extremely well for a very long time.

CHAPTER 5

PLACE-KICKERS

The most important quality a place-kicker can have is the ability to produce under pressure. If a kicker can hit from 40 yards and out, great. But I'd rather have a consistent kicker from 30 yards, especially one who can come through in the clutch, than an inconsistent, unpredictable kicker with greater range.

A winning team takes advantage of a high percentage of its scoring opportunities. When you get the ball in scoring range, you want seven points if you can get it, but you want to come away with at least three. When you get nothing it is destructive to your momentum and morale.

The place-kicker is critical to a team's success. And when he can come through with a field goal from 25 or 30 yards in the last minute with a game on the line, he is one of the most valuable players on the team.

It doesn't matter if he doesn't do anything else for you, though it is certainly a big plus if he fills another role. The two top place-kickers on my list filled other roles successfully. But I wouldn't have picked them if they hadn't been the best at their specialty.

Some coaches underestimate the importance of the kicking game. The place-kicking game puts many points on the board for you and cannot be overestimated. Very often the place-kicker is the difference between victory and defeat . . . the highest scorer on the team.

The glory goes to the guys who kick the 50-yarders, and if they can kick the 25-yarders, too, I'm all for them. But if not, I'll take the guys who can kick the 25-yarders consistently and come through in the pressure situations for me every time.

Needless to say, they have to kick extra points successfully every time, or very close to it. There's little margin for error here.

Another important quality a place-kicker should have is the ability to put the ball into the end zone consistently on kickoffs. The long-range guys do this most often, of course. It is helpful to cut down on potentially dangerous runbacks as much as possible.

Even if a place-kicker does not play another role, his is among the most difficult and demanding jobs in the game. He doesn't get many chances in a game so he has to make the most of those he does get. Very often he must come through with the game on the line, sometimes a title on the line.

It is a pressure-packed position. The great ones seem almost immune to pressure. They are poised, cold-blooded characters with a lot of confidence. The great ones do not slip into long slumps, though most place-kickers do. Merely good ones bounce from team to team, up and down from season to season, sometimes from game to game.

Place-kickers have to be able to get off their kicks fast and high to avoid blocks, but if they're not accurate it doesn't matter how fast they kick or how high their kicks travel. There has to be a good snap and a good hold for a good kicker to do his job consistently, so the smarter coaches have this specialty practiced more than do others.

In recent years we have turned to soccer-style kickers, often from foreign countries where soccer is a major sport, because of the added force these fellows seem to generate with their sidewinder style. But the first two I picked were old-fashioned, straight-on fellows. I don't care how a kicker kicks as long as he does the job.

In my mind, the following place-kickers did the best job.

1.
George Blanda

George Blanda kicked more field goals (335) and more extra points (943) than any other placement man in the history of pro football. That's 1,948 points scored. Add nine touchdowns and his point production soars to 2,002, more than 500 ahead of the next highest total.

Blanda played for 26 seasons—longer than any man in history—and was 48 years old and a hero of middle-age America when he retired in 1976. His career can be divided into three distinct sections. The first one began in 1949 and lasted 10 years with the Chicago Bears, for whom he served mostly as a backup quarterback and regular kicker. Then, with the emergence of the American Football League in 1960, Blanda moved to the Houston Oilers, doubling as the league's best passer and its best kicker. That phase lasted until 1967, when he was traded to Oakland and returned primarily to kicking.

When he retired, Blanda had played in four different decades and either tied or owned outright 16 regular-season and 21 championship-game records.

Blanda was an efficient quarterback, leading the NFL in attempts and completions in 1953 and stringing three straight years (1963–65) in which he paced the AFL in those same departments. But it was as a kicker that he is best remembered. When the Raiders acquired him in 1967 at the advanced football age of 40, he proved his foot was still young. He produced three straight 100-point seasons. Five times in nine seasons with the Raiders he led the league in extra points, giving him a record eight PAT titles for his career. Included in that streak was a record 64 conversions in 65 attempts for Houston in 1961.

The 6-2, 215-pound Blanda played in four Pro Bowl games and was named Male Athlete of the Year in 1970 when, at the age of 43, he pieced together a remarkable streak of five straight games in which he pulled out either victories or ties for Oakland with late-game heroics, either by passing or kicking or both. He is a member of the Pro Football Hall of Fame.

The fact that George Blanda played 26 years of professional football probably accounts for much of the fact that he kicked more extra points and more field goals and scored more points by far than any other player. But the 26 years is by far the longest pro football career ever, and the more I think about it the more awed I am by it. He not only kicked, he also threw the ball. He was a player.

George has to have been one of the most amazing athletes of all time. He played until he was almost 50. He played quarterback until the last year or two of his career. He was past 40 when he had maybe his greatest season, with a string of last-minute victories, kicking or passing, that was darn near unbelievable.

The big thing right here is that George rates being No. 1 as a place-kicker. He hit field goals long as well as short and he hit consistently. Most important, he hit under pressure. And he almost never missed an extra point. Maybe there have been better pure kickers, but none better under pressure. I look at it this way: If a game was on the line I'd sooner have Blanda going for the winner than anyone else I can think of.

George did not make my list of the greatest quarterbacks. If I thought he rated it, I'd have put him there as well. I picked a position for others who were deserving at more than one position, but I consider kickers and punters specialists and considered them separately.

A couple of my punters made it at other positions. They made it as punters strictly on their ability as punters.

However, the fact that a place-kicker or punter was outstanding at other positions was a plus in my estimation. And George was an outstanding quarterback and passer. He was smart. He called a good game. He had a rubber arm.

George Blanda

George came into pro ball with the Bears when they had several star quarterbacks and he wasted a lot of years, but he proved himself as a passer in the AFL and later back in the NFL.

George was like old leather. He was slick and tough as he could be. He was confident and cool under pressure. You could count on him. He came through in the clutch countless times. He was a terrific competitor. There's no way I wouldn't list him among the 100 best pro football players.

2.
Lou Groza

Lou Groza was more than just "the Toe"—the nickname he carried because of his fabulous place-kicking ability. He was a quality kicker, but when he started his pro career in 1946, rosters were limited to 33 men and teams couldn't afford the luxury of carrying a player who did nothing but kick. In fact, for quite a while Groza's kicking was little more than a sideline, an added duty to his regular responsibilities as an offensive tackle.

That was Groza's position—tackle. And he was efficient at the job, a quality blocker on the great Cleveland Browns teams assembled by Coach Paul Brown. And for 21 years, Groza also provided the Browns with one of the game's most accurate kickers. When he retired after the 1967 season, he held 10 NFL and 24 Cleveland records and had ended the last link between the modern Browns and the team that began play in the old All-America Conference back in 1946.

The 6-3, 250-pound Groza and Brown first crossed paths at Ohio State in 1941. World War II interrupted Lou's college career, but he continued to play football while in the service and developed his kicking style, thanks to a supply of footballs sent to him by his old coach. In 1946, Brown had moved from college coaching to organize the Browns, and Groza signed on early. In his rookie season, he kicked 13 field goals and 45 of 47 extra points, breaking existing pro records in both categories.

After four years in the AAC, the Browns were absorbed into the NFL in 1950. That year they played Los Angeles for the championship and the game provided Groza with his greatest thrill. He had missed an extra point early and Cleveland was trailing by that single point, 28—27, until the final minute. An intercepted pass gave the Browns one last shot and Groza converted a 16-yard field goal with 28 seconds left on the clock, giving Cleveland the championship.

For his career, Groza kicked 264 field goals, 810 extra points, and scored one touchdown for a total of 1,608 points. He was an All-Pro selection six times, played in nine Pro Bowls, and was chosen the league's Most Valuable Player in 1954. He is a member of the Pro Football Hall of Fame.

Lou Groza

Lou Groza, like George Blanda, got extra consideration from me because he was more than just a kicker. Groza was an outstanding offensive lineman, one of the great tackles, and a superb blocker on both passes and runs. He didn't make my list of the most outstanding offensive linemen of all time, but he came very close. But if he had just been a kicker he still would have made my list of the greatest kickers. He was one of the most consistent kickers ever and he came through in the clutch.

Lou didn't start out as a kicker. But he became the kind of kicker you could count on under all circumstances, including championship games. He won a championship game for Cleveland one year with a last-second field goal. That's the kind of thing you remember about the great ones, and he was a great one who won a lot of games for the Browns over the years. One year he kicked close to 90 percent of his field-goal attempts successfully, setting an NFL record which stood for many years until a couple of years ago, when Jan Stenerud broke it. One year Lou was selected Most Valuable Player in the league, which I think is the only time such an honor has been won by a kicker or an offensive lineman.

Lou was a big guy, strong and durable. He played 21 years, including four in the AAC. Despite the punishing play in the line, Lou never was too tired to kick effectively. He was efficiency-plus on extra points, deadly at almost any distance on field goals, and he booted the ball into the end zone on his kickoffs regularly.

3.
Jan Stenerud

No field goal kicker in National Football League history has enjoyed a more accurate season than Jan Stenerud did with the Green Bay Packers in 1981. Stenerud attempted 24 field goals and converted 22, a .917 percentage that smashed the NFL record of .885 held by Lou Groza since 1953.

Stenerud also kicked 35 extra points and finished the season with 101 points. That was his sixth 100-point season, tying Gino Cappelletti, George Blanda, and Bruce Gossett for the record. Stenerud's 1,344 career points left him sixth on the all-time NFL scoring list. He is the leading active scorer, and his 304 career field goals tie him with Jim Turner for second place on the all-time list, trailing only Blanda's 335.

Not bad for a guy who came to this country as a skier.

Born in Norway, Stenerud attended Montana State on a skiing scholarship and it was there that he began kicking footballs. He mastered the task well enough to be drafted by the Kansas City Chiefs in 1967, and was the club's placement specialist for 13 seasons, setting a number of team records. Among them are most points in a season (129 in 1968), most points after touchdown (394), most consecutive PATs (155 from 1968 to 1973), most field goals (279), most field goals in a season (30, twice), most field goals in a game (five, three times), longest field goal (55 yards), and most consecutive field goals (16, in 1969).

He played 186 straight games for the Chiefs before being released in 1980. But there still were some kicks left in Stenerud's right foot and he joined the Packers midway through that season.

Stenerud, a 6-2, 190-pounder, holds two other important kicking records. His 48-yarder in Kansas City's 23–7 victory over Minnesota in Super Bowl IV is the longest in that series' history. He also kicked a 48-yarder in the Pro Bowl that year, setting the record for that series as well.

Aside from George Blanda and Lou Groza, there have been additional outstanding place-kickers who were standouts at other positions. Gino Cappelletti and Bobby Walston, who were excellent ends, stand out in this respect. But neither really rates with the 100 top pro football players.

I wanted at least one pure place-kicker on my list. I had some outstanding ones to pick from. These included two who also were excellent punters, Sam Baker and Tommy Davis.

I had one of the top pure place-kickers ever at Washington, Mark Moseley. Jim Bakken was a great one. So was Jim Turner. Fred Cox was incredibly consistent. And Garo Yepremian certainly was one of the best ever.

Jan Stenerud

My choice is Jan Stenerud, who has been spectacular and consistent for 15 years and has come through again and again in big games and at big moments. He seldom missed an extra-point conversion all these years, seldom missed a short field-goal attempt, and hit more than his share of long ones. His range extends to 50 yards or so and he often has hit the long ones in the clutch.

Where Blanda and Groza were old-fashioned, straight-on kickers, Stenerud is a sidewinding, soccer-style kicker who played some soccer in his native Norway. In the old days there were some great dropkickers. Ken Strong is one who comes to mind. But Stenerud seems to me to have been a kicker who has stood apart from most others over the years.

PART II

THE
DEFENSE

CHAPTER 6

DEFENSIVE LINEMEN

The main thing I look for in a defensive lineman is the ability to rush the passer. It is a talent that has grown in importance over the years as the passing game has grown in importance. The earlier players could not be measured as much by this yardstick. I have taken this into account in selecting the defensive linemen who rank among the 100 greatest professional football players. And throughout these selections I have tried to measure men against the game they played and the other outstanding players of their day. The really great player could have played in any game on any day. The really great player of the early days would have learned the modern techniques. But I do think that as the years have gone by we have been getting bigger yet faster and more agile men in the defensive line, better all-around athletes, especially at the ends—and there have been more standout defensive linemen in the past 20 years than there were in the preceding 30 years.

For many years now pro teams have been beaten more by the pass than by the run. Ball control won't defeat pro teams as easily as it will college teams because the sophisticated pass offenses of the pros can get back in a play or two what took the other side's ground game 10 or 15 plays to achieve.

In preparing game plans, pros involve all 11 defensive players in guarding against the pass, while only the front men are involved in primary defense against the run. I always spent much more practice time preparing my teams to defense the other teams' passing game than their ground game.

It is harder for a team to play effectively against the pass than against the run. Teamwork is more critical against the pass. The defensive linemen rushing the passer and the defensive backs covering receivers may be operating far apart, but if they're not doing their jobs, if any one of them fails, the whole defense fails. Individually, players have to react faster against the pass and cover more of the field.

Many more players can play effective defense against the run than against the pass. It is simply much easier. I do not mean that it isn't important for a defensive lineman to be able to overcome interior blocking, mix it up in the middle, get to the ball carrier, and be able to bring down the strongest and toughest of them. I considered this ability very heavily. But sheer size, strength, and determination give a guy a good chance against the run. It takes much more quickness and agility, finesse and intelligence to get to the passer. I do not mean the greatest tackles have not had the intelligence of the greatest ends. Not by any means. Some of the brightest men I've known have been tackles. Perhaps they did not have the quickness or agility to play end. But no one has succeeded at end without intelligence. You have to outmaneuver the blockers. Much of it is a mind game.

The greatest pass rushers have the moves of running backs. These pass rushers have been the first men off the snap of the ball. They have combined quickness and agility and maneuverability to get by the blockers and get to the passers and either rush them so they cannot throw well or bring them down. Hurrying them is almost as important as sacking them.

As the passers have become bigger and stronger, quicker and more agile—and this is what coaches are looking for in passers in recent years—it has become increasingly difficult for pass rushers to be effective. Rules changes I discussed in the chapters on quarterbacks and receivers have made it increasingly easy for the passer and receiver and increasingly difficult for the pass rushers and defensive backs. It may be that fewer great defensive ends will develop in the NFL because the rules restrict them. A defensive end will have to be more outstanding than ever in order to shine.

The truly great defensive end has had to be outstanding against the run as well as the pass. It's just that a defensive end's primary responsibility is to rush the passer. The truly great defensive tackle has had to be able to rush the passer as well as defend against the run. It's just that a defensive tackle's primary responsibility is to defend against the run. I have looked for all-around ability in selecting the greatest defensive linemen—end or tackle—of all time. And in looking over my list I find that I have picked fewer ends than tackles. I think that is because it takes something a little extra to play defensive end, and fewer have it. But three of the first four I have picked were ends. They had that something extra even other great defensive linemen didn't have.

Statistics on things like sacks are recent developments in football and have not been available for long. Since a player's statistics often depend on the help a guy gets, they can be misleading, too. There really are no statistics to measure a lineman's ability. Both offensive and defensive linemen are tested by top opponents. Coaches play the best against the best. I judge a pass rusher more by what he is able to achieve against a great blocker than against an ordinary blocker, for example, and vice versa.

I have weighed what I have seen, primarily in person, along with (though less heavily) what others have seen, but the fellow who has lasted a long time and consistently been picked for the All-Pro teams or the Pro Bowl deserved extra consideration. Consistency counts a lot in my book. The fellow who played as well at the end of games and in big games as at the beginning of games or in ordinary games also ranks high in my book. The fellow who played with injuries and enjoyed a long career and was still playing well in his last years ranks high in my book. This is as true for defensive linemen as for offensive linemen. It is very tough in the line.

Frankly, I look for a little meanness in a defensive lineman, just as I look for poise in an offensive lineman. I don't favor a dirty player. I favor one who hits cleanly, but you have to hit hard to gain the respect of and a psychological advantage over your rivals if you are a defensive player. Un-

fortunately, the dirty player may be more feared and so, sometimes, more effective than the clean player.

In any event, I think to be enormously effective a defensive player has to play with a certain reckless abandon and have a certain devil-may-care attitude about hurting anyone, or, for that matter, getting hurt out there on that field. Sometimes I have thought the greatest defensive players have not only had at least a mean streak and played as though angry, but even took a certain pride in playing in pain and outlasting their rivals at a trade in which it is tough to last long.

Beyond the passers, receivers, and runners, who can be and must be measured (at least in part) by statistics, the rest must be measured much more subjectively. So here are the greatest defensive linemen as I judge them.

1.
David (Deacon) Jones

Even if he had not been one of the finest defensive ends ever to play pro football, Deacon Jones would own an important slice of the game's history. That's because he contributed to the language of the game when he coined the term "sack" to describe the technique he performed so efficiently—trapping the quarterback behind the line of scrimmage.

Few people were better at achieving sacks than Jones, who adopted the name "Deacon" when he came to the Los Angeles Rams in 1961. He figured that name was more memorable than his given one—David.

Jones played college football at a couple of small schools—South Carolina State and Mississippi Vocational. It was the thorough film study of a couple of Ram scouts, Eddie Kotal and Johnny Sanders, that led the Rams to Deacon. They were interested in a running back but, watching the films, they focused on the big defender who seemed to outrun their prospect every time he had the ball. That made Jones worth a gamble as a fourteenth-round draft pick in 1961.

Jones quickly established himself in the pros as a big man who could move. He was 6–5 and 250 pounds, but unlike some defensive linemen, he was mobile, often going from sideline to sideline on a single play. And he specialized in sacks, a major factor in the success of the Rams' "Fearsome Foursome," the nickname given to the defensive line. In 1967, for example, Ram quarterbacks were sacked 25 times all year, but Jones alone recorded 26 quarterback sacks that season.

From 1965 to 1970, Jones was picked for the All-Pro team six straight times. There also were eight Pro Bowl appearances, and Jones was an overwhelming choice for the NFL's All-Pro team of the decade of the 1960s.

Jones played for 14 seasons in the NFL, spending 11 years with the Rams, two with San Diego, and a final season with Washington before retiring in 1974. He was named to the Pro Football Hall of Fame in his first year of eligibility (1980), a tribute to his accomplishments.

Besides his playing ability, Jones is remembered for his flamboyant style. Once, playing against Washington, he found himself chasing Bobby Mitchell, one of the game's fastest players, on a pass play. He caught Mitchell, but only after matching strides with him for 10 yards. Jones' explanation later was he just wanted to see if he was as fast as the receiver with sprinter speed. He was.

In my mind it is very close between Deacon Jones and Gino Marchetti as the best defensive lineman. For a while I was thinking I should pick Gino because I coached Deacon and might be prejudiced, but my real prejudice is toward great players and I leaned a little to Deacon all the while. They were the two best defensive ends of all time and I feel Deacon was more responsible for developing the way the defensive line should be played.

Deacon was tall, but not as heavy as some defensive linemen. He was quicker and more agile than the other defensive linemen of his day and led the trend toward quicker, more agile defensive linemen. If you're going to try to outmuscle massive offensive linemen it's going to take more time than you can afford to give the runner or passer.

David (Deacon)
Jones

Deacon Jones was such a great athlete he'd have been a great linebacker, or even a great defensive back, I believe. I never knew a defensive lineman who was as quick getting off at the snap of the ball as the Deacon. Or as quick at getting to the quarterback. He devised ways of getting past the blocker, like the helmet slap. He'd swat the side of his opponent's helmet so hard it knocked him off balance. Boom! Deacon was past him. Deacon had better footwork and faster hands than any defensive lineman, anyway, and he'd outmaneuver one in a hurry.

Opposing passers started off each play with one eye on Deacon. When a player is good enough and gets a good enough reputation he makes his opponents nervous and they often are beaten before the play begins. Deacon caused opposing quarterbacks to hurry their passes. He came at them like an attack dog. He was so agile the most elusive of passers found it difficult to evade him. And they found it difficult to slip away from such a sure tackler.

Deacon was better against the pass than against the run, but he was a pass defense all by himself. Opposing teams used to double-team and triple-team him in a desperate attempt to contain him. In an attempt to confuse them I'd flip-flop him with Merlin Olsen or the other tackle, or line up Deacon over the center because he could rush effectively from any position. Olsen was a good pass rusher, too, and a great run defender. He and Deacon had to be the best defensive duo ever and they'd work stunts beautifully.

Other teams really did some desperate things to try to contain Deacon. One team lined up a tackle against him, brought in a tight end to try to block him from one side, and then brought in a defensive back, John David Crow, to block him from the blind side. It was dirty football, born out of desperation, but it didn't work. Nothing really worked well against Deacon.

Deacon just loved to play. He was the single best practice player I ever coached. He went as hard in practice as in games. He drew blood from his teammates in practice. He went hard on every play of every game. He played in pain. I don't recall once having to call a time-out because of an injury to Deacon, and he suffered plenty.

He was at his best in big games because he had a big ego, and he loved being known as the best and loved being in the spotlight. But we also won a couple of those meaningless Playoff Bowl games of those days between the conference runners-up because of how well he played in them, and I remember he was MVP of one of them.

I made him my team's captain with the Rams and he never let me down. He was an enthusiastic, inspirational leader of his teams for 14 years and no one ever played a position better.

2.
Gino Marchetti

If it had not been for 300-pound Gene (Big Daddy) Lipscomb, Gino Marchetti would have owned a record streak of playing in 11 consecutive Pro Bowl games.

Marchetti, a defensive end, played in 10 of those postseason All-Star games, from 1955 to 1965. The only one he missed was in 1959, and his absence was caused by Lipscomb, his teammate on the Baltimore Colt defense.

In the 1958 NFL championship game between Baltimore and the New York Giants, Marchetti made a crucial tackle on Frank Gifford. Lipscomb arrived at the scene a moment later and his bulk landed squarely on Marchetti's ankle, breaking it. The injury cost Marchetti his postseason Pro Bowl streak, but the tackle halted a Giant drive and helped the Colts gain

Gino Marchetti (#88)

possession for their pulsating march to the tying field goal in that famous overtime game won by Baltimore.

That was Marchetti's style for 14 pro seasons. He always seemed to be in the middle of the most crucial defensive plays, throwing his 6-4, 245-pound frame into passers and ball carriers. From 1956 to 1964 he was chosen for the All-Pro team eight times, missing only in 1963.

After serving with the Army in World War II and seeing action during the Battle of the Bulge, Marchetti attended the University of San Francisco, where one of his teammates was running back Ollie Matson. Drafted by the New York Yanks, Marchetti played the 1952 season in Dallas, which inherited the faltering Yanks' franchise. A year later, the club was transferred again, this time to Baltimore. It was there that the team finally found a home as the Colts.

By then Marchetti also had settled in on defense. He had been tried as an offensive tackle in his first pro days but it quickly became obvious that Marchetti belonged on defense. He was chosen to the All-Pro squad for the decade of the 1960s and, in 1972, was named to the Pro Football Hall of Fame, inducted at the same time as his old college teammate, Ollie Matson.

Gino Marchetti came along a little before Deacon Jones and wasn't as inventive or influential as Jones, but Marchetti was a great pass rusher. He wasn't as fast as Deacon, but he was meaner and fast for his size. He just overpowered blockers and blasted in on the passer and when he got to him he really pounded the guy. I can still see him in my mind blowing in and then blowing over the passer. Marchetti usually gave him an extra lick, too. To be honest about it, Gino wasn't the cleanest player ever. He intimidated opponents. But as I have admitted, I always liked meanness in a defensive player. Most coaches do.

I think because he was quicker Jones was the best defensive lineman I ever coached, but Marchetti was the best I ever coached against. You put your best blockers against him and double-teamed him and triple-teamed him and just tried to slow him down a little, or take him out of a play here and there. But that was the best you could hope to do. You could hurt him, but he was so strong and so tough and so determined you never could completely stop him. He was very good against the run and just great against the pass.

I coached Gino in a Pro Bowl game once and I can't forget how dedicated he was. A lot of good players don't devote themselves too much to the Pro Bowl. A lot skip out on it. A lot who go there don't give it much. It comes after the season is over. It doesn't count in any standings. The players are tired and sore and ready for a rest. But a coach wants to win every game and so do the best players. This is the best against the best, it's an honor to be picked, and the players with a lot of pride want to play well. Gino never missed a team meeting, practiced as hard as he played, and played as if it was a championship game. I gained a lot of respect for him then.

With the Colts, Gino played in numerous championship games and he was always at his best in those games. He was a winner. He played 14 years and I don't think anyone who ever played the game was more difficult to contend with on the field.

3.
Bob Lilly

Bob Lilly's pro football career with the Dallas Cowboys ran the full spectrum. He tasted the ashes when the Cowboys, as a new expansion team, took their lumps, and then drank champagne when they became Super Bowl champions. Lilly experienced both extremes and almost everything in between during 14 NFL seasons.

Lilly was Dallas' first draft choice, its first All-Pro selection, its first Pro Bowl player, and its first Hall of Famer.

Selected out of Texas Christian University in 1961, Lilly became the cornerstone of the Dallas defense. But "Doomsday," the nickname the Cowboys' defense would proudly wear eventually, was not constructed overnight. A variety of players moved in and out of the line while Lilly remained in place, the basic element in the unit.

Lilly was a defensive end in his early days with the Cowboys and he was efficient enough at the job to be selected Rookie of the Year in 1961 and named to the Pro Bowl game the next season. But it was when he was switched inside to defensive tackle that he began to blossom as a truly awesome player. The move freed him from the responsibility for containing plays and he was able to let loose from the tackle slot. He flourished in the position and, at 6-5 and 260 pounds, he had perfect size for the assignment.

Selected for 11 Pro Bowl games, Lilly also was an All-Pro choice for six straight years, from 1964 to 1969, and again in 1971 and 1972. He played in 292 professional games, including 196 straight regular-season contests. He saw action in five league or conference championship games between 1967 and 1972 and played in Super Bowls V and VI.

Lilly scored four touchdowns during his career, three of them on recovered fumbles and the other on an interception. He recovered 16 fumbles, often fighting off double and triple coverage to get at the ball carrier.

When he started with the Cowboys, the team was a struggling expansion club. They had gone 0−11−1 in their first season. They were 4−9−1 in his rookie season and did not reach .500 until 1965, his fifth season. That's why it meant a little something extra to Lilly when the Cowboys won the world championship in Super Bowl VI. The champagne tasted much better than the ashes had.

Bob Lilly

Bob Lilly was the greatest defensive tackle ever, in my book. He would have been one of the greatest defensive ends, but he was moved inside early in his pro career. Most good pass rushing comes from outside, but some top players are able to provide it from inside. Lilly was one who did.

Lilly was sort of a combination of Deacon Jones and Gino Marchetti. Lilly was a little bigger than either, but almost as quick as Jones and almost as strong as Marchetti. Lilly was almost as good a pass rusher as either, but a better run defender than both. He made plays all over the field.

Lilly lacked the meanness of Marchetti. And Lilly didn't have the enthusiasm of Jones. But Bob was the smartest, coolest defensive lineman I ever faced. We tried everything against him but we couldn't confuse him or contain him.

When my teams played Dallas the two things we worked on most were double-teaming Bob Hayes, because he was so fast and dangerous as a receiver, and double-teaming Bob Lilly, because he was the key to their defense.

Dallas didn't have as many outstanding players as most of the other great teams I've known. But they had a lot of good, smart players who were coached well by Tom Landry and played as a team. Lilly was a great team man, but he also was a great individual player.

Like Jones and Marchetti, Lilly played 14 years and wore very well. I doubt that he missed very many games or even very many plays. He was a massive man and seemed indestructible. He was extremely consistent from game to game and did exceptionally well in big games. It is significant to me that he played as well when the Cowboys were a bad team as when they became a great team.

4.
Doug Atkins

For 17 years, Doug Atkins terrorized opposing quarterbacks. He was a 6-8, 275-pound mountain of a man who spent considerable time in enemy backfields. Not bad for a guy who was traded by the Cleveland Browns because they felt he'd never be good enough for the demanding world of pro football.

Atkins was drafted in the first round by the Browns in 1953 and spent two seasons with them. But the ex-Tennessee star was traded to Chicago in 1955 because head coach Paul Brown was convinced that Atkins would never achieve success in the NFL. An ulcer had cut Doug's weight considerably that year and, stretched over that large frame, he looked almost emaciated.

By 1957, the defensive end had developed into a Pro Bowl performer and he appeared in eight of those All-Star contests, including seven in a row. He was named Lineman of the Game in the 1958 contest, his second Pro Bowl. He was also a three-time All-Pro selection and was voted into the Pro Football Hall of Fame in January 1982.

Doug Atkins

But Atkins' relationship with Pappa Bear, George Halas, might best be described as strained. The two had some celebrated contract battles in the dozen years Atkins spent in Chicago. Finally, the Bears traded Atkins to New Orleans in 1967 figuring that, at 36, the old man was finished. But Doug responded with three more standout seasons for the Saints, retiring at age 39 after 205 NFL games. When he completed his career Atkins trailed only Lou Groza in terms of NFL longevity.

Pro football was no bed of roses for Atkins. He survived a long list of career-threatening injuries, including two knee operations, a fractured collarbone, two broken hands, two sprained ankles, a torn bicep muscle, a torn groin muscle, and an assortment of cracked ribs. But he always came back for more.

Atkins was chosen to the All-Pro team of the decade for the 1960s, but he received consideration for the decade team of the 1950s as well. That's how long he was around and how well he played.

Most men Doug Atkins' size can't carry that kind of weight well enough to be a standout defensive end, but Doug was as tall as a basketball forward, a fine basketball player, a fine high jumper, a fine all-around athlete. He went to college on a basketball scholarship, though that was before he gained 60 pounds or so. Even so, he was fast on his feet for a man his size and became one of the great defensive ends.

I coached Doug in Chicago and always thought he was one of the most underrated players ever. He won many honors, but not as many as some of the others on my list. So I was pleased to see Doug make it to the Pro Football Hall of Fame in 1982. He was so big he was awesome and when

*he came at a man he was frightening. He intimidated opponents, domi-
nated games, and was one of the most effective players I've ever observed.*

*Whereas most defensive ends move from the outside, off their inside
shoulder, Doug was unorthodox and moved to the inside, off his outside
shoulder, and this made him difficult for blockers to deal with. He had a
feel for traps and was difficult to catch off guard.*

*He blew over most blockers. He actually was tall and agile enough to
hurdle some who bent down to block him; I saw him do this numerous
times. He had long arms and seemed to surround passers who sought to
elude him. He fell on them with terrific force. I think they felt like the side
of a building had fallen on them. He was a great pass rusher but also a
great run defender. He caved in blockers, closed holes, and jumped on
runners. He forced fumbles. He made his foes make mistakes.*

*At his best, Atkins was almost as good as the best, but he was a little
inconsistent. To be at his best he needed a little inspiration. As big as he
was, it is fortunate for his opponents that he wasn't meaner. Vince Lombardi always told his Packers not to do anything to Doug to make him mad.
I hate to think what Doug would have done to the guys who get away with
all the holding today. I remember that a Redskin held Doug after he'd been
warned by Doug not to do it anymore. Doug knocked him down and kicked
him so hard in his helmet his face mask flew off.*

*Doug was smart, too. And dedicated. He kept a notebook in which he
jotted down tendencies and analyzed opponents. He studied films. He was
always prepared to play. He suffered more serious injuries than most
players, but he kept playing. He played 17 years, until he was almost 40,
which is one of the longest careers pro football has had.*

5.
Bill Willis

Bill Willis was a trailblazer—in more ways than one.

He was among the first black men to play professional football, breaking
into the game in 1946, a year before baseball's Jackie Robinson made
headlines in Brooklyn. And he proved that one doesn't have to be a giant to
play defense.

Willis was just 6-2 and 215 pounds, but few men played middle guard
better than he did for eight pro seasons, all with the Cleveland Browns.

The Browns were being organized in the All-America Conference by Paul
Brown in 1946. Brown had coached at Ohio State during World War II and
one of his stars on the Buckeyes' 1942 national championship team was
Willis. After graduation from Ohio State, Willis became football coach and

athletic director at Kentucky State College, a small black school. But his interest in pro football was whetted when he heard about the formation of the new league in which his former coach was involved. He asked for a tryout and earned a job almost immediately because of his catlike moves on defense.

Willis was so quick getting off the ball in practice that Brown decided that his speed would better suit him for work at guard instead of tackle, where he had played in college. Eventually Willis became the Browns' middle guard, playing in the center of a five-man line. Occasionally he would drop back from the line, essentially pioneering what would become the middle linebacker's position.

The Browns swept to four straight AAC championships before the league folded. In three of those seasons, Willis received All-League recognition.

In the NFL, Willis was named to All-Pro teams in each of his four seasons, 1950–53. So, in eight years as a pro, Willis was chosen as an All-Star seven times. He also played in the first three NFL Pro Bowls.

Willis also was named to the All-Pro squad of the 1940s and was selected for the Pro Football Hall of Fame in 1977, testimony that stardom in football doesn't depend on size, or, for that matter, race.

Bill Willis was the quickest lineman I ever saw. He was quicker than Deacon Jones. Of course, Willis wasn't as big as Deacon. Willis was small for a lineman, even in the 1940s. But he was so quick and so aggressive he hit like a 250-pounder. Speed adds to impact. This is true of a golfer swinging a driver, a baseball player swinging a bat, a boxer throwing a punch. A smaller man whose hands move faster hits harder than a bigger, slower man.

Willis played middle guard in the five-man line in the the 5-2 defense they played in those days. Usually he lined up over the center. Sometimes he dropped back off the line a little and so became the first middle linebacker. But he'd be right back playing middle guard—or nose tackle, as they call it—in the three-man line, in the 3-4 defense with four linebackers they're playing a lot these days. He was the greatest middle guard ever, the finest lineman of the 1940s.

Offensive linemen are much bigger today than they were yesterday, so I suppose Bill would have had to play linebacker today, but he was quick and that made up for a lot. They used to think that he cheated because he got across the line so fast. But what he did was watch the center's hands and move as soon as they tightened on the ball, even as the center first started to snap the ball. I don't think that anyone else ever picked this up and it gave Bill a split second on everyone else.

Willis was extremely smart and mobile. He seemed to make a different kind of pass rush each time. He was one of the first great pass rushers and was equally effective against the run. He moved laterally real well and was one of those players who made plays all over the field. He was like a cat, pouncing on people. He was the first black player in the old All-America

Bill Willis (#30)

Conference, endured dirty tactics and racial slurs and, with Marion Motley, helped to break the color barrier in professional football. Willis was an individual of great tolerance and dignity and had exceptional character.

Willis was a leader of those great Cleveland clubs and helped to make them successful when they moved into the NFL. He played only eight years of pro ball, but that was because he didn't get his chance until four years after his college career ended. A number of offensive-line immortals, including Jim Parker, said he was the most difficult opponent to deal with they ever faced.

6.
Leo Nomellini

Leo Nomellini was one of those unique players who achieved levels of excellence on both offense and defense, enabling him to be selected for All-Pro honors on both units. The Pro Football Hall of Fame tackle, who spent 14 seasons with the San Francisco 49ers, was an offensive All-Pro in 1951 and 1952 and was picked as a defensive All-Pro in 1953, 1954, 1957, and 1959. In his first 12 seasons, Nomellini was selected for the Pro Bowl 10 times and twice recovered fumbles in those games, helping the West All-Stars to victories.

Nomellini was San Francisco's first draft choice in 1950, the year the 49ers were absorbed into the NFL from the All-America Conference. He played 174 consecutive regular-season games, establishing what was at

Leo Nomellini

the time the league's iron-man record. Nomellini never missed a game and, with preseason, playoff, and Pro Bowl appearances, his total reached 266.

Born in Lucca, Italy, Nomellini grew up in Chicago. He served with the Marines in World War II and then went to the University of Minnesota, where he was a consensus All America selection in both his junior and senior years. At 6-3 and 264 pounds, Nomellini won the Big Ten heavyweight wrestling championship at Minnesota. Later he wrestled professionally during the off-season from football.

Nomellini had plenty going for him in football. He always reported to training camp in shape. That's one of the reasons he was able to play until he was 39 years old.

Early in his career, Nomellini established himself as a skilled blocker, opening holes for the 49ers' fleet of running backs such as Hugh McElhenny, Joe Perry, J. D. Smith, and John Henry Johnson. But Nomellini's defensive skills at tackle, such as his rushing the passer, were so great that San Francisco had to place him on that unit as well. In 1955, when injuries devastated the club, Nomellini became virtually a 60-minute-per-game player all season long.

One of the reasons Nomellini chose Minnesota for his college football was the fact that his idol, fullback Bronko Nagurski, had played there. Eventually Nomellini followed Nargurski all the way to the Pro Football Hall of Fame.

Leo Nomellini was a wonder. He was tall, but he seemed as wide as he was tall. When I see that bull busting through windows and walls in those beer commercials on television I think of Leo because that's the way he looked when he came busting through a line. He was agile for a big man. He had good footwork and fast hands, especially for a fellow of his build. He was as good a blocker as he was a tackler. I would have had to find room for him among the greatest offensive linemen if I hadn't placed him among the greatest defensive linemen.

He's the first I've picked for this list who was better against the run than the pass. He was a tackle and he threw blockers around, stood his ground, and made the center of his line almost impossible to penetrate. He just beat on the men who tried to block him. I saw him play over center one entire game and by the end of the game the center looked like he'd gone 15 rounds with Rocky Marciano. And Nomellini never seemed to get hurt.

There were some other remarkable defensive linemen in the 1950s who did not make my list but well might have. Ernie Stautner was one. The Moose lasted 14 years and was as tough as a steel spike. Art Donovan was another. The son of the great boxing referee of the Joe Louis years, Art was a war hero, a real fighter on and off the football field, and had a dozen great seasons.

Nomellini made it and deserved it. He had rare all-around ability as an athlete and complete dedication to his sport.

7.
Len Ford

The Cleveland Browns were using a six-man front when Len Ford joined the club in 1950 as a refugee from the defunct Los Angeles Dons of the old All-America Conference. Ford had been a two-way end in the AAC, good enough on offense to have caught 67 passes for 1,175 yards and eight touchdowns in two seasons. But with the Browns he was assigned to the defensive unit and quickly evolved into a devastating rusher. He was so quick that the Browns decided to reduce their rush line from six players to four so that Ford would not get caught in traffic. Cleveland pulled its linebackers back, tightening the front line and moving Ford closer inside where he could get a better shot at the quarterback and the ball carrier.

At 6-5 and 260 pounds, Ford was an awesome defender whose mere presence often forced the offense to design plays away from him. He missed almost all of the 1950 season because of a broken nose and fractured cheekbone. But he returned for the championship game against Los Angeles and, wearing a specially designed protective cage attached to his helmet, he turned in an outstanding performance as Cleveland won the title. In the next seven years, Ford was chosen to the All-Pro team five times and selected to play in four Pro Bowl games. He finished his career at Green Bay in 1958 and was named to the All-Pro team for the decade of the 1950s, as well as to the Pro Football Hall of Fame in 1976.

Ford recovered 20 fumbles in his career, and that constituted an NFL record at the time of his retirement. He always seemed to have a nose for the ball, perhaps a leftover trait from his pass-catching days with the AAC Dons. In the 1954 NFL title game against Detroit, Len intercepted two passes, returning one of them 45 yards for what was, at the time, a championship-game record.

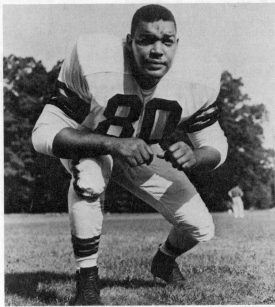

Len Ford

Ford played college football at Michigan and starred in its 49–0 Rose Bowl victory in 1948 over Southern California. He had transferred to Michigan from Morgan State because he wanted a chance to play in the Rose Bowl. That game was something special to Ford, long after he became something special in the NFL.

Another great player of the 1950s, another great Cleveland Brown, another who helped break the color barrier was Len Ford. He also was a pioneer at defensive end and as a pass rusher, showing the way the position should have been played before Gino Marchetti and then Deacon Jones came along to really develop the position to what appears now as its full potential.

Ford was one of the fastest big men ever. Lenny was not as fast as Deacon Jones, but bigger. Ford was a fast-moving mountain. Actually he was an outstanding offensive end and might have gone on to greatness as a receiver had Paul Brown not surprisingly settled him on defense and designed a defense around him. What a tight end he'd have made! Lenny Ford performed as a 60-minute, two-way player in his early years as a pro.

Ford was the first great pass-rushing defensive end. He was as agile as he was big. Like Doug Atkins, if he caught an opponent crouching or down he hurdled him. He got past blockers with fancy footwork and enormous strength and chased passers with wild determination. If he got caught off balance by a rushing play, he could reverse himself in the blink of an eye and get back into the play. He was all over the field. He was a ball hawk who always seemed to be around a football when it was fumbled and who picked off passes the way few defensive linemen ever did.

As I remember him, Ford was sensational in title games. I remember he returned from the injured list to play in one title game with a mask to protect his face, which had been mashed in. He was sensational. He was a pressure performer who put tremendous pressure on defenses.

8.
Joe Stydahar

Only when football helmets became mandatory equipment did Joe Stydahar agree to wear one regularly. He preferred to play the rugged game of pro football bareheaded—no small bit of courage for a man who earned his living in the game's trenches, playing tackle for the Chicago Bears.

Stydahar did an excellent job with and without benefit of the helmet. In nine seasons with Chicago, he played on five division championship teams, and three of them went on to capture the NFL title. Stydahar, who wore uniform No. 13, anchored the Bears' line and was named to the NFL's All-Pro team for the decade of the 1930s.

When the NFL started its college draft in 1936, Stydahar was the first player chosen by Pappa Bear George Halas. A strapping 6-4 and 230 pounds, Jumbo Joe had developed into an outstanding college tackle at West Virginia, where he also captained the basketball team.

Stydahar made Halas' judgment seem flawless, gaining All-Pro recognition in each of his first four pro seasons. He was a two-way performer but was especially outstanding on defense and quickly developed into one of the game's all-time greats at defensive tackle.

His pro career was interrupted by Navy service during World War II, which cost him two seasons. He retired after the 1946 season and joined the Los Angeles Rams as an assistant coach the next year.

Stydahar served as head coach of the Rams for two seasons, taking the team to the NFL title game in both 1950 and 1951. He was caught in the middle of the Rams' quarterback controversy involving Norm Van Brocklin and Bob Waterfield, solving it for a time by having the two eventual Hall of Famers alternate by quarters. That satisfied neither man but the fact remains that the Rams were winners when Stydahar coached the team. Joe was immortalized in the Pro Football Hall of Fame in 1967.

Joe Stydahar

Joe Stydahar would have made my list as an offensive tackle if I hadn't placed him at defensive tackle. He was another of those old two-way, 60-minute guys, but they all weren't equally effective on offense and defense. Joe was. He was big and strong. He may not have been the biggest lineman of his day, but he certainly was one of the strongest. He was quick. He was tough. He was smart. And he was mean. He was a football player through and through. He looked like a football player.

Joe was a great tackle against the run. It was very hard to move him. He'd plow through people to get to the runner. He hit very hard and runners seldom broke his tackles. He was a little less effective against the pass, but he was effective. On offense he was one of the strongest, surest blockers I've seen. He didn't just get in the way, he knocked opponents over.

There were many outstanding defensive linemen in the 1930s who came close but did not make my list, or who started their careers too early to qualify. Among the early ones were Buckets Goldenberg and Emerson Glover. One I remember with great admiration was Turk Edwards of the Redskins. He was as wide as a house and sometimes took down two men at a time. I thought about him a lot for my list.

But Stydahar was one of the exceptional ones. He was another of those who looked like all brawn, but he had a lot of brains. He was a real leader.

He captained the Bears when they were the best. He coached the Rams when they were one of the best. Although a lineman, he produced high-powered offenses. Later he assisted me with the Bears. I have a lot of respect for Joe. Although he had to take time out to serve in World War II, he had a terrific career.

9.
Al Wistert

No football recruit at Michigan ever will wear uniform No. 11. That's because the Wolverines retired the jersey after the last of the remarkable Wistert brothers finished playing tackle there. There were three of them—Francis, Albert, and Alvin—each of them an All-American who set a standard for the position. Only one, however, Albert, moved on to stardom in the National Football League.

Al Wistert came out of Michigan in 1943 and was drafted by the Philadelphia Eagles, who operated in that wartime season as a combined franchise with the Pittsburgh Steelers. The Steagles divided their season between the two cities and introduced two outstanding rookie tackles, Wistert and Frank "Bucko" Kilroy.

The next year, the teams split and Philadelphia drafted running back Steve Van Buren. Lined up behind those effective tackles, Van Buren would flourish as one of the top ground gainers of his era.

Wistert, nicknamed Big Ox, hardly was giant-sized. He stood 6-1½ and played at 219 pounds, small by today's lineman standards. But he was an outstanding blocker and a key man in the Eagles' advance to three consecutive NFL championship games from 1947 to 1949. Van Buren averaged better than 1,000 yards a year in those seasons at a time when reaching that plateau was considered remarkable. Many of those yards came behind Wistert's blocking.

In 1947, Wistert was named captain of the Eagles. That was one of three straight seasons in which he was named to the All-Pro team, a string of standout play that led to his selection to the All-Pro team for the decade of the 1940s.

There were no Pro Bowl games during most of Wistert's career. When the modern version of the game was introduced in 1951, Wistert was selected to play for the American Conference team. That was to be his final season in pro football.

Al Wistert was one of the smartest players I ever watched operate on a football field. He was a pretty good-sized tackle for his day and a master of technique. He was very quick and he outmaneuvered and outwitted his

Al Wistert

opponents. He never seemed to make a mistake. He was another excel-lent two-way player.

Wistert seemed to be born with perfect balance. He always played in perfect position and seldom was off his feet. He was a superb pursuit man and seemed somehow to get in on every play. He was a sure tackler. He maybe was best against the run, but he was among the good early pass rushers. He was as fine a blocker as you could want. He didn't have the size to overpower people on the pass block, but he was a master of every kind of block.

It was very close between Wistert, as good as he was, and several others from the 1940s who were given my very serious consideration. Bruiser Kinard of the old Brooklyn Dodgers of the NFL and later the New York Yankees of the All-America Conference was a real bruiser, a hard nut to crack on both offense and defense. Bruno Banducci of the San Fran-cisco 49ers of the All-America Conference and the NFL was another bruiser who went both ways equally well. Al Blozis of the Giants was a real giant and would have gone on to greatness in football if he had not been killed in World War II.

Wistert stands out in my mind. He was skilled, determined, consistent, and resourceful. He showed the highest sort of leadership qualities and was very much a high-quality player.

10.
Willie Davis

It happens so often. Scouts are attracted to a game to watch one athlete and instead become mesmerized by another. That's exactly how Willie Davis won a ticket into the NFL.

Davis had been an NAIA All-American at Grambling College but had not generated much enthusiasm among the pro scouts. Then, near the end of his senior season, Davis' Grambling team went up against Florida A&M. The scouts were out in force, examining some of the A&M pro prospects. But the best player on the field in Grambling's 28–21 upset victory was Davis, who made 19 tackles and assisted on 16 others.

That was good enough for Cleveland, which drafted Davis on the seventeenth round in 1956. Before he could report to the pros, there were two years of Army service. Then, for two seasons, the Browns shuffled him from one position to another and from offense to defense. In 1960 he was traded to Green Bay, considered at the time to be the Siberia of pro football. But Vince Lombardi soon would change that and Davis became a vital part of that change.

Lombardi installed the 6-3, 245-pound Davis at defensive end. There would be no more position shifts for him after that. He had found a home and Green Bay had found a future Hall of Famer. In 10 seasons with the Packers, Davis was chosen for the All-Pro team five times—those selections all coming within a six-year stretch from 1962 to 1967. He was a Pro Bowl selection for five consecutive seasons and was chosen for the All-Pro squad of the decade of the 1960s.

Davis appeared in six NFL championship games and the first two Super Bowls, playing an integral role in the Green Bay dynasty.

He played in 162 games, never missing a start, and in his 12 pro seasons he recovered 21 opponents' fumbles, just one short of the all-time record at the time. Davis' greatness was recognized when he was inducted in the Pro Football Hall of Fame in 1981.

Willie Davis was as important a part of Vince Lombardi's great Green Bay Packer teams of the 1960s as anyone because he was the bellwether of that team on defense, and because defense was as important to the success of that team as anything else.

It is the combination of size, strength, and quickness that enabled a few of these fellows to rise above the rest, and Davis had these things in ample amounts. He also had great toughness and incredible balance.

We never could knock the guy off his feet, no matter how many men we hit him with or how hard we hit him. He could drive over or around block-

ers so you never knew what to expect from him. He was smart. Later I offered him coaching jobs, but he was a big success in business.

Davis was a strong pass rusher and a steady run defender. He took care of his side of the line and turned a lot of plays in. It was very difficult to get outside of him. He diagnosed and anticipated plays extremely well. He was one of the best defensive ends at anticipating and picking off passes.

Deacon Jones, Gino Marchetti, Bob Lilly, Merlin Olsen, and Davis were All-Pros out of the 1960s. Massive Roger Brown and Alex Karras were absolutely overpowering tackles at times but lacked the consistency to be among the very best.

The Packers of that period had a powerful defense. They had especially good defensive backs and linebackers. And a big tackle, Henry Jordan, was another good one on the defensive line with Willie Davis. But without Davis that line would not have been good enough to take as many titles as the team did. He was the only unstoppable player they had on the defensive line.

He played 12 years and he played every game and he played almost every play on defense in every game. I don't think I ever saw him play a bad game and I know he played his best in the big games, the title games.

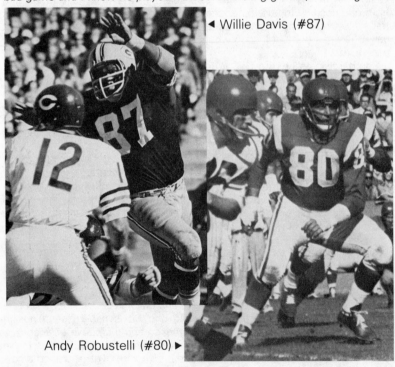

◄ Willie Davis (#87)

Andy Robustelli (#80) ►

11.
Andy Robustelli

His height and weight statistics weren't exactly impressive. He was merely mortal-sized at 6 feet and 230 pounds, hardly the behemoth type one expected in a defensive lineman. He played his collegiate football at tiny Arnold College, whose enrollment once was as low as 350 and hardly qualified as a developer of many standout football players. He was selected in the nineteenth round of the 1951 draft, when most of the players picked are strictly afterthoughts and are considered to have little chance of making the grade in pro football.

But Andy Robustelli made it all the way to the Pro Football Hall of Fame as one of the game's premier defensive ends, first with the Los Angeles Rams and later with the New York Giants. Robustelli played for 14 seasons and was an iron man, missing only one game during that span. He was an All-Pro selection seven times and also played in seven Pro Bowl games.

In college Robustelli had developed into an outstanding offensive end but when he arrived at his first pro training camp, he found the Rams set at that position with future Hall of Famers Tom Fears and Elroy (Crazylegs) Hirsch. So the rookie moved to the defensive unit and made a home for himself there, achieving stardom at end.

After five years with the Rams he was traded to New York and became a leader of the Giants' defensive platoon. He played nine more seasons in New York and in 1962 was chosen by the Maxwell Club in Philadelphia as that season's outstanding NFL player, a unique honor for a defensive player.

Robustelli's last three years with the Giants, 1962–64, saw him in the dual role of player-coach and he later returned to serve in the club's front office during the 1970s.

During his career, Robustelli played in eight NFL championship games and was a leader on the field and off. Coaches often singled out his enthusiasm for the game and his determination as major reasons for his success.

Robustelli did better than his alma mater. Arnold College drifted out of existence and was absorbed by the University of Bridgeport in Connecticut. And this tough defensive end with a zest for football is the only Arnold alumnus ever to make it to the Pro Football Hall of Fame.

Again, intelligence set a player apart. Andy Robustelli had good but not great size. He had good but not outstanding quickness. However, he was a very smart player. He studied the game. He studied films. He diagnosed opponents. He diagnosed plays. He came to every game ready to play to his full potential, and he played every game to its limit. He played in a lot of championship games, and played his best in those games.

Some of the players on my list made it on size and strength, raw ability, and a love of playing. A defensive lineman has to love to hit or he's not going to be that good, because hitting is the defensive game and you're going to take a lot of hard licks, too. Others made it on smart play. They had to have outstanding talent, too, but many players did a lot less with a lot more talent.

Robustelli is one who had good size and good ability but great intelligence and who made the most of himself. He wasn't as mean as some on my list but he was a sure tackler and he played with an enthusiasm that shone through.

Andy was a great pass rusher and excellent run defender. He turned plays in on his end and moved all over the field to make plays. He was extremely consistent and the inspirational leader of a very consistent, inspired Giant defense that took the team to the top in the 1950s and early 1960s. Jim Katcavage was the other end. Rosey Grier and Dick Modzelewski were the tackles. Andy made the line work. Sam Huff was the key linebacker, flanked by Cliff Livingston and Harland Svare. Emlen Tunnell, Jim Patton, and Dick Nolan were the defensive backs. The fourth was Tom Landry for a while, but later he coached some of them.

12.
Merlin Olsen

Merlin Olsen wasn't perfect. He played defensive tackle for 15 years in the NFL with the Los Angeles Rams and was named to the Pro Bowl squad 14 times. He missed the designation for the only time in 1976, his last season. Otherwise, he would have batted .1000—perfect.

No man has played in more Pro Bowl games than Olsen. Drafted out of Utah State University on the first round in 1962, Olsen won a regular job in training camp and started 210 consecutive games. He was a unanimous All-Pro choice five times and was selected as a member of the NFL's All-Pro squad for the decade of the 1960s. During his career, Olsen was named the Maxwell Club's NFL Player of the Year once, the Rams' Most Valuable Player twice, their outstanding defensive player four times, and was named a member of their all-time team.

Olsen was one of the key men in the Rams' "Fearsome Foursome"— ranked among football's all-time best front lines. He teamed with Lamar Lundy, Roosevelt Grier, and Deacon Jones in destroying enemy offenses. The unit dominated football in the mid-1960s.

Merlin Olsen (#74)

Ironically, it was Jones who drove Olsen to the Rams' defensive unit in the first place. When Merlin reported to his first LA training camp, there was a tug-of-war between the offensive and defensive coaches over this 6-5, 270-pound giant. He was playing guard in one scrimmage, working against Jones, when Deacon came roaring by, nearly ripping off the rookie's head. Shortly after that, the coaches decided that Olsen fit in better on defense, working alongside Jones instead of across from someone like him.

Olsen, a member of Phi Beta Kappa in college, always was an interesting postgame interview. When he retired, it was an easy transition to the broadcast booth, where he became a regular for NBC as its top football color analyst. He also has done a great deal of acting and, in 1981, played the title role in the NBC television series *Father Murphy.* Earlier he became a regular on *Little House on the Prairie,* another popular TV series.

Merlin was voted into the Pro Football—not the entertainers'—Hall of Fame in January, 1982.

I coached Deacon Jones and Merlin Olsen during the time they were part of the "Fearsome Foursome" defensive line of the Los Angeles Rams of the 1960s. It had to have been one of the greatest defensive lines of all time, and Jones and Olsen had to have been one of the most destructive defensive duos ever.

Merlin was one of those massive men, bigger than but not as quick as Deacon. Olsen was a tackle, Jones an end, but they used to flip-flop positions at times and work highly successful stunts, alternating on the pass rush and keeping the opposition off balance. When they both went at the passer, he was in real trouble.

Deacon was a better pass rusher, but Ole was very, very good at it and was outstanding against the run. For a man his size he was amazingly agile. Whereas Deacon was an instinctive, enthusiastic player, Ole was calculating and collected. Olsen was one of the most intelligent men ever to play the game. He knew what was going on at all times and took advantage of every weakness the opposition had and every mistake that was made.

Merlin used to drive us crazy in team meetings. He worried about everyone else as well as himself. He'd ask who was going to cover the back coming out of the backfield or who was going to pick up a receiver 35 yards downfield, and the guys would break up. I'd point out that if he took care of rushing the passer it wasn't his job to worry about covering a receiver. He took a lot of kidding about this stuff, but he did care.

One of the moments I remember about Olsen was a game we had to win from the Giants in Yankee Stadium to have a chance to win our conference. Merlin had a bad knee, didn't practice all week, and wasn't expected to play on Sunday. But he got the doctor to OK him and he turned up on the field. I played him and he destroyed people and we destroyed the Giants.

Sometimes I think a defensive lineman is better off being instinctive than intelligent, better off being mean than poised, but fellows like Olsen had the desire to be superior and he used his exceptional size and strength very well. Usually I don't want a defensive lineman analyzing problems. I prefer he attack them, but Ole thought his way through and played exceptionally well for 15 seasons.

13.
Alan Page

In 15 pro seasons, Alan Page never missed a game, playing in 218 consecutive contests on the defensive line. Drafted out of Notre Dame by Minnesota in 1967, he spent 11 seasons with the Vikings followed by four years with the Chicago Bears.

Defensive linemen don't have the usual statistical testimony of yards and points to comment on their careers. They depend, instead, on items such as blocked kicks, sacks, and tackles. Few linemen had more impressive numbers than the ones Page recorded. For his 15 NFL seasons, the 6-4, 225-pound tackle totaled 173½ sacks and 28 blocked kicks — excellent accomplishments.

Page retired after the 1981 season at age 36 and went out strong. In his final year with the Bears, he had 9½ sacks and three blocked kicks. Of those sacks, 3½ were recorded in his final game.

In 1971, Page enjoyed a singular honor. He became the first defensive lineman in NFL history to be selected as the season's Most Valuable Player. He compiled 10 sacks, six forced fumbles, three fumble recoveries, and 147 tackles, 111 of them solos that year. Three years later, in 1974, Page set a Viking record with 137 solo tackles. He was involved in a career-high 172 tackles that year and also had a career-high 15 sacks.

Page was named to the Pro Bowl squad nine straight years from 1969 to 1977 and was selected for the All-Pro team nine times in his first 11 seasons. The only other defensive linemen honored that frequently were Joe Greene and Gino Marchetti.

During his career as one of the NFL's most feared linemen, Page went back to school, pursuing his law degree at the University of Minnesota. He passed the Minnesota bar exam in 1979 and spent his last three NFL seasons as a full-fledged attorney. He was selected in 1981 by the United States Junior Chamber of Commerce as one of the country's 10 Outstanding Young Men of the Year for his charity work with organizations such as the American Cancer Society, the National Multiple Sclerosis Society, and the United Negro College Fund.

Alan Page was an astonishing all-around athlete. He was big, though not enormous, strong, quick, and so agile as to be almost acrobatic. At their peak in the 1960s and 1970s he and Carl Eller were another of the out-

Alan Page (#82)

standing defensive duos of all time when they were with the Minnesota Vikings, and Eller was one of the last players cut from my list. Carl was enormous, instinctive, savage, and he endured 15 seasons. Page also lasted 15 seasons, never missed a game, and was, I think, a little more consistently effective than Eller, possibly because Page was a little quicker. Page was as good a pass rusher and, I think, a little better run defender than Eller.

Page had tremendous desire. You could block him, but you couldn't keep him blocked. I remember one big game against the Vikings when I was with the Rams. Tom Mack, who was an outstanding offensive guard, blocked Page to the ground, but he got up and intercepted a pass from Roman Gabriel. It was an incredible play and later, after studying films, I still couldn't believe Page had gotten up so fast and moved so well he could make that interception.

Page intercepted a lot of passes. He recovered a lot of fumbles. He blocked a lot of punts. He sacked passers many times. He may have been capable of making more varied plays than any player ever at his position. He was one of those who was always all over the field.

The game I mentioned against the Rams was a playoff game on an icy field in Minnesota in snowy, bitter-cold weather. Page was a big-game guy and adverse conditions didn't bother him. He came through with a big play in a way that few defensive linemen, even some of the best, have been able to do.

14.
(Mean) Joe Greene

When Coach Chuck Noll began the reconstruction of the Pittsburgh Steelers, his first building block was a huge tackle out of North Texas State named Joe Greene. Noll picked Greene on the first round of the 1969 NFL draft, and the 6-4, 260-pound tackle became the anchor of Pittsburgh's "Iron Curtain"—one of the finest defensive lines in pro football history.

Mean Joe maintained that important position for most of his 13 seasons with the Steelers, until his retirement after the 1981 NFL season.

Greene got his nickname because North Texas State was called the Mean Green Machine and it was just a short step from there to Mean Joe Greene. Teammates and opponents said he was tough on the field but gentle off it. Greene resented the nickname a bit but endured it anyway.

Joe quickly developed into a high-quality player, and his nine selections for the Pro Bowl game represent an AFC record. He was a 10-time All-Pro choice and a unanimous pick for the NFL's All-Pro team for the decade of the 1970s.

Only one man played more games for the Steelers than the 181 Greene logged in his 13 seasons. He is Ray Mansfield, who played only one more game during his career.

Certainly Mean Joe was an integral part of the rebuilding of the team, which was 1–13 in his rookie season but developed into a four-time Super Bowl champion. Greene was one of the club's most recognized players, a leader both on and off the field.

His best season may have been 1972, when he was named the Defensive Player of the Year as the Steelers began a run of eight straight playoff appearances. Greene totaled 11 quarterback sacks that season, a team and career high. Five of those sacks came in a single game against Houston. He also recovered an Oiler fumble in that game. He repeated as Defensive Player of the Year in 1974, when he began the unique practice of lining up at an angle between the center and guard. Greene proved difficult to contain using this technique, and he enjoyed one of his finest campaigns.

(Mean) Joe Greene

He was the central character in one of television's most successful commercial campaigns for Coca-Cola and won a Clio—the advertising industry's version of the Hollywood Oscar. The commercial led to a television film, starring Greene, in 1981.

When he announced his retirement from football on February 10, 1982, Joe said he wanted to be remembered "as a good football player who wasn't really mean."

Although people talk about what a nice guy Joe Greene is off the field, I can assure you Mean Joe Greene earned his nickname on the field. He was mean, nasty, and intimidating. He is a big guy and he threw his weight around fiercely. Sometimes he was too reckless. He got taken out of plays from time to time. But he also made tremendous defensive plays. He turned games around. He was one of those few defensive players who could dominate games. His only drawback was that he was a little inconsistent. He played some ordinary games. But his ordinary games were better than outstanding games by some others. And he always was up for the big games.

Pittsburgh had more than its share of success in the 1970s, and Greene was the cornerstone around which the Steeler defense was constructed. He was an extremely powerful player on a powerhouse team. He and L. C. Greenwood were the strongest players up front, backed by a couple of other stars, Jack Ham and Jack Lambert. It was very difficult to run an offense which wasn't disrupted by these guys. And Greene always was the one who scared you the most.

Maybe because of his colorful nickname, Joe got a lot of publicity. He was a flamboyant player, anyway, who attracted a lot of attention. And his television commercial made him famous outside of football. Because of all this, there was a tendency on the part of some to regard him as overrated. Not in my book. Greene was one of the really dominating players in NFL history.

15.
Randy White

They call Randy White "Manster—half man, half monster." That's because the Dallas Cowboy tackle plays defense with a vengeance. He is one of the hardest hitters in pro football, and he's the Cowboys' strongest player. He lifts weights and routinely bench-presses 475 pounds. But at 6-4 and 250 pounds, he does not sacrifice speed for strength.

In college at Maryland, White played defensive end and was a consensus All-America in 1974, when he won both the Outland and Vince Lombardi trophies as college football's top lineman. He was the second player chosen in the 1975 draft, the Cowboys utilizing a pick acquired in a trade with the New York Giants.

At first the Cowboys tried White at linebacker, but after two seasons as a backup there, head coach Tom Landry moved him into the trenches and he flourished. He has been named to the Pro Bowl for five straight years beginning in 1977 and he has been an All-Pro for four straight years, beginning in 1978.

In 1977, his first season at tackle, White shared MVP honors for Super Bowl XII with defensive end Harvey Martin. White recorded 12 quarterback sacks that season and increased that total to 16 in 1978, sharing the club lead with Martin. White also fell one short of the team lead in solo tackles that year, recording 75.

Cowboy coaches insist that White's sack and tackle totals are misleading because he is double- and triple-teamed so often. But that just frees other Dallas defenders.

White is one of those players Landry calls "gamemakers"—individuals who are such outstanding performers that they can control the outcome of a game by themselves. Landry and the other Cowboy coaches say White doesn't have any bad games. And there are plenty of people around the NFL—most of them offensive linemen—who agree.

Randy White (#54)

There were many outstanding defensive linemen in the 1970s. Claude Humphrey, Bubba Smith, Jack Youngblood, Elvin Bethea, L. C. Greenwood, and Carl Eller were remarkable ends who belong with the best ever. Eller and Alan Page were a dynamic twosome for the Vikings' many title contenders. Page made my list, Eller narrowly missed. Greenwood and Greene were a dynamic duo for the Steelers' four-time Super Bowl title teams. Greenwood didn't make it, though Greene and other Steelers did. Some fine players had to be left off.

Harvey Martin and Randy White have been a dynamic duo for the Dallas Cowboys. Reluctantly, Martin was left off my list. White has played just long enough to establish himself as a player who ranks among the finest of all time. He has been the successor to Bob Lilly as the heart of the Dallas "Doomsday Defense," sort of a second group of great teams turned out by Tom Landry. I am especially proud of the success I enjoyed against Tom because he is such a great coach and always is so consistently difficult to defeat. I know how tough Lilly was to contain and it looks to me like White is almost equally difficult to deal with. You can put two or three good men on him and not stop him.

Randy seems to get bigger every year. He didn't look big to me when he first broke into the league, but he seems enormous now. I hear he's built himself up. I sense he's a very dedicated player. He has a lot of quickness to go with his size and seems exceptionally strong. He is agile and has developed marvelous moves. He is a great pass rusher, but he may be an even better run defender. He varies his charges and cannot be blocked cleanly or held out of a play for long. He gets into plays and gets to passers and runners. He seems to surround them and is as sure a tackler as I've seen.

CHAPTER 7

LINEBACKERS

The most versatile players in football are the linebackers. They have to defend against the pass and the run. They have to be mobile enough to charge upfield and rush the passer and range downfield to cover the receivers, yet big and strong enough to back up the line and tackle the runner who has powered through the line. They also have to be smart enough to read offenses to adjust to complicated coverage. The middle linebacker usually is the defensive quarterback who has to anticipate and read offenses and call the signals for the entire defense.

The linebacker is the link between the linemen and the backs on defense. Successful football requires a coordinated effort. If the linemen don't rush the passer effectively, the backs won't be able to cover the receivers effectively. And if the linebacker doesn't do a little bit of both effectively, the defense will come apart completely.

Many offenses are designed primarily to neutralize the linebacker. Play-option passes are designed to freeze the linebacker in place in expectation of running plays while receivers move behind him to take passes. Many passes are designed to isolate a slower linebacker on a faster receiver. Many passes to tight ends are designed to put these big guys against smaller linebackers. Draw plays are designed to cause the linebacker to drop back to cover a pass that turns out to be a delayed run into territory he has vacated.

In many ways I think it is more fun to play linebacker than any other position. The linebacker usually is freer to roam the field and use his own judgment than players at other positions. He gets to express a wider range of abilities than players at other positions. He rushes the passers, tackles the ball carriers, and knocks down passes. Since he covers passes so much, he has more opportunity to intercept them and run the ball on returns than the linemen.

There is no question that the quarterback is the single most important player on the offense. They call the passers, receivers, and runners the "skilled" players. But I think the linebackers are the most important players on defense. And playing the position requires enormous skill. On a given team with a great pass rusher such as Deacon Jones or Bob Lilly, a defensive end or tackle may be the most important defensive player. But generally speaking, the linebacker fills the key role.

Some of the greatest athletes ever in professional football have played linebacker. While I tried to find the logical positions for the 100 greatest players, whatever their position, I think the linebacker list is the strongest of all my lists, with the possible exception of the running backs. And it was a more difficult task for me to pick the first, second, and third best and so forth among the linebackers than even among the running backs.

Here, then, are my top linebackers.

1.
Chuck Bednarik

Chuck Bednarik was football's last iron man, a two-way performer who was a 60-minute-per-game player for the Philadelphia Eagles. On offense he played center. On defense he switched to linebacker. The remarkable part of Bednarik's performance, though, is that he was still playing both ways long after the two-platoon system had been introduced to the sport.

Bednarik, a native of Bethlehem, Pennsylvania, played for 14 seasons with the Eages after achieving All-America status at the University of Pennsylvania. He was a seven-time All-Pro choice and was selected for the Pro Bowl game eight times, six as a linebacker and twice as a center. In 1954 he was chosen as the outstanding player in the Pro Bowl, an unusual honor for a lineman. But Bednarik was an unusual lineman.

The Eagles drafted Bednarik on the first round in 1949. Service in World War II had delayed his college career and he was 24 years old as an NFL rookie. His arrival forced Philadelphia to move All-Pro center Vic Lindskog to another position and Bednarik won a starting job on defense as well.

Chuck Bednarik

Linebackers

Bednarik, a 6-3, 230-pounder, delighted in bone-jarring tackles and is remembered for two devastating hits, both delivered during the 1960 season. The first one leveled Frank Gifford of the New York Giants and forced him into a one-year retirement. The second merely nailed down the world championship for the Eagles.

Philadelphia was facing Green Bay in the 1960 NFL title game at Franklin Field, Philadelphia. Bednarik, who was then 36 years old, was on the field for 58 minutes and as time was running out, the Eagles hung on grimly to a 17–13 lead. The Packers were marching downfield, racing the clock and moving relentlessly toward the Philadelphia end zone.

On what developed into the final play of the game, bulldozing Jim Taylor carried the ball for Green Bay. As he moved toward the end zone, he was met head-on by Bednarik. The Eagle iron man made the tackle one-on-one, saving the victory and the championship for Philadelphia.

Chuck Bednarik not only was the best linebacker I ever knew, he also was the best offensive center of the past 30 years and would have ranked right up there with Mel Hein and Bulldog Turner among the offensive linemen had I chosen to put him on that list.

But hitting was Bednarik's game and he belongs with the defensive specialists primarily. He was the surest, strongest snapper I've ever seen and an absolutely brutal and unbeatable blocker. But his hits are what one remembers best about him.

Bednarik was a big man, but it was his desire and viciousness that made him one of the two hardest-hitting tacklers I've ever seen. Dick Butkus was the other. They had so many of their opponents so afraid of them it gave them a great psychological and competitive edge over others.

Two famous tackles by Bednarik—the one that knocked Frank Gifford unconscious for 36 hours and into a year's retirement and the other on Jim Taylor that saved the title game in 1960—were clean but classic hits which saved big games. Gifford admits he has not been able to forget his. Neither can Bednarik. He describes it with pride.

If not actually dirty, Bednarik was mean. He did what he had to do and if he hurt people along the way, I guess he just accepted it. When he tackled them, they stayed tackled. They seldom slipped away from him. He drew a bead on opponents and battered into them with frightening force.

I think some others had greater range. A few were superior on pass coverage. But Bednarik more than made up for it with his determination, hustle, and recklessness. Wherever the ball was, he was there. He made plays all over the field. He made the big plays in the big games.

Bednarik was the right name for him. It sounds tough. He was tough. He came from one of those Pennsylvania steel towns. His father worked in a steel mill. Chuck was a gunner on a bomber during World War II. He played 14 years in the NFL, until he was almost 40. He dominated games in a way that few defensive players ever could.

2.
Bill George

The manner in which they played defense, yielding yards grudgingly, earned the Chicago Bears the nickname "Monsters of the Midway." And one of their finest defenders was Hall of Famer Bill George, largely responsible for defining the position of middle linebacker.

George was an All-America tackle at Wake Forest. He was so proficient that the Bears drafted him in the second round in 1951, even though he still had a year of collegiate eligibility remaining, a rule later rescinded. When George reported in 1952, he moved into the defensive lineup at middle guard in the five-man front used by all pro teams in those days. Included in the responsibilities of players assigned to that position in passing situations was the job of bumping the center from his three-point stance before dropping back on coverage. George observed that passes were being completed just beyond his reach and decided that if he dropped back instead of engaging the center first, he could pick off those passes. The first time he did it, the pass hit him in the stomach. The next time, he made the first of 18 career interceptions and it didn't take long before other teams were adopting the innovation. That's how the position of middle linebacker was born.

George was an All-Pro middle guard in 1955 and 1956. By 1957 the position was dropped from All-Pro teams and replaced by middle linebacker. Appropriately, George was named to the All-NFL team at that position for five straight years, from 1957 through 1961.

Chicago's defense was designed around George. He called the Bears' defensive signals for a decade, and his ability as a blitzer dominated Chicago's strategy when opposing teams had the football.

Besides his 18 interceptions, George recovered 16 fumbles. He was an eight-time selection for the Pro Bowl and, early in his career, he was used as a place-kicker. He booted four field goals and 14 extra points.

The 6-2, 230-pound George played for 14 seasons with Chicago—the longest time any player stayed with the Bears. After one wrap-up season with Los Angeles, he retired after the 1966 campaign and, eight years later, was named to the Pro Football Hall of Fame.

Bill George was the smartest defensive player I ever coached. He called defensive signals for the Bears when they were at their best defensively. He studied films, kept a notebook of his own, did his homework every week, and always prepared to play his best. He always saw to it that his teammates were prepared to play their best, too. He was the captain and real leader of the team through most of the 1950s and well into the middle 1960s. I was with the Rams by then and picked him up because he could

Bill George (#61)

still contribute to a team with his intelligence even when his body was beat up.

George was a big, strong guy and he took care of his body. He kept a dumbbell by his locker and was always working out with it at times others wouldn't even think of it. He was big enough and strong enough to have played up front in the defensive line. Actually, he came up as an offensive player, which is why he was assigned No. 61, which he wore throughout his career. However, he became a middle guard in the old 5-2 defenses and dropped back to play middle linebacker in the new 4-3 defenses so he could cover the short pass over the middle better. George practically invented the middle-linebacker position and the 4-3 defense.

George covered the short pass as well as any linebacker ever and came up with a lot of interceptions. He had a nose for the ball and also had many fumble recoveries. He was always in the thick of the action. He was fast enough to cover short receivers and to blitz the passers very effectively. He also was extremely effective against the run. He had been a wrestler in school and manhandled people. If not quite the savage hitter Chuck Bednarik or Dick Butkus were, George had good hands and was a sure tackler who didn't let ball carriers slip away. He made as few mistakes as any player I've seen.

George suffered with a shoulder injury through much of his career, but it never stopped him from playing better than the other guys. He played 15 years of superb pro ball and there hasn't been anyone I've admired much more.

3.
Dick Butkus

If one had to construct a model for a pro football middle linebacker, he might start with Dick Butkus' dimensions (6-3, 245 pounds) and playing disposition (unfriendly).

Butkus brought a zest to the task of being the central figure of his team's defensive alignment. He was an exceptional performer, first at the University of Illinois, where he was a two-time All-America and finished third in the 1964 Heisman Trophy balloting, and then with the Chicago Bears, where he starred for nine seasons.

The Bears won an NFL-AFL bidding war for Butkus with the Denver Broncos, mostly because the ex-Illinois star wanted to play in his home state. In the College All-Star game before his rookie NFL season of 1965, the husky linebacker was in on 15 tackles and blocked an attempted field goal. He succeeded 14-year veteran Bill George in the middle-linebacking post with the Bears and stamped himself for stardom in his very first pro game when he made 11 unassisted tackles in the opener against San Francisco.

That season Butkus led the Bears' defense in both fumble recoveries and interceptions, a rare double for a linebacker. But Butkus was a rare linebacker. He was blessed with enough speed that enabled him to cover the field from sideline to sideline and football instinct that, more often than not, led him to the play.

Dick Butkus

Linebackers

A torn-up right knee terminated his pro career in 1973 and led to a lawsuit against the Bears. Butkus charged the team with improper handling of the injury, and the suit eventually was settled out of court. The episode hardly diminished his accomplishments on the field, however, and he was elected to the Pro Football Hall of Fame in 1979.

He finished his career with 25 opponents' recovered fumbles, second best in NFL history, and 22 interceptions. There is no record for fumbles forced, but Butkus owned his share of that, too. He was, well, just what you'd want a middle linebacker to be—6-3, 245 pounds, unfriendly, and superb.

Dick Butkus succeeded Bill George as middle linebacker of the Bears. Butkus came in and took over in George's last year with the team. And he was darn near as good as George. Of them all, only Bednarik hit as hard as Butkus. Butkus played with the ferocity of an angered animal. He was mean. Like Bednarik, Butkus had a name that sounded like the man he was.

Not that he wasn't smart. I think he was more of an instinctive player, while George was more of a calculating player, but both were students of the game. We were short-staffed when I helped coach the Bears and I had a lot of jobs to do. I couldn't get the scouting reports ready before Thursdays. Butkus was always wondering why he couldn't get them on Wednesdays. He would study them on the plane flights to road games while the others played cards.

I mentioned in my chapter on the running backs that I drafted Gale Sayers and Butkus on the first round in 1965. The Bears had accumulated three first-round picks that year. The third player I picked was Steve De-Long, a lineman. But we lost him to the AFL. We almost lost Butkus to the AFL, too. He and his agent, Arthur Morris of Chicago, came to the Bears' office to talk terms with George Halas. Butkus and Morris left furious.

Halas could be a little close with a buck. For example, when Morris said Butkus wanted a car for a bonus, Halas hemmed and hawed and said he'd look around for a used car. This was before the pros paid unproven rookies big bucks. But the AFL was driving up prices. And Butkus knew he was good. And I knew he was good. They stormed out of Halas' office with Butkus growling profanities. I intercepted them in the corridor and had the darndest time pacifying them. I promised to make Halas see reason. I had the darndest time with Halas. But Butkus got his car; we got Butkus a new one.

We needed Sayers to replace Willie Gallimore and we needed Butkus to replace Bill George. Both Sayers and Butkus deserved to be All-Pro as rookies and went on to become all-timers. I recall clearly that on his first day of practice with the Bears Butkus was knocking his own teammates down left and right. Veterans like Doug Atkins vowed to get even with him. But throughout his career, players always were vowing to get even with Butkus and no one ever did. Butkus always got the better of every player he faced. He scared people and nothing ever scared him. I hate to say this, but I think he enjoyed hurting people. He really enjoyed playing.

Butkus was a brute on the blitz. He was very quick for a big guy and he hurled himself at anyone with the ball. He was always around the ball and terrific on pass coverage. He made plays all over the field. I'd be looking at films and wondering who the heck that was 40 yards downfield and it would be Butkus. He fell short of lasting 10 years with the pros because of a bum knee. I tried to get another year out of him with the Redskins but he couldn't pass the physical. If he had, he might still be playing.

4.
George Connor

It's hard enough to be picked for one unit of an All-Pro team, but George Connor of the Chicago Bears went that achievement one better when he was named to the squad on both offense and defense for three straight seasons in the early 1950s.

Connor's All-Pro term began in 1950, when he was named to the team for his work as an offensive tackle, the first of four straight years during which he was honored for his performance on that unit. Then, starting in 1951, he also won All-Pro honors for his defensive work, the first year as a tackle and the next three as a linebacker. Counting both units, Connor was named to eight All-Pro squads in five seasons at three different positions, no small accomplishment.

Connor's difficult All-Pro double should have been expected. He was, after all, an All-America selection at two colleges, achieving that status first at Holy Cross and then at Notre Dame after World War II naval service interrupted his college career.

Connor spent his entire eight-year pro career with the Bears, although he passed briefly through the hands of the New York Giants and Boston Yanks. The Giants drafted him in 1946, when his original Holy Cross class graduated. They swapped him to Boston and the Yanks passed him along to the Bears when Connor, a native of Chicago, made it clear he would not play elsewhere.

It was a happy marriage between the 6-3, 240-pound versatile Connor and the Bears that started in 1948. He was a standout tackle on both offense and defense, as his All-Pro selections prove, but it was at linebacker that he really excelled. He was an expert at reading plays and stopping them before they had a chance to develop.

Actually, Connor's introduction to the linebacker position came almost by accident. In 1949, the Philadelphia Eagles were the NFL's best team and the Bears were trying to develop strategy that would contain the power sweeps of running back Steve Van Buren. They decided Connor's size made him a good candidate to pull back from the line and contain the plays. It worked. The Bears beat the Eagles—Philadelphia's lone loss that season.

Connor played in four straight Pro Bowl games from 1951 to 1954 and was named to the Pro Football Hall of Fame in 1975. If there were two wings in the Canton, Ohio, shrine, one for offense and the other for defense, they might have needed two plaques for him.

George Connor

George Connor makes it three straight linebackers from the Bears, three of the first four on my all-time list. Well, that's just the way it is. The Bears had the best linebackers for many years. I have still another Bear linebacker on my list, Joe Fortunato. And I could have put on others, like Larry Morris. Connor belongs with the best. I could have put him with the offensive linemen. He was a great blocker, maybe the best ever. He was an outstanding two-way player. He was always an all-star, wherever he was.

Connor had everything. He was tall, heavy, and strong. He was quick and agile. He was as smart as Bill George. He may not have been as mean as Chuck Bednarik or Dick Butkus, and Connor didn't hit as hard as they did, but he had tremendous technique on his tackles. He had long arms and good hands and was a very sure tackler. Connor preceded Bill George, who preceded Dick Butkus. What a group of stars at linebacker! Connor could play inside or outside. He was very versatile. He was better against the run than against the pass, but he was very good against the pass. A linebacker didn't have to defend as much against the pass as against the run in Connor's day, but I'm sure he could and would have adjusted to today's offenses.

The position of linebacker is a relatively modern development in football. There really wasn't such a position in the 1930s, though Bronko Nagurski for one, and Clarke Hinkle, for another, played something approximating the position. Both were brilliant at it, but both are on my offensive unit. In the 1940s, Bulldog Turner and Bill Willis played linebacker at times, but both also are on my offensive unit. Although Chuck Bednarik really refined the way the position should be played, George Connor goes back farther than any linebacker on my list.

The one drawback to Connor was that he only played eight seasons. Otherwise he might have been No. 1 at one position or another. But he was so good he had to be high on some list. He was a wonderful all-around athlete, a 60-minute man, and one of the finest football players who ever lived.

5.
Joe Schmidt

At the University of Pittsburgh in the early 1950s, Joe Schmidt established a reputation for being injury-prone. He suffered two broken ribs as a freshman, a fractured wrist and a shoulder separation as a sophomore, a wrenched knee as a junior, and torn knee cartilage and a concussion as a senior. So even though he had seemed to be a reasonably efficient middle guard, most pro teams greeted his draft availability with a shrug. Detroit chose him on the seventh round in 1953. It turned out to be a very lucky seventh-round selection for the Lions.

Schmidt had come to Pitt as a fullback but was switched to middle guard there. When he reached the NFL in 1953, the pro game was beginning to evolve from traditional five-man defensive fronts into the 4-3 alignment. Schmidt switched again, this time to middle linebacker. Few men played the position more efficiently.

Chosen to the All-Pro team eight times, Schmidt played in nine consecutive Pro Bowl games from 1955 through 1963. He developed into one of the Lions' leaders and was selected the club's Most Valuable Player by his teammates four times.

At 6 feet and 222 pounds, Schmidt was not exceptionally big. And he had only ordinary speed. But he was like a defensive quarterback, calling signals and directing traffic. He was strong against running plays and made 24 pass interceptions during his career.

Joe Schmidt (#56)

Schmidt played for 13 seasons with the Lions and then served as the club's head coach for six more years. In 1973 he was inducted into the Pro Football Hall of Fame.

Any one of my first five linebackers could have been No. 1. It was very hard to pick among them. Joe Schmidt was just about as good as anyone who ever played the position. Schmidt was almost like a coach on the playing field for the Lions for 13 years, then their head coach on the sidelines for six more. He was an exceptionally smart man, a great player and a good coach.

Schmidt wasn't as big as other linebackers on my list, but he was sturdy and strong. He was a middle linebacker who played his position perfectly and called defensive signals brilliantly. He studied his opponents and diagnosed plays as well as anyone ever did. He blitzed passers and covered passes superbly. He was always on the runner and seldom missed a tackle or made a mistake. He had finesse as well as fury. He was a very active player who played all over the field and dominated games.

Schmidt and Bobby Layne were the inspirational leaders of the Lions in the 1950s. Both were outspoken characters who weren't afraid to criticize their teammates. Between them they fired up those great Detroit teams. It was Schmidt who provided a profane pep talk to his teammates in the dressing room at halftime of one of the most famous playoff games ever, the 1957 Western Conference title game against the 49ers when the Lions came from behind, 27–7, to win, 31–27.

Joe was dedicated to winning. He was also intense, inspirational, intelligent, and talented.

6.
Sam Huff

The year was 1960 and pro football was beginning to make its move on America's sports psyche. One of the major developments in the movement came when CBS television devoted a half-hour documentary to the game. The network decided the most effective way to present the program was to wire a middle linebacker during a game. That's how "The Violent World of Sam Huff" came about.

Huff was the middle linebacker for the New York Giants, a big, hard hitter who came out of West Virginia's coal-mining country to achieve stardom in the NFL. He was in his fifth season in the NFL when CBS helped popularize his name and the dangers inherent in playing his position. The microphone picked up all of the action, the crunch of bodies, and the impact of helmets and pads. It was a realistic example of what goes on when pro football players collide.

Drafted from West Virginia in 1956, Huff beat veteran Ray Beck out of the starting job and helped the Giants win the NFL championship that year.

Sam Huff

He remained as the club's defensive pivot at middle linebacker until 1963, when he was traded to Washington. He played for five more seasons with the Redskins.

Huff is perhaps remembered best for his one-on-one confrontations with Cleveland's Jim Brown, the greatest running back in the history of pro football. The Browns and the Giants were fierce rivals in those days, often battling each other for the NFL Eastern Conference championship. Much of the rivalry was spotlighted in the showdowns between Brown, leader of the Cleveland attack, and Huff, around whom New York's defense revolved. There was a five-game stretch between 1958 and 1960 when Brown could manage only 50 yards or less a game against the Huff-led Giant defense. In the 1958 Eastern Conference playoff game—the one leading up to the famous overtime championship game between the Giants and the Baltimore Colts—Brown carried the ball seven times against the Giants and managed only eight yards, mainly because of Huff's defensive excellence.

Huff, a 6-1, 230-pounder, was a five-time Pro Bowl selection and was named to the NFL's All-Pro squad for the decade of the 1950s. He was voted into the Pro Football Hall of Fame in January, 1982.

Some say Sam Huff was overrated. They've said it so much he became underrated. He got a lot of recognition because the New York media are so large and so influential. But he deserved all the attention he attracted, and he earned the Hall of Fame selection he got in 1982. He was a marvelous middle linebacker, active and aggressive, and a key man on those outstanding New York Giant teams of the late 1950s and early 1960s.

Huff was the key figure in the defense Jim Lee Howell devised to stop the great Jim Brown of the Cleveland Browns. It worked as well as any special strategy ever has worked, primarily because Huff often stopped Brown so the Giants were able to beat Cleveland. Brown was hit on every play, whether or not he had the ball, and Huff did most of the hitting.

I was a coach with the Bears when we played the Giants in Toronto in an exhibition game during which Huff was wired for sound for a television documentary that made him famous all over the country. He played a heck of a game and it made a heck of a film. Up to then defensive players didn't get much recognition, but that film made fans realize how important defense is. I sure didn't see anything wrong with that. Huff was a flamboyant type who attracted attention, but I didn't see anything wrong with that, either.

Sam did a terrific job. He was a smart and a physical player. He was better against the run than against the pass, but he did a little bit of everything extremely well. He had a great career, most of it with the Giants, but the last part of it with the Redskins. After he'd been retired for a year, Sam was brought back for one last year, the only season Vince Lombardi coached the Redskins, much as I brought back Bill George with the Rams. But by the time I got to the Redskins Huff had retired. I wish he hadn't. He was the kind of player a coach wants on his side.

7.
Ray Nitschke

In the years when the Green Bay Packers were dominating the NFL, their defense played a major role in the team's success. Three times from 1960 through 1967—the height of the Green Bay dynasty—the Packer defense had the lowest point yield in the NFL. At the heart of that defense was middle linebacker Ray Nitschke, who played his position with a zest that earned him selection to the NFL's All-Pro squad for the decade of the 1960s.

The 6-3, 235-pound Nitschke spent 15 years with the Packers after being selected on the third round of the 1958 draft. He came out of the University of Illinois, where he had played fullback on offense and linebacker on defense. He was primarily a blocking back in college, but he did gain 943 yards rushing in three years and averaged 6.5 yards per carry on 79 attempts as a senior. But there was little doubt that his football future was on defense. Few performed the assignment better.

It was not until 1962 that Ray really began blossoming into a star under coach Vince Lombardi. Nitschke had been in and out of the lineup until then but when Lombardi gave him full-time work, the balding linebacker flourished. The Packers beat the New York Giants in the NFL title game that season and Nitschke was named the Most Valuable Player after deflecting a pass for an interception and recovering two fumbles.

For his career, Nitschke made 25 interceptions, many with catlike moves on pass defense.

Although often overshadowed by Green Bay's large cast of offensive stars, Nitschke was selected to the Pro Football Hall of Fame in his first year of eligibility, 1978.

Ray Nitschke is one of those players who rarely received the recognition he deserved during his career. The number of times a player was picked All-Pro was one of the guides I used in narrowing my lists, but Nitschke was named only three times in 15 seasons. He was picked to play in the Pro Bowl game only once. I have no idea how this could have happened. In my mind, Nitschke was one of the ten greatest linebackers ever. I know many of my coaching contemporaries would agree wholeheartedly.

Nitschke was a key Packer on five NFL championship teams. He called defensive signals. He was smart and alert and one of the all-time leaders among linebackers in interceptions and fumble recoveries. He was big and strong yet quick and agile. He was equally good on pass as on run coverage. He was one of the hardest hitters I've seen. And he always seemed to make a big play or two in a big game. He was a money player on a team that always had the stakes piled high on the table.

Ray Nitschke (#66)

The Packers had a lot of great players through the 1960s. Many of them made my list. None deserved it more than Nitschke. A few others might have made it. Another linebacker who well could have been on this list was Dave Robinson, a rangy, rugged guy who came along on the Packers a little after Nitschke. But Nitschke was one of those special players who did things others didn't do. When I was with the Bears we named one of our defenses "47 Nitschke" because it was copied from the way Ray played a certain situation. Naming a defense after a player is a pretty high compliment in my book.

When Nitschke got wound up he could take apart an offense all by himself. He seemed to go a little crazy at times, a wild man who was almost impossible to contain. But the people who were really a little nuts were those who left him off some of those All-Pro teams.

8.
Ted Hendricks

Ted Hendricks owns two impressive but little-known NFL records—very good for a linebacker. Players at that position do not usually compile impressive statistics the way offensive performers such as running backs, quarterbacks, and wide receivers do.

Hendricks has a record four safeties in his career, tops in NFL history, and has blocked 21 kicks—punts, field goals, and extra points.

A six-time Pro Bowl and five-time All-Pro selection, Hendricks was a three-time All-America at defensive end for the University of Miami and became the first sophomore in the school's history to gain that honor. He was picked in the second round of the 1969 draft by the Baltimore Colts and, at 6-7 and 225 pounds, became an immediate factor on defense. His tall, thin frame, accentuated by his flailing arms, earned him the nickname "the Mad Stork" as he roamed Baltimore's defense.

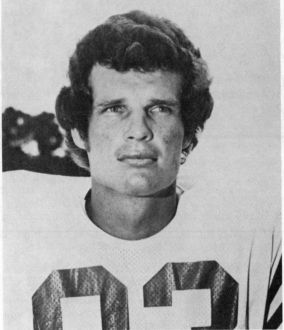

Ted Hendricks

Hendricks became something of a free-lancer behind the line of scrimmage, roving from one side to the other, red-dogging sometimes, dropping back on pass defense sometimes, but always a factor. In 1974 the Colts made one of the least advantageous trades in NFL history, swapping Hendricks and a second-round draft pick to Green Bay for a linebacker named Tom MacLeod and an eighth-round draft pick.

Hendricks played just one season for the Packers, leaving as a free agent in 1975. Oakland, often regarded as the last stop for pro players who have had problems elsewhere, grabbed the big guy, happily paying two first-round draft choices to the Packers as compensation. It proved to be a bargain. Hendricks responded with an All-Pro season in 1976 and has been a leader of the Oakland defense ever since, helping the Raiders emerge as winners of Super Bowl XV in January 1981.

For his career, Hendricks has recovered 11 fumbles and scored two touchdowns on blocked punts, and his 26 interceptions are fourth best among all NFL linebackers.

Hendricks has never missed a game in 13 NFL seasons and had a consecutive-game streak of 190 through the 1981 season.

Ted is quiet, but he owns a distinct sense of humor, as evidenced by the time he showed up for a Halloween practice wearing a hollowed-out pumpkin on his head.

Ted Hendricks is the first great linebacker who is not built in the mold of a linebacker. You know, second basemen are supposed to be a certain size, and point guards are supposed to be a certain size. But players come along who change the concept. Hendricks just didn't look like a linebacker, and when he came into pro ball they said, "Hey, we've got to put some weight on him or play him somewhere else." Holy mackerel, Green Bay didn't even give him a chance before he went to Oakland.

He could play well somewhere else. Defensive end, certainly. But he's become one of the most unusual and one of the most outstanding linebackers we've ever had. Talk about players who are all over the field! With his height and long arms, his quickness and mobility, he's high on the all-time list in interceptions and fumble recoveries and holds the record for blocked kicks. He's the most opportunistic player I've seen. He forces as many mistakes as anyone ever did, and he takes advantage of mistakes as well as anyone ever did.

Although he looks tall and skinny, Ted is strong and tough. I don't think most teams play him right. You have to block him just like you would a down lineman. He's very elusive, but you have to get in his way, you can't let him just roam free and follow the play. Any offensive game plan against Oakland should start with neutralizing Hendricks as much as possible. That's the mark of a great player—that he requires special handling.

The Raiders have been in a lot of big games, and no one has played better in them than Hendricks. He's an amazing athlete and he's changed our concept of what a linebacker has to be, which is another mark of a great player—that he brings something new to his sport.

9.
Joe Fortunato

He wore a fullback's jersey—No. 31. That's because, if he hadn't been one of football's best linebackers, he probably could have made it in the backfield. Joe Fortunato knew how to run with the football almost as well as he knew how to tackle somebody else who ran with it.

Fortunato played college football at Mississippi State, working as a running back on offense and a linebacker on defense. He was an All-American and, in 1952, he rushed for 779 yards, an average of 6.1 per carry. The

Joe Fortunato

Chicago Bears drafted him in the seventh round in 1952 as a future pick. He finished at Mississippi State in 1953 and then went into military service for two years. Playing service football at Fort Benning, he showed that his running abilities were no fluke, averaging 6.0 yards per carry.

When he reached the pros in 1955, though, head coach George Halas decided that Fortunato's future was on defense. It turned out to be a wise decision, because Fortunato became a key member of the Bear linebacking crew for 12 seasons, playing in 155 games. He was selected for five Pro Bowl games and was a unanimous All-Pro selection for three straight years from 1963 to 1965.

Fortunato was credited with 21 fumble recoveries and made 16 interceptions in his career. That total of 37 takeaways is third best in Bear history.

After retiring as a player in 1966, he remained with the team, first as defensive assistant coach and then as defensive coordinator. Only 6-1 and 225 pounds, Fortunato nevertheless was one of the most important cogs in Chicago's defensive alignment.

Fortunato's college ball-carrying achievements did not go unnoticed in Chicago. In 1957 he was asked to carry the football twice. On one of those carries he barreled into the end zone on a one-yard plunge for a touchdown. After that he returned to defense, preventing TDs instead of producing them.

Joe Fortunato called defensive signals for our 1963 championship team in Chicago when we set a modern record of only 144 points allowed in 14 games. He, Bill George, and Larry Morris formed one of the standout linebacking groups any team ever had. They were powerful, far-ranging players, undoubtedly our greatest strength that season.

Fortunato played a dozen seasons and seldom missed a play. He was one of the smartest players I ever knew. He read films real well and spotted a lot of things others missed. He picked up keys out on the field others missed. He always seemed to be in the right place at the right time. He had good hands and is among the all-time leaders among linebackers in interceptions and fumble recoveries.

Joe wasn't too tall, but he was wide, built like a tank. He had been a runner in college and the Bears drafted him as a running back—before I got there. I believe he could have been a fine fullback in pro ball. Or a great tight end. He certainly was an outstanding linebacker. He ranged all over the field, played the pass as well as the run, and hit tremendously hard. When he picked off an interception he ran with the ball like a running back.

I believe Joe was underrated. He was overshadowed a bit by Bill George. Bill had the bigger reputation, and the people who pick those All-Pro teams don't want to pick two linebackers—or two at any position—from the same team. But it just happens that the Bears had two or three of the outstanding linebackers of all time at one time, and I'm not going to leave Joe Fortunato off my list just because Bill George already is on it.

Fortunato played in the late 1950s and early 1960s. There were a lot of outstanding linebackers in this period. Larry Morris was one I have mentioned. Les Richter was another. Jack Pardee was yet another, one of my personal favorites, one of the most courageous and one of the most underrated players ever. A standout Green Bay Packer, Dave Robinson, came close to making the list. No one came much closer than Tommy Nobis, who was really something. But they were not as talented as Fortunato in my opinion.

10.
Chris Hanburger

NFL teams had sifted through 243 of the 252 college players they would draft on December 6, 1964, when the Washington Redskins decided to take a chance on a smallish linebacker from North Carolina. And that is what led to a brilliant 14-year professional career for Chris Hanburger.

Chris battled his way into the Redskins' starting lineup 10 games into his rookie season and stayed there until 1978, when he retired. At 6-2 and 218 pounds he was rather light for a pro linebacker but he made up for any problems in size with speed, trigger-quick reactions, and determination.

Nine times in his career, Hanburger was selected to play in the Pro Bowl. He was the NFC Defensive Player of the Year in 1972, when the Redskins went to their only Super Bowl, and he was chosen to the NFL team of the decade for the 1960s.

Not bad for the 244th player selected in the draft.

Hanburger, son of a career Army officer, enlisted and served three years in the Army before moving on to play college football. So he was older than most rookies, reporting to his first Redskin camp when he was 24 years old. He was assigned veteran linebacker Sam Huff as a roommate and quickly developed into the special teams' version of Huff, bouncing bodies around with little concern for health and welfare. Eventually the aggressive style caught the eye of the coaches, and Hanburger became a starter.

Hanburger played 135 consecutive games for the Redskins before an appendectomy suffered just before the start of the 1977 season cost him nine games that year. After playing the full 16-game schedule in 1978, he retired.

For his career, Hanburger intercepted 19 passes, recovered 12 fumbles, and scored five touchdowns. Three of those TDs came with recovered fumbles, tying him with nine others for second place on the all-time list. The only man with more recovered-fumble TDs is Bill Thompson, who played as a defensive back for Denver.

Chris Hanburger (#55)

Some people are going to be surprised to see Chris Hanburger's name on my list. But I think he was one of the great ones. He was named to a lot of All-Pro teams. And the coaches picked him to the Pro Bowl just about every year. Yet his reputation isn't as good as some others'. But his play was of the highest kind.

Chris was a little light for a linebacker. He's another who didn't fit the mold. He was seldom knocked off his feet. He had real good balance and excellent agility. But quickness was his biggest asset. He could really rush the passer and he covered a lot of ground on pass defense.

Chris was as important to my Redskins as anyone. He was smart. I think that's a quality all of the great linebackers have, because a player has so much freedom at the position and has to know what he's doing out there or he won't get the job done. He was a real student of the game. He was always prepared to play.

Chris was out most of one season after an operation, but otherwise he did not miss a game in his 14 seasons. As you can see by now, the great ones are durable, and despite his lack of size, Hanburger endured. He played the right side as skillfully as almost anyone I ever saw. I think the right side is the correct place for the lighter linebacker to be, and Chris certainly was the right man for the job.

Whenever we'd bring in a young linebacker with the Redskins, I'd tell him that even if he wasn't playing yet, he could learn a lot about playing the linebacker position just by watching Chris Hanburger. "Keep your eyes on Chris," I'd say, "and you'll see how it's done." He was a picture player.

11.
Jack Ham

When the NFL decided to select teams of the decades, it turned the chore over to the Hall of Fame Selection Committee. The assignment was difficult, considering the outstanding players who have passed through the league. When they got to the 1970s, however, the selection committee had an easy time at one of the linebacker positions. Jack Ham of the Pittsburgh Steelers scored a clean sweep, receiving every vote cast. No other defensive player was a unanimous choice.

The total agreement of the voters was understandable. Drafted out of Penn State's linebacker factory in 1971, he was selected for eight straight Pro Bowl games and was a mainstay in the "Steel Curtain" defense that delivered four Super Bowl championships to Pittsburgh during the decade.

The 6-1, 225-pound Ham has been a starter from his first game as a pro. He came to the Steelers with impressive credentials, a near-unanimous All-America pick in 1970 and chosen as the outstanding player on defense

Jack Ham (#59)

in the Hula Bowl. He quickly established himself as the anchor of the "Steel Curtain."

No NFL linebacker has been selected for the Pro Bowl as frequently as Ham, whose eight-game streak began in 1973. Two seasons later, he was chosen as the NFL's Defensive Player of the Year.

Ham's 31 career interceptions tie him with Detroit's Stan White for the lead among active NFL linebackers in that department. The ex-Penn State great also has 18 career fumble recoveries, tops for active Steelers. The only linebacker in NFL history with more interceptions is Don Shinnick of the Baltimore Colts, who picked off 37 from 1957 to 1969.

Four times in his career, Ham has had two interceptions in a single game. His most important "double" was achieved in the AFC championship game in 1974 against the Oakland Raiders. The Steelers won the contest and went on to capture the first of their four Super Bowl titles.

Almost everything I said about Chris Hanburger goes for Jack Ham. He's small for a linebacker, but quick, smart, and tough. You could use him as a model for other linebackers to copy. He's played the outside position about as perfectly as possible. He blitzes at the right time, and he drops back at the right time. He picks off a lot of passes, and he recovers a lot of fumbles. He seems to me to be one of the more intelligent, resourceful players.

Unlike Hanburger and some others, who came into pro ball from the late rounds of the draft, Ham was a high pick out of Penn State, one of many outstanding linebackers Joe Paterno has developed there. But there's a story that when Ham turned up at the Steelers' dressing room the first day of preseason practice Art Rooney, Jr., a vice-president of the club, told him deliveries were made at the side entrance. Ham looked like a kid. He may not look like a football player, but he's been one of the great ones.

It's one thing to win one championship. It's another thing to win more than one. A good team can have a hot year, get the breaks, and have a great season. But it takes a great team with real pride in its performance to be a consistent winner and to win more than one title. Winning four Super Bowls put the Steelers right up there with the best of all time. And Jack Ham was one of the great players on that team. I think that when Ham got hurt, the Steeler defense started to go down and the team started to slump.

But Ham has played 11 seasons so far and he didn't miss many games when he and the Steelers were at their peaks. At one time he, Jack Lambert, and Andy Russell were one of the greatest sets of linebackers ever. Ham always seemed to come up with the big play. There were those two passes he intercepted in the fourth quarter of a conference championship game against Oakland. And the tackles he made in a Super Bowl when Minnesota was held to just 17 yards rushing.

He has been a big-play guy on a big-play team.

12.
Jack Lambert

Jack Lambert belongs in Bartlett's *Familiar Quotations*. It was Lambert, the ruggedly efficient linebacker of the Pittsburgh Steelers, who summed up in a single sentence the philosophy of players who spend their lives on the defensive platoon.

An innocent interviewer asked Lambert what changes he'd like to see in football. The Steeler linebacker had a casual suggestion. "They ought to put the quarterbacks in dresses," he said.

That exemplifies Lambert's approach to his job fairly well. His skills can be measured by a streak of seven straight Pro Bowl selections.

Lambert joined the Steelers in 1974 as a second-round draft choice from Kent State and proved to be the final cog in the construction of the "Steel Curtain," the defense that would carry Pittsburgh to four Super Bowl championships in his first six years with the team. At 6-4 and 220 pounds he is not extremely big, but Lambert is one of football's hardest hitters. He has led the Steelers in tackles in all of his eight NFL seasons.

Since 1977, Lambert has served as captain of the Steelers and is considered among the indispensable players on the team's defensive unit. He had six interceptions in 1981, pushing his career total to 25.

Twice selected as the NFL Defensive Player of the Year, Lambert also was named the Steelers' MVP twice by his teammates and is a six-time All-Pro. He made All-Pro and the Pro Bowl game for the first time in 1975, when he set an AFC record by recovering three fumbles in the championship game against Oakland.

Lambert played a key role in each of the Steeler Super Bowl victories. In the last one, Super Bowl XIV at Pasadena against the Los Angeles Rams, it was his late-game interception deep in Pittsburgh territory that shut down LA's threat to take the lead.

No one has hit much harder than Jack Lambert. He has been a punishing player, mean and nasty, who has put a lot of players out of commission. He is tall, tough, quick, a good pass defender, and a great run defender. Jack Lambert and Jack Ham have been a terrific combination of linebackers for the Steelers.

What Ham does on intelligence, Lambert does on instinct. I'm not saying Lambert isn't smart. What I am saying is that he's been a natural, a fellow who obviously loves to play, who plays with enormous enthusiasm, who loves to hit, who takes pride in playing hurt. He's almost like an animal the way he throws himself around out there. He's aggressive and he snarls at you all the time.

Jack Lambert

There were many outstanding linebackers in the 1970s. Bobby Bell, who began his career in the 1960s but concluded it in the 1970s, was certainly one. One of the great all-around athletes and a super player who came out of the American Football League, Bell was one of the last players eliminated from my list of 100, and I feel bad I couldn't find a place for him. Willie Lanier, also a fine AFL product, was another. Bill Bergey was a consistently superior player. Randy Gradishar and Robert Brazile have been outstanding players in recent years.

But Lambert has been a real standout. On standout teams. My only reservation about him has been his lack of longevity. But he completed eight seasons in 1981 and it was significant to me that he played as well in the Steelers' poorest seasons the past two years as in any of their most successful seasons. While I like those players who make teams into big winners, I also respect those players who play well for teams that aren't big winners. Jack Lambert is a winning-type player and would be one even if he was playing for a consistent loser.

13.
Maxie Baughan

When Maxie Baughan was drafted out of Georgia Tech in 1960 and signed as a second-round selection by the Philadelphia Eagles, he admitted that he didn't know what to expect in pro football. There were no NFL teams in Alabama, where Baughan was born and raised. So he played in the first pro game he ever saw in person. It was memorable, to say the least.

Baughan, as a rookie linebacker, was on the bench when Eagle veteran Ed Khayat was kicked in the back of the head by San Francisco's Hugh McElhenny. Baughan raced after McElhenny, and in no time the game turned into a full-scale brawl. When it was over, Baughan had established himself firmly in the hearts of his teammates. The team went on to win the NFL championship in that 1960 season.

Baughan was the only first-year starter on that Eagle squad and was placed at a difficult outside-linebacker spot. He was victimized now and then, as all rookies are. On one play, Frank Gifford of the New York Giants caught him out of position and completed a pass for a long gain. Soon Gifford returned to the same zone, shopping for another big gainer. This time, though, Baughan intercepted the pass, helping Philadelphia to a vital touchdown. The youngster was a quick learner.

Baughan spent six seasons with the Eagles and was selected for the Pro Bowl game five times. He then was traded to the Los Angeles Rams in 1966 in exchange for three players and spent five more years there, where he was chosen for four more Pro Bowl games. After three years on the

Maxie Baughan

sidelines, he returned for one more fling, in 1974 with Washington. A four-time All-Pro selection, Baughan was just average-sized, at 6-1 and 230 pounds.

After his playing career ended, Baughan served as an assistant coach at his alma mater, Georgia Tech, before returning to the pros as an assistant at Washington, Baltimore, and with the Detroit Lions.

One thing that all great linebackers have had is toughness. Maxie Baughan sure had it. I can remember games when he was hurt and no one thought he could play. But he not only played, he also performed as well as ever. He was another of those standout linebackers who wasn't as big as some, but he was very quick and tenacious, had a lot of finesse, and used his size real well.

Of course, size doesn't mean that much if you don't have ability. And toughness isn't that important if you don't have ability. Maxie Baughan had an abundance of ability. And he was smart enough to make the most of it, even though he had a terrific temper. Once in a while, he went wild. He always played with reckless abandon. But he always played well.

I brought Maxie to L.A. when the Eagles thought he was losing a little something. But I love those experienced players who know how to perform, and I think all they need is the opportunity to prove they still can play. I had a lot of confidence in Maxie, and he responded to it by having five more great years. I have to admit he was one of my personal favorites. But I've left off my list some real personal favorites I could have picked, like Ron McDole.

Maxie enjoyed the physical game. If he couldn't overpower blockers, he could outwit them and outlast them. He never gave up on a play, and he wound up getting back into plays he seemed out of. He hated to lose and never gave up on a game. He had a lot of leadership in him and fired up his side, game after game. No one loafed while Maxie was around. He was a fiery fellow who would have been any coach's favorite. I think he's been a little underrated. Maybe he didn't receive all the honors he deserved. But he rates this one.

CHAPTER 8

DEFENSIVE BACKS

In some ways defensive back may be the most difficult position to play. It may not take as much skill to play as quarterback, but it takes considerable skill. The defensive back is going to be beaten from time to time. The best of them is going to be burned. He's going to be made to look bad. He's going to be frustrated and embarrassed. So he has to have good character. He has to have confidence in himself and courage, tenacity and the spirit to fight back.

Basically, of course, the defensive back has to cover receivers. Although defenses are designed that try to give defensive backs help in the critical areas and against key receivers, and although each defensive back has to be able to team up well with the linebackers and the other defensive backs, the defensive back basically has to be able to cover the best receivers one on one. Since the receiver knows where he is going and the defender doesn't, the advantage is to the receiver.

The defensive back's primary job is to knock down the pass, not tip it where someone else can catch it. And not intercept it. Interceptions can turn games around and are enormously valuable, but the defensive back has to know when to go for one and when not to. The gambler who intercepts a lot of passes but gets burned by a lot of receptions can hurt you more than he helps you. The great defensive backs all have had a lot of interceptions, but not at the expense of a lot of receptions. Tips involve a lot of luck. You practice picking off tipped passes. The good defensive back doesn't tip the ball into the air, but he is alert to pick off those tips that do occur.

The good defensive back knows his assignments, stays with his man, anticipates and diagnoses the pass better than others, and makes it tough for the receiver to get good position. He also knocks down the pass, has the timing and toughness to hit hard enough to knock the ball loose at the instant of the catch if he can't prevent it, and makes the tackle if he can't prevent the catch or knock the ball loose. Once the ball is in the air, he has to be mobile enough to move to it to help out a teammate if the ball is not going to the receiver he is covering. Or if the play has turned into a run, he has to be mobile enough to move upfield to make the tackle. He has to be able to make tackles upfield and downfield.

Because of the mobility and agility required, most good defensive backs are smaller players. I haven't known many good ones much over six feet tall or over 200 pounds, but there have been a few and I'm sure others will come along who do not fit the mold. Usually they are smaller men who often have to tackle heavier men, so these defensive backs have to have good toughness and technique. They have to have very good timing. Quickness is probably the biggest physical asset they can have. Straight-away speed helps, but quick reactions and movements are more impor-

tant. And, as I have suggested, they have to be mentally tough and mentally quick, too.

The great defensive back can play any position in the defensive backfield. Basically, the cornerbacks cover the short passes, the safeties the long passes. So the cornerbacks cover more passes than the safeties. And the cornerbacks have to make more tackles. But the safeties have to cover a wider area of ground with less help, have to cover the more dangerous passes, and they have to help out more. Usually, the smarter, quicker players play safety, especially free safety; this man roams a lot and is on his own a lot. He's your center fielder. The strong safety is usually the more physical player. Certain physical tools may dictate a player's position. The bigger, stronger guy may be better at cornerback than safety.

Most of the rules changes in recent years have been designed to increase scoring. They help the offense more than the defense. The design is to make the game more appealing to the public. But it's been getting tougher to defend against the passing game. The rushers are restricted in what they can do to the blockers and to the passers. The linebackers and defensive backs are restricted in what they can do to the receivers. Only one bump is permitted now, and that within five yards of the line of scrimmage. You have to stay with the receivers while staying away from them. If you do break up the pass, you may get called for pass interference if you made any contact at all with the receiver or got in his way in any way once the ball was in the air. I hate to see pass interference called because of incidental contact downfield. I guarantee you it is called many more times on the defensive player than on the offensive player.

The rules are not right, but they're the ones we have to live with. Because of these rules you're going to see more passes thrown, more passes completed, and more passes completed deep than ever before. Because of these rules it's going to be more difficult for defensive backs to do a good job and gain recognition in the 1980s. Because players went both ways and backs were picked primarily for offensive skills and the passing game was not sophisticated, there were not many great defensive backs developed in the 1930s and 1940s, though there were a few. Most of the most effective ones performed in the 1950s, the 1960s, and the first part of the 1970s. Here are my selections.

1.
Herb Adderley

When the Green Bay Packers used their No. 1 draft choice in 1961 to select Herb Adderley, they figured they were getting some offensive backfield insurance. Adderley, after all, had been an All-Big Ten running back at Michigan State. Herb delivered handsomely in the pros, but he did it in the defensive backfield.

Adderley served his internship on the Packer special teams, training ground for so many rookies, and backing up two pretty good runners, Jim Taylor and Paul Hornung. When cornerback Henry Gremminger was injured on Thanksgiving Day in 1961, coach Vince Lombardi reached for Adderley as the replacement. It was the start of a brilliant defensive career. He intercepted a pass in his first game on the job and by the next season he was a full-time cornerback in a career that lasted a dozen seasons, nine of them with Green Bay and the last three with Dallas.

Adderley, a 6-1, 200-pounder, had a knack for the big play. In 1963, Green Bay was trailing Minnesota, 28—27, when Fred Cox got set to kick a chip-shot 10-yard Viking field goal. Adderley blocked the kick, and the Packers recovered the ball and returned it for a touchdown—a 10-point turnaround on a single play.

In Super Bowl II against Oakland on January 14, 1968, Adderley picked off a Raider pass and returned the interception 60 yards for a touchdown—the first TD interception in Super Bowl history. Between his years with Green Bay and Dallas, Adderley played in four of the first six Super Bowls and was on the winning team in three of those games.

For his career, which ended in 1972, Adderley recorded 48 interceptions, returning them 1,046 yards for an average of 21.8 yards per runback. He scored seven touchdowns, second best in NFL history for a defensive back. Included among his 120 kickoff returns was a 103-yarder in 1962 and a 98-yarder the next year.

He was named to the Pro Football Hall of Fame in 1980.

Herb Adderley was the ideal defensive back. He would have been an outstanding offensive back, too. He was smart and quick, strong and tough. He had fast feet and good hands. Boy, did he have good hands! It wasn't a gamble when he went for the ball. When he went for it, he caught it. And when he got it, he could really run with it. He also made great runs returning kicks. He was dynamite.

Adderley played left cornerback. The defensive left side is the more difficult side because most players are right-handed and most offensive plays go to the offense's right. You usually put your best defensive linemen, linebackers, and defensive backs on the left side. Adderley played in an era when the cornerback did not get a lot of help, although Willie Wood, his safety, came up to help him at times. Basically, Adderley was in one-on-one coverage, but it was difficult for the best receivers to beat him.

Herb Adderley

When I helped coach the Bears we used to play the Packers three times a year, including a preseason game. When I coached the Rams we played the Packers twice a year. Willie Davis at left defensive end and Adderley at left cornerback all but took the left side away from our offense. Adderley and Willie Wood made a lot of big plays in the many big games the Packers won in the 1960s, when they were the dominant team in the NFL. If I'd had room for one more defensive back on my list of 100 greatest professional football players it would have been Willie Wood.

Adderley anticipated plays superbly. He was where the ball was. If it was a pass, he was the best at single coverage I ever saw. If it was a run, he came up and got into it. Gosh, was he physical! He really put it to a receiver or a running back when he hit him. Adderley didn't make mistakes, and he wasn't burned very often. He was very consistent, always on top of things. He played 12 years, he played hurt, and he hurt people.

After Green Bay thought he was through, Dallas got a lot out of him. He was always in shape. He was a terrific competitor, and he wanted to win as much as any player I ever saw. Usually a defensive player doesn't help you to win, he helps you not to lose. But Adderley was one defensive player who helped you to win.

2.
Dick (Night Train) Lane

Dick Lane was working at an aircraft factory in Los Angeles in 1952 when he decided to change careers. He had played some junior college and military service football, and one day he showed up at the offices of the Los Angeles Rams, seeking a tryout. And that was how the Hall of Fame career of one of the game's greatest cornerbacks was born.

Lane sought to make the team as a receiver behind the great Tom Fears. However, Lane wasn't making much progress and it seemed he might not survive training camp. Then he got a break.

Injuries depleted the Los Angeles defensive secondary, and Lane was pressed into service there. By then he had picked up the nickname "Night Train" because of the popular record of the day, and when the Rams moved him from offense to defense, the Train found his station on the football field.

In his first season, he set a league record with 14 interceptions, returning two for touchdowns. Even though the NFL regular season now stretches four games longer than the 12 that Lane played, that 14-interception record still stands.

Los Angeles traded Night Train, a 6-2, 210-pounder, to the Chicago Cardinals in 1954, and his 10 interceptions that season gave him the league title in that department for the second time in three seasons.

Occasionally the Cardinals would use Lane at his original position as a receiver. In 1955, he tied a record by being on the receiving end of a 98-yard TD pass play. Chicago swapped him to Detroit in 1960 and, with the Lions, he was an All-Pro choice four straight years.

Lane played in six Pro Bowl games, and his 68 career interceptions are third on the all-time list. He had 1,207 yards returned, for a 17.8 average and five TDs. He once intercepted passes in six straight games. He was voted to the all-time NFL team in 1969 and is a member of the Pro Football Hall of Fame.

Night Train was married to the legendary blues singer Dinah Washington until her death in December, 1963.

Sometimes it seems to me that good defensive backs are made, not born. It's as though no one wants to be a defensive back. The great defensive backs have been superb athletes who might have been outstanding at other positions. The first two I have picked on my list of the greatest defensive backs both were trying it at other positions—Herb Adderley as a runing back, Dick Lane as a receiver—when injuries to others caused their coaches to try them in the defensive backfield. No one knew him as Dick Lane. He's always been Night Train Lane. Seldom has a nickname stuck so tight to a player. A colorful name for a colorful character and a colorful player.

He was, I admit, a gambler, but he got away with it. He had guts and when he went for the ball he usually got it. He played on instinct and he had a feel for the play. Somehow he always seemed to get good position on the receiver, which only the better ones do. He didn't have much background in football, much less at defensive back, but he was a natural and learned on the field. He became a classic cornerback. He was quick and had almost acrobatic ability. He'd come out of nowhere to get to the ball. Or he'd twist and turn in some way to get into the play just when he seemed out of it.

It was very hard to prepare a passing offense against one of Lane's teams because you never knew what he would do. You just knew he would hurt you in some way. He did hurt people. While he was a fun-loving fellow off the field, he had a streak of meanness in him on the field. He was a headhunter. Tackling, he went for the head. Sometimes he yanked people down by the face mask. They had to make that a penalty. And he'd clothesline them by swinging his straight arm across their neck. Not very admirable, but he had opposing receivers so wary of him half his job was easier for him.

I don't know if Night Train was hard to handle. Or too undisciplined. Or too much of a gambler. Two teams let him go. All I know is he played for

Dick (Night Train) Lane (#81)

three teams—the Rams, the Cardinals, and the Lions, and was an All-Pro for all three. He played for 14 years as though he loved it and with a delight in disrupting offenses that seldom has been matched in his sport. He was a terrific competitor, the kind of player who made things happen and could turn a game around for you.

3.
Jack Christiansen

The Detroit Lions were a bit hesitant about drafting Jack Christiansen in 1951. He was coming out of Colorado A&M, a rather obscure football school, and his college playing weight was just 162 pounds, hardly big enough to withstand the heavy-duty responsibilities of an NFL running back. But they risked a sixth-round pick on him and learned quickly that they had come up with a star.

Jack Christiansen

Because of his size, Christiansen was assigned to defensive-backfield and punt-return duties, and he made his mark there in a hurry. In his rookie season he set an NFL record by returning four punts for touchdowns. Two of the returns came in a game against Los Angeles, and two more occurred in a contest against Green Bay. A year later, he had two more touchdowns on punt returns and an average punt return of 21.5 yards, the second-best single season production in NFL history. In eight NFL seasons, Christiansen set a record with eight TD punt returns.

Installed at safety on the defensive unit, he quickly became the leader of the secondary, which included another Hall of Famer, Yale Lary, plus Jim

David and Carl Karilivacz. The group was called "Chris' Crew" and in the eight years they played for the Lions, they totaled 130 interceptions. The 6-1 Christiansen, whose playing weight soared to 185 pounds later in his career, had 46 of those thefts, leading the league with 12 in 1953 and 10 in 1957. In both seasons Detroit won the NFL championship.

Christiansen's early days in college were dominated by track. A shooting accident which immobilized his left arm and almost cost him his life during his senior year in high school prevented him from playing contact sports for a while and it was not until his junior year in college that he resumed playing football. He averaged 8.1 yards per carry and once rushed 183 yards in a single game. He also returned a punt a record 89 yards. Those credentials led the Lions to him in 1951.

In his eight pro seasons, Christiansen played in five Pro Bowl games and was a five-time All-Pro selection. Chosen to the All-NFL team for the decade of the 1950s, he also is a member of the Pro Football Hall of Fame (1970).

Jack Christiansen was the best safety I ever saw. He was one of the fastest men in a football uniform I ever saw. I never saw a receiver outrun him. Boy, could he run! He could have been a great pro running back. He was a fine running back in college. And when he intercepted a pass or took a punt or a kickoff he returned it as well as anyone ever did.

But he was drafted for defense in the early 1950s, just when the passing game was getting to be sophisticated and there was a need for passing defenses becoming sophisticated. They didn't know how to coach pass defense in those days, and players like Christiansen were pioneers who learned as they played. He practically invented the position of free safety. He would still be a great model for others to copy.

He was very alert, looked for clues, and anticipated plays beautifully. He figured out receivers' moves and routes and always seemed a step ahead of them. He wasn't a gambler and his first concern always was to break up the pass, but he had good hands and instincts and intercepted far more than his share of passes.

Christiansen was tall and skinny, didn't look like he could be much of a hitter, and wasn't too mean. He admitted he didn't like to hit those big backs like Marion Motley and Steve Van Buren by the time they got into the secondary and had a head of steam going. But he did hit them. He had determination and courage. He saved one championship game against Cleveland when he came up to hit the great Jim Brown so hard on third down that it shook the ball loose.

Although Christiansen wasn't mean, he could be sneaky. He used to throw handfuls of dirt or mud in a receiver's eyes and, no matter how much the receivers would gripe, the officials never seemed to catch him at it. Christiansen did whatever he could to do his job well. He was inventive, versatile, enormously effective. He played only eight years, but they were eight great years.

4.
Emlen Tunnell

When assistant coach Tom Landry constructed the famous "Umbrella" defense for the New York Giants early in the 1950s, one of its most important elements was Emlen Tunnell, who joined the team as an obscure free agent.

Tunnell had played his college football first at Toledo and then at the University of Iowa, but he was unhappy with his defensive role for the Hawkeyes. He wanted to score points, not prevent them, and so he decided in 1948 to leave Iowa, where he had one year of eligibility remaining, and seek a job with a pro team. A friend suggested the New York Giants, and Tunnell became one of the most successful walk-ons in pro football history. The irony, of course, is that he made the Hall of Fame as the first purely defensive player. No wonder Iowa wanted him playing on that unit.

Besides working at safety, Tunnell returned kicks to satisfy his ball-carrying desires. He was so good at the assignment that he quickly became known as the Giants' "offense on defense." Frequently his yardage totals exceeded those of the star running backs and receivers whose job it was to move the football. For example, in 1952 Dan Towler of Los Angeles led the NFL in rushing with 894 yards on 156 carries, an average of 5.7 yards per attempt. The figures were impressive for the era, but they paled

Emlen
Tunnell

compared with Tunnell's 923 yards on just 52 carries for a 17.8 average. Of course, all of Tunnell's yardage was assembled on punt, kickoff, and interception returns, but the fact remains that his total yardage was greater than that of the league's leading rusher.

The 6-1, 200-pound Tunnell always was among the top yardage producers for the Giants. He finished second on the club only to pile-driving fullback Eddie Price in 1951 and trailed only quarterback Charley Conerly in 1953.

Tunnell played for 11 seasons with the Giants, from 1948 to 1958, and then completed his career with three years at Green Bay, where his former assistant coach on the Giants, Vince Lombardi, was rebuilding the Packers. Tunnell finished his career with records for interceptions (79 for 1,282 yards) and punt-return yards (2,209), both of which have since been surpassed.

Chosen for nine Pro Bowl teams and selected to the All-Pro squad four times, Tunnell was picked for the All-NFL team for the decade of the 1950s and was the first black elected to the Pro Football Hall of Fame. He also was the first member of his race to coach in the NFL, joining the Giants as an assistant following his retirement.

For some reason, defensive backs often have been used to return punts in the NFL. On my all-time team, Jack Christiansen and Emlen Tunnell would return punts and running back Hugh McElhenny would return kickoffs. Tunnell was the best punt returner I ever saw. He was a gifted runner with a fine feel for the open field. I know he held records for yards gained returning kicks. He was a running back originally and always wanted to be a running back. This skill was a big plus in my assessment of Emlen, but he was close to the top as a defensive back, anyway.

Tunnell was pretty big for a safety, but he was quick and agile. He was an intelligent player who anticipated plays very well and always seemed to be in position to handle the pass. He wouldn't gamble unnecessarily, but he had one of the highest totals of interceptions. He had very good technique on his tackles and took pride in his ability to tackle. Emlen was a complete player, a very dedicated player, very competitive, and he rose to the big occasion.

Emlen played with Tom Landry in the Giants' defensive backfield and later with Dick Nolan and Jim Patton under Landry in the mid-1950s when Tom developed the "Umbrella defense" and the Giants were a power in the NFL. These were all extremely smart men. Landry has been one of the great coaches, while Nolan has been a good coach. Emlen was the first black player on the Giants. He was a modest man of strong character.

Patton was a super player I considered seriously for this list. Jack Butler of Pittsburgh was another really fine player I considered. Tunnell had enormous natural talent and the dedication to make the most of his ability. After many fine years in New York, he was grabbed by Green Bay when Vince Lombardi was straightening out the Packers and wanted veterans who knew how to win.

5.
Yale Lary

Yale Lary was a double-duty star for the powerful Detroit teams during the 1950s—a skilled safety in the defensive secondary and the team's punter, whose booming kicks regularly maintained good field position for the Lions.

Lary came out of Texas A&M a two-sport star. He played four seasons of minor-league baseball and 11 years in the NFL. Drafted in the third round in 1952, he began his pro football career as an offensive back. That didn't last long, though. Trying to block All-Pro defensive end Leon Hart in a Lions' scrimmage proved so frustrating that Detroit coach Buddy Parker quickly moved Lary to the defensive backfield. The move paid immediate dividends. Lary fit in immediately there and Detroit won the NFL championship in his first two seasons, and again in 1957.

After two years in the NFL, Lary's football career was interrupted by service in the U.S. Army for two years. He returned to pro football in 1956 and played through 1964. When he retired, he had 50 interceptions, fifth best in NFL history at the time. And, although his work as a pass defender was exemplary, Lary's punting talents contributed as much to the success of the Lions.

For his career, he punted 503 times, averaging 44.3 yards per kick. That is less than a yard short of Sammy Baugh's all-time record average of 45.1 yards. Lary's 48.9 average in 1963 was the second-highest single-season average in history, trailing only the 51.4 posted by Baugh in 1940. Lary led the league in punting three times—1959, 1961, and 1963. He missed a fourth championship in 1962, finishing second to Tommy Davis by a razor-thin average of just 3.6 inches.

Lary's punts had long hang time as well as distance. In 1960, for example, opponents averaged less than one yard return on his kicks.

A four-time All-Pro selection, the 5-11, 189-pound Lary played in nine Pro Bowl games and was selected to the All-NFL team for the decade for the 1950s. He was named to the Pro Football Hall of Fame in 1979.

The year after the Detroit Lions drafted Jack Christiansen, they drafted Yale Lary. Together they were the best pair of safeties any team ever had at any one time and they played together for seven seasons. With the brilliant Jim David they formed an outstanding trio of defensive backs. With them, the head coach, Buddy Parker, pioneered the "prevent defense," where you drop five men in the middle and three deep to protect against the long passes in the late stages of games to protect a lead. That was 30 years ago. Christiansen and Lary played major roles in the evolution of pass defense.

Defensive Backs

Yale Lary

Lary was a superior athlete. He was one of the greatest punters ever and is included on my short list of the three top punters on my list of 100 players. He is one of two players—Sammy Baugh is the other—whose name appears twice on the list, though each is counted only once. Yale was a great runner. As a punter, he knew when to run. It is my understanding that he decided to run instead of punt ten times in his career and that he made the first down nine of those times. He had great instincts. As a pass defender he was superb. He seemed to know where the receiver was going. He was smooth and graceful, always in balance, a well-coordinated athlete, and a classic competitor.

The Lions were one of the dominant teams of professional football in the 1950s. Bobby Layne was one reason. Jack Christiansen and Yale Lary were two others. Others contributed, such as Doak Walker, Hunchy Hoernschmeyer, Lou Creekmur, and Les Bingaman. These were marvelous pressure performers.

Three of the first five defensive backs I've picked played for the Lions—Christiansen, Lary, and Lane. That's just one of those things that happen. A fourth might well have made my list, the spectacular Lem Barney, who came along later. Jim David and Don Doll were other fine defensive backs who played for the Lions.

6.
Larry Wilson

As his first NFL training camp was nearing its conclusion, Larry Wilson sent word to his wife, Dee Ann, to meet him in San Francisco, where his St. Louis Cardinals would be playing their final preseason game. He had been benched for the better part of three weeks after being victimized for three touchdown passes by Baltimore's Raymond Berry, not the best way for a rookie defensive back to win a job. Wilson figured he would be released after that final preseason game and that having his wife there would soften the blow. Besides, he reasoned, they could have a short vacation before driving back home.

 Larry Wilson

But the Cards decided to give Wilson one more look in that last exhibition game and, when he held R. C. Owens, the 49ers' star receiver, without a catch, Larry made the team. Dee Ann drove home alone, and Wilson embarked on a Hall of Fame career as a free safety.

Wilson, a 6-foot, 190-pounder, played the position with the Cardinals for 13 years, from 1960 to 1972, and mastered the defensive technique called the safety blitz. The late Chuck Drulis, then the Cardinals' defensive coordinator, helped Wilson develop the play which brings the safety swarming after the quarterback for a sack. The Cardinal playbook labeled the maneuver "Wildcat," and that soon became Wilson's nickname because he did the play so well.

By 1966 he had established himself as one of the best defensive backs in the league, and he certified that by leading the NFL with 10 interceptions that season. Included in the total was a streak of seven straight games in which he picked off passes. In the sixth game of the string he intercepted three passes, returning one for a touchdown in a 21–17 victory over the Chicago Bears.

Drafted out of Utah, Wilson developed a reputation for being one of the toughest players in the game. He often played through injuries. In 1965 he broke his left hand and a finger on his right hand in one game against the New York Giants. The next week, against Pittsburgh, he showed up with both hands in casts, blocked a pass, caught the ball on the way down, and took it 35 yards for a touchdown.

A six-time All-Pro, Wilson appeared in eight Pro Bowl games and was named to the All-NFL team for the decade of the 1960s. His career totals include 52 interceptions for 800 yards returned, a 15.4-yard average, and five touchdowns.

Larry Wilson was the kind of guy who'd come from out of nowhere to dump the passer on one play and be 40 yards downfield to take the ball away from the receiver on the next play. He didn't have a lot of speed, but he had a lot of heart and he hustled on every play. He was smart and he had great instincts.

Gee, was he tough! He was as hard as a nail. He played 13 years and he played hurt. He practically invented the safety blitz and he just loved to flatten the passer. He loved to tackle and he hit a ton. He had good hands and always seemed to be picking off passes. He seemed to be all over the field and it was difficult to design an offense that would take him out of the play.

Wilson played for the Cardinals through the 1960s and into the early 1970s. They weren't a very good team, and although you might not usually point a game plan at a defensive back, he was their best player and opposing coaches attacked him. They seldom defeated him.

We always tried to do things to get around him and keep him from hurting us, but he always got into the play and he hurt you. I admired enormously how well and how hard he played for a down team.

7.
Ken Houston

For a defensive player, Ken Houston made his way into the end zone for a score a remarkable number of times. He returned nine of his 49 career interceptions for touchdowns, setting an NFL record. In addition, he returned one punt for a TD in 1974 and went 74 yards with a blocked field goal in 1967 for another one. That's 11 TDs, not bad for a player who was paid to prevent them, not score them.

Houston played his college football at Prairie View in Texas and was a linebacker on the team that won three consecutive national small-college championships. In the first universal draft after the pro football merger in 1967, Houston lasted through eight rounds before he was selected, appropriately enough, by Houston. It was a perfect match and Houston, the player, made Houston, the team, and moved into the secondary at safety. In 1971, his fifth year in the league, he made it into the record book. He returned four interceptions for touchdowns, setting a record that was tied a year later by Jim Kearney of Kansas City. Two of those interception TDs came in a single game against San Diego, tying another record.

That was Houston's best season, and a year later, when he failed to pick off a single pass, the Oilers soured on him. They traded him to Washington for five players in 1973. The deal turned out to be a steal for the Redskins. Houston went on to play eight more seasons for Washington and became a perennial All-Star. He was selected for 12 straight Pro Bowls, the last one despite a fractured forearm, which prevented him from playing. The injury ended an impressive consecutive-game streak, which had stretched to 182.

A high tackler, Houston always played his position aggressively and, if he could intimidate an opponent, he intimidated him. Those qualities didn't make him terribly popular but he was respected by opposing players and coaches.

The 6-3, 198-pounder was selected to the NFL's All-Pro squad for the decade of the 1970s and returned to Houston after his retirement in 1980 to coach high school football.

For his career, Ken totaled 49 pass interceptions for 898 yards returned, an 18.3-yard average.

Kenny Houston had played six seasons for Houston in the AFL and the NFL when I traded five players to get him for my Washington Redskins in 1973. Everyone said I had given too much to get him. Well, he gave me five years the others wouldn't have given me combined. He not only was still an outstanding player, but he also was a tremendously positive influence on my team. It's a cliché, but he was the first to the practice field and the last to leave. He never missed a practice, never missed a game. He worked with our younger players. He was a complete team man. He became captain of our team. I consider things of this sort critical in evaluating a player.

Kenny was, I think, the outstanding defensive back of the 1970s. He had quick feet and soft hands. A safety, he roamed far and wide to make plays. He always seemed to be in the play and he always made the play. Usually a linebacker calls defensive signals for you, but when Chris Hanburger was hurt, I had Kenny call them for us and he did very well. He anticipated plays. He was quick and determined.

You know, I mention determination a lot in this book, but then I'm talking about the best, and that's a quality you must have to be one of the best.

Ken Houston

All professional football players are not determined. They have natural ability or they wouldn't be in the big league, but they'd all be All-Stars if it was easy. It takes something extra to play hurt, to go hard when you're losing, and to get up and get back in the play when you've been knocked down. Kenny Houston had that something extra.

He took a beating in his 14 years in pro football, but, as far as I know, he never complained. He may have been better physically when he was with Houston, but he played as well as ever with us. He was a terrific team man, totally unselfish, and a marvelous player who cared a lot more about team victories than he did about individual glory.

8.
Willie Brown

Willie Brown played cornerback in the NFL for 16 seasons, from 1963 to 1978. In each of those years, he intercepted at least one pass. No other defensive back in history has ever produced that type of long-term consistency.

Brown finished his career with 54 interceptions, No. 10 on the all-time list. Included were four in a single game on November 15, 1964, giving him a share of another record. And in Super Bowl XI, while playing for Oakland against Minnesota, he picked off a pass and returned it 75 yards for a touchdown and another record.

All of that is impressive, of course, but Brown's major contribution to pro football was the development of a defensive strategy that changed the concept of his position. He was the first defensive back to use the bump-and-run technique on receivers, disrupting pass patterns and changing the way the position was played.

A tight end in college at Grambling, Brown went undrafted when he graduated. He signed as a free agent with the Houston Oilers in 1963, but did not play for them and drifted to Denver, where he played for four seasons. In 1967 the Broncos traded Brown to Oakland, and he spent the next dozen years as a key part of the Raiders' secondary.

Willie Brown

In 16 seasons, Brown played in nine All-Star games—five in the AFL and four Pro Bowls following the merger. He was selected to the all-time AFL team and was a five-time All-Pro choice.

Brown's best season statistically was his second as a pro, when he intercepted nine passes and returned them for 140 yards for Denver. But the figures after that are somewhat deceptive. Brown, a 6-1, 190-pounder, never had that many interceptions again, but it is because quarterbacks were less likely to work on his sector of the field. He was an expert at coverage, and in 1971 Raider statistics showed that only 10 opponents' passes had been completed in his area of responsibility.

Willie Brown lasted longer than almost all of the other great defensive backs. He had a lot of the flamboyance of Night Train Lane in him. Willie was a gambler who loved to intercept passes, but he also was a wonderful competitor who just enjoyed playing. His enthusiasm showed through in everything he did.

Willie was a cornerback, and he was a complete player. He had fast feet and fast hands and was acrobatic in his ability to twist and turn in midair. He could keep up with almost any receiver, and if Willie lost position on him he had a knack of getting back into the play somehow. A lot of desire showed through in his play. He just stuck to you. He had a world of confidence and didn't believe anyone could beat him. Few did.

One of the interesting things about Willie was that he didn't seem to lose his speed. Many of the really great players who had outstanding speed were able to sustain it throughout their careers. Maybe Willie wasn't quite as fast at the finish of his career, but he really had a remarkably long career and he seemed to me to be about as quick as ever at the end. He played through some of the 1960s and most of the 1970s with those great teams Oakland had, and he was always outstanding in the many important games they played. He was a strong tackler who obviously liked to hit and didn't mind the bumps and bruises.

9.
Ed Meador

Ed Meador didn't look the part. He was a baby-faced 5-11, 190-pounder, but put him in the defensive secondary and he turned into a tiger. For 12 seasons, from 1959 to 1970, he played free safety and some cornerback for the Los Angeles Rams, and every year he either led the club in tackles or was close behind one of the better-known linemen, either Merlin Olsen or Deacon Jones.

Meador not only was a tough tackler but also a brilliant pass defender. His 46 career interceptions are a Ram club record and almost 20 better than the No. 2 mark in team history.

In college at little Arkansas Tech, Meador was an offensive back. The Rams drafted him in the seventh round in 1959 and he came into the pros with impressive credentials. Among other honors, he was selected as Arkansas' top amateur that year.

He had never seen an NFL game in person before reporting to the Rams' camp that summer. By the time the team played its preseason opener against Detroit, it was clear that Meador would be an important part of the club.

By 1964 he had developed into the team leader on defense and was named the Rams' Most Valuable Player that year and again in 1965. Meador was named the Rams' outstanding defensive back seven times, and he was selected for the Pro Bowl five times. When the Pro Football Hall of Fame selectors picked an All-Pro team for the decade of the 1960s, Meador was on the roster.

Besides his duties in the defensive secondary, Meador often was used to run back punts for the Rams and also was the holder for extra-point and field-goal attempts.

Meador produced 547 return yards with his interceptions and scored five touchdowns. Late in his pro career he was inducted into the NAIA Hall of Fame, a tribute to his collegiate play that set the stage for a great NFL career.

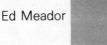

Ed Meador

Ed Meador was a great player with the bad teams the Los Angeles Rams had in the first half of the 1960s and with the great teams we had in the last half of the 1960s, after I got there. As I've said before, I have to admire a player who plays great for a bad team, who doesn't give up, who gives his best. That's the kind of player you can win with. I studied films of the Rams and really admired Eddie. I felt he was one of the players I could build a winner around.

Eddie was smart, tough, and had good hands. He was a bit of a gambler. He gambled on an interception against Bob Hayes, missed, and got burned for a long score. He didn't gamble against guys like Hayes again. Eddie had such good hands he held for our extra-point and field-goal tries, and one time he went on his own, took the ball, and ran with it for a first down. But he almost didn't make it. He had to break a tackle to make it. And, afterward, he admitted to me he'd made a mistake. He laughed and said there was no way he wasn't going to make it because he knew I'd have killed him otherwise.

Sometimes you had to go with a guy like Meador because he wanted to win so much he'd do anything he could to do it. He was very resourceful and inventive. He made plays you didn't think he could make. He covered deep passes real well and came up to double on short coverage. He was a good-technique tackler and wasn't afraid to lay into a man. He played 12 seasons and he gave it everything he had every play of every game.

He had real leadership qualities and captained the Rams for me. I'm not sure if I know every one who was a captain, but it's amazing to me how many of these all-timers captained their teams.

10.
Pat Fischer

There was no logical explanation for Pat Fischer. With his dimensions— 5-9, 170 pounds—he should have been beaten regularly by the big, swift wide receivers of the NFL. But somehow the little cornerback survived. In fact, he not only survived, he also flourished through 17 seasons in the NFL.

Fischer intercepted 56 passes, tied for seventh place on the all-time list, and returned four of them for touchdowns. He also had 19 fumble recoveries, taking one of them 49 yards for another TD. Not bad for a little guy.

In college at the University of Nebraska, Fischer was a quarterback and a halfback. His size probably was a factor in St. Louis waiting until the seventeenth round of the 1961 draft to select him. He clearly wasn't a high-priority prospect.

But Pat, one of four Fischer brothers to play football at Nebraska, battled his way into the Cardinals' starting lineup on defense and was the team's starting left cornerback until 1967. He played out his option with St. Louis that year and signed with Washington as a free agent in 1968. The Redskins surrendered a second- and a third-round draft choice as compensation, but Fischer was worth the price. He played 10 more seasons for Washington and was a valued member of the "Over-the-hill Gang" that went to Super Bowl VII in 1973.

Critics kept complaining that Fischer was too old, too small, and too slow, but he kept getting the job done. His best stretch came earlier in his career, during the 1963—64 seasons, when he picked off 18 passes for the Cardinals. He still was a capable player when he retired after the 1977 season at the age of 37. By then he had made his mark. Chosen for three Pro Bowl games, he was selected to the All-NFL team for the decade of the 1970s and proved that there is a place in football for players who are neither tall nor heavy.

Pat Fischer

One of the most amazing athletes I've ever seen was Pat Fischer. He was short, but he could really leap and somehow was able to cover the tallest receivers on the highest passes. He tore into the biggest guys on tackles. I saw him drop a lot of big guys in their tracks. One I remember was MacArthur Lane, the old Cardinal, who weighed about 220 or 230 pounds. Pat dropped him dead. And laughed about it later. He had a great sense of humor.

Pat was like a bantam rooster. I remember he started a fight with Roy Jefferson in practice one time. Pat wasn't afraid of anyone or anything. He was a battler. He may have been small, but he played big. He played left corner, the difficult side. He could deal with tight ends. He could go deep or come in. He could play the pass or the run. He was very quick, really agile, and just loaded with desire.

Pat was a tough cookie. He was a real bump-and-run guy. I don't know if he could play today because he believed in contact. He'd bump 'em so hard they couldn't run. I don't care how big they were, he'd put the ax to them. They had to fight him for the ball. He was so tough he even put stickum on his mouth—not because he expected to catch the ball in his teeth or eat it, but because it was easier to get his hands on it from his mouth than from his pants or somewhere else. Even Lester Hayes didn't do that.

Pat had a heart as big as his body. He had an operation on the lumbar region of his back—this type of injury is sort of treacherous for an athlete—but he came back after that and continued to play as well as ever. He played in what I guess was pretty bad pain at times. You couldn't get him out of the lineup. He played 17 years, even longer than Willie Brown, which is really remarkable. Pat spent seven fine seasons with St. Louis, then 10 more with Washington. I was happy to have him, I'll tell you that. When you add up 17 years of tough, tenacious, skilled football you have one of the best ever.

11.
Bob Boyd

It seemed obvious that Bob Boyd simply was too small to play in the National Football League. At 5-10½ and 192 pounds, Boyd was something of a shrimp roaming defensive secondaries. Photographers delighted in posing him next to giants such as Big Daddy Lipscomb and Gino Marchetti, who worked up front on Baltimore's defensive platoon while Boyd patrolled the pass routes.

And yet, despite his size limitation, Boyd survived well enough to intercept 57 passes, sixth on the all-time list. He ran back those interceptions for 994 yards, a 17.4-yard average.

Bob Boyd

Boyd was something of a surprise to the Colts. A split-T quarterback at Oklahoma, he was drafted in the tenth round of the 1960 collegiate grab bag. He was moved into the defensive backfield in training camp and became an immediate starter for Baltimore.

Boyd was tested in his first year, as all rookies are, and he responded by intercepting seven passes, establishing himself as a quality defensive back. It wasn't easy, though, and Boyd confided later that the development of plays was often a confusing blur in his first year in the league. But he was determined to survive and began keeping his own book on passers and receivers, trying to determine their tendencies in particular situations.

That insight helped him overcome the limitations of his size to excel in the NFL for nine seasons, from 1960 to 1968. Chosen for four Pro Bowl games, Boyd was named to the All-Pro team for the decade of the 1960s and was selected for three straight All-Pro teams, from 1964 to 1966.

A tough, crafty runner and a hard tackler, Boyd emerged as one of the leaders of the Colts and was the club's defensive captain, assigned to call signals for all those big guys who played with him.

Bob Boyd was small, but he was a lot heavier than Pat Fischer. Boyd wasn't the fastest fellow, but he was quick enough. The Colts—Don Shula—used him very well. They used him in a lot of zone defenses and he was maybe the best zone defender I ever saw. He was never out of position and he covered his area perfectly. He reacted real well as a play developed and he made excellent adjustments as he went along.

He was a main man on those fine Baltimore teams of the 1960s and one of those who always seemed to make a big play in a big game when his side needed it most. I feel like I've used the term "big play in a big game" much too much, but I don't know how else to put it and it really is a quality all the great players share. If they didn't have it, they fell short of greatness. The true test of an athlete comes in the clutch, and the great ones came through.

Boyd was solid all the way through his career, very consistent, and a fine competitor. I had him in the Pro Bowl right after the Colts had lost to the Jets in that big Super Bowl upset. I had three of the Colts and they were all disappointed at what had happened in the Super Bowl and I'm sure really didn't want to play in a Pro Bowl game just then. They were down during the week in practice and weren't giving me a good performance.

I called them together and told them I was sorry they had lost the Super Bowl, but I didn't want to lose the Pro Bowl and told them if they didn't play any better in the game than they had in practice they were just going to add sorrow on sorrow. I asked them to perform with pride. And they did. I was pleased. I was especially pleased when Boyd came to me afterward and told me he appreciated the pep talk and thanked me for waking him up. From an All-Pro that was something. Bob Boyd was an all-time All-Pro.

12.
Jake Scott

Jake Scott wasn't in the very best of shape to play in Super Bowl VII in January 1973. The Miami Dolphins' safety had missed two weeks of practice because of a separated shoulder and was listed as doubtful for the championship game against the Washington Redskins.

The shoulder wasn't Scott's only problem. He had played most of the 1972 season with a painful neck injury. In addition, a week after the Super Bowl game, during a routine physical for the Pro Bowl, it would be discovered that Scott had two hairline wrist fractures, which explained the pain he felt there.

But the Dolphins were working on a perfect season, and little aches and pains weren't going to keep Scott out of the lineup. The 14–7 victory over Washington made it 17–0, the first perfect year in modern pro football. And the hero of the victory, the Most Valuable Player of Super Bowl VII, was the safety who wore No. 13, the guy who was so banged up, Jake Scott.

The 6-foot, 188-pound Scott intercepted two passes in the game, returning one of them 55 yards after the Redskins had driven to the Miami 10-yard line. It was appropriate for a member of the defensive unit to be selected as MVP because that group had been largely anonymous all season, called the "No-name Defense," and operating in the shadow of offensive stars such as Larry Csonka and Earl Morrall.

Scott spent six seasons with the Dolphins, from 1970 to 1975, and played in three Super Bowl games. He moved to Washington in 1976 and played with the Redskins for three years, finishing his NFL career in 1978. For nine NFL seasons he intercepted 49 passes, returning them for 551 yards.

Scott played his college football at the University of Georgia, leaving after his junior year to play for the British Columbia Lions of the Canadian Football League. He spent just one year in the CFL, 1969, and then took a $5,000 pay cut to sign with the Dolphins.

Jake Scott was another big-play, big-game guy who produced under pressure, a key man on one of the great teams of all time, the Miami Dolphins of the early 1970s.

Jake Scott played for the Dolphins for six seasons; then I brought him to Washington and he played for the Redskins for three years. I remember he arrived at midnight at training camp and reported right to me. He wanted me to give him something to work with right away. I gave him four defenses. The next day he ran all four in practice perfectly. I was amazed. He

Jake Scott

was extremely bright and determined. He did his homework. I never saw him make many mistakes.

Jake lacked speed, but he made up for it by playing smart. He read keys extremely well, anticipated developments, and always was in position to make the play he had to make. He had good balance and good strength. He used his strength to discourage receivers. He had good hands and held onto the ball when he outmuscled a receiver for it. He never got discouraged.

Jake was an outstanding competitor, extremely tenacious, extremely tough. He never seemed to get tired, or at least he could play tired. He was at his best in the last minutes of games when the other side was trying to pull out a game and he frustrated many a two-minute rally almost all by himself. When you needed him most, he was there—which is another good definition of an all-timer.

13.
Cliff Harris

Very few defensive backs hit harder than Cliff Harris, who played free safety and sometimes strong safety for 10 years with the Dallas Cowboys. And Harris' zest for hitting didn't end with opponents. He banged heads with teammates in practice, too. In fact, Harris' hits caused teammate Golden Richards, a wide receiver, to present him with a crash helmet equipped with a flashing red light and a battery-operated siren. It was designed to warn pass catchers when Harris arrived in their patterns.

Harris, a 6-1, 192-pounder, was an example of what a thorough scouting system can sometimes miss. He slipped through the NFL net, probably because he attended tiny Ouachita Baptist University in Arkadelphia, Arkansas, not regarded as a developer of outstanding football talent. He was playing minor-league football with the Southern California Rhinos in 1970 when the Cowboys heard about him and signed him to a free-agent contract.

He became a starter in his rookie season, but his pro career was interrupted when he was called into the armed service. He was back a year later and regained his first-string job with an impressive training camp. He remained a starter for the remainder of his career, teaming for a long time with strong safety Charley Waters to give Dallas the best deep-pass coverage in the league.

Ironically, it was Waters who replaced Harris when Cliff was called to military duty. When Harris returned, head coach Tom Landry decided to keep Waters on a regular job and the pair blossomed, complementing each other perfectly.

Harris' philosophy of defense was that if a receiver got hit hard enough, he'd be looking for the defender the next time down the field and might not concentrate quite as well on making the catch. It seemed to work.

For his career, Harris intercepted 29 passes and recovered 18 fumbles. He played in six Pro Bowl games and was a four-time All-Pro selection. An integral part of five Dallas Super Bowl teams, Harris left the Cowboys following the 1979 season—the same year Roger Staubach retired. Dallas had a replacement waiting to take Staubach's job. Replacing Harris, however, was more difficult.

Both Cliff Harris and Charley Waters were remarkable players who made pressure plays, and it was difficult to choose between them. I'd have taken them both if I'd had room.

I'd have taken Lem Barney, too, if I could. Boy, he was spectacular! Or Willie Wood. I feel bad because I left off Jim Johnson. And Dick Anderson.

211

Pat Thomas has been terrific. And Nolan Cromwell is starting to build an impressive career. If Mike Haynes had been around a little longer I'd have had to find a place for him because I really like him. Paul Krause is the all-time leader in interceptions, but as an all-around performer I couldn't fit him in.

You just don't have room for every player you've admired at every position on a list of the 100 best over 50 years. Cliff Harris is the last defensive back I picked. He was a key cog in a marvelous Dallas machine that won and won, but that wouldn't have won nearly as often without him. They didn't win over my teams very often, but I can't say we beat him very often. He was the kind of guy who made an interception or made a tackle and forced a fumble just when you thought you had a touchdown. You had to play like heck to play through him.

He played free safety and he really was a wide-ranging centerfielder. He played strong safety, too, and he was a hard hitter. You just couldn't discourage him. You couldn't keep him down. He was smart and skilled and extremely resourceful. You had to figure out ways to deal with him, and it wasn't easy. The great ones always made it hard on you.

Cliff Harris

CHAPTER 9

PUNTERS

If a punter boots the ball 60 yards and the receiver returns it 60 yards, the punter hasn't done a thing for his side. I'd rather have a punter who can consistently kick the ball 40 yards without a runback. That means the punter has to boot the ball high enough for his teammates to get downfield to cover the kick. Thus height is as important as distance. When his team has to kick the ball, a coach loves the fair catch. Even better, no catch on a good punt. But the coffin-corner kick has virtually died. Where has it gone? It is pretty much a lost art. But the punter who could put the ball out of bounds inside the other team's 10-yard line was very valuable, and those kicks often meant the difference between victory and defeat. Pinning the other side inside its 10 (where a fumble or an interception could mean a touchdown, and good defensive play would at the least give you good field position) is what wins games.

I have said I think coaches underestimate the value of the kicking game. That is true for punting as well as for place-kicking. I think field position decides more games than any other factor. That is why I favor defense over offense. Your defense gives you good field position and gives you a chance to use your offense effectively. Or it doesn't. Your punter is a key person in your defense. If your defense keeps you out of trouble, he can put the other team in trouble. If it doesn't, he can get you out of trouble.

If a punter can play another position for you, fine. Danny White of Dallas is a good quarterback and a fine punter, for example. He is one of the few punters around today who attempts and is successful at coffin-corner kicks. But the smart coach goes for the best punter he can get, whether or not he can play another position. Whether or not he also place-kicks.

Few can punt and place-kick equally well. I think Tommy Davis and Sam Baker could. But I'm not picking combination punters-place-kickers. Doing one or the other well enough is enough for me. Ray Guy of Oakland is a powerful punter and a powerful place-kicker, but the Raiders have been smart enough to use him strictly as a punter because they had more consistent place-kickers.

I am a great believer in special teams. I think I pioneered the special coaching of special teams. Special teams operate on place-kicks —kickoffs and field-goal and extra-point attempts —and on punts, on both offense and defense. The one is trying to execute the kick successfully, the other attempting to make it unsuccessful. Blocked punts, field goals, extra points, and long returns of punts and kickoffs often turn games around. You have to execute these things effectively and provide protection properly for your people to perform successfully.

You have to put good people in key positions and practice to points of perfection. I haven't picked anyone from suicide squads for my greatest 100 list because you don't dare send your top players on these murderous missions. But if you don't think Deacon Jones or Dick Butkus wouldn't have been the best on these squads, you're mistaken.

Like the place-kickers I picked among my 100 greatest pro football players, two of the three punters I picked played other positions well. In fact, two of the punters were among the all-time best at other positions, one the very best. So, while they are only counted once among the 100, they are the only ones whose names appear twice. But they were picked as punters here. Now for the best ones.

1.
Sammy Baugh

As both my all-time No. 1 quarterback and all-time No. 1 punter, Sammy Baugh occupies a unique position among all players on my list of 100. If you wish to conclude that this makes him the No. 1 player on the entire list, I won't argue with you. He also was an outstanding defensive back, remember, good enough to have made my list of the best defensive backs if I had been listing players other than the specialists at more than one position. But Sammy Baugh was the best punter we've had, period. He'd be here if he wasn't elsewhere.

Sammy Baugh

Baugh booted the ball long and high. There may have been punters who kicked the ball higher, but none who kicked the ball longer. Look at the record book. Forty years later Sammy is still the all-time leader in punting average for a game, a season, a career. And he had to kick more in those days than most do today. The game was more defensive, with fewer long marches and less scoring. No one ever led the league as many seasons in average distance per punt. Yet Baugh booted the ball out of bounds inside the 10 consistently. A runback of a Baugh boot was rare, a good runback even rarer. Baugh got off his punts fast and seldom had one blocked. He was the perfect punter. And close to the perfect player.

2.
Yale Lary

Yale Lary was almost as good a punter as Sammy Baugh was. And Lary was one of our greatest defensive backs ever. This would have earned him extra consideration for my list of best punters, but he didn't need it. Baugh booted the ball farther, but Lary kicked it higher. Ray Guy is supposed to punt the ball higher than any kicker ever, but I'm not at all sure he kicked it higher than Lary.

I read once that during one season, six straight opposing teams failed to return 32 straight punts a single yard off Lary's booming boots. The punts allowed plenty of time for complete coverage and usually had to be fair-caught. I can believe it because I saw it time and time again—his soaring punts spiraling far downfield, the returner waiting helplessly as tacklers closed in on him.

Yale Lary

Yet, for all his height, Lary averaged close to 45 yards a kick in his career, Baugh only a little more. But Baugh was much more expert at the old and valuable coffin-corner kick. Only Baugh led the league more often in average distances per kick.

Lary loved to punt. You could see it in his actions after a good one. He'd skip downfield, prepared to join in a coverage that seldom was needed. Baugh and Lary were players, unafraid to make a tackle, able to make a tackle, unlike so many modern punters. Lary seldom made a mistake, seldom made a bad punt, seldom left his side in a hole. Lary got off his punts fast and they seldom were blocked.

Like Baugh, Lary was at his best in big games. In one championship contest against Cleveland, Lary took a low snap on two hops, evaded tacklers, and got off a punt on the run that covered 74 yards.

There have been other great punters who did more than punt, notably Norm Van Brocklin, one of the great quarterbacks and passers. Also Glenn Dobbs, one of the outstanding all-around athletes of all time in pro football but who played pro football for four years only. But Yale Lary was simply exceptional.

3.
Ray Guy

When the Oakland Raiders chose Ray Guy in the 1973 college draft, it marked the first time a pro team selected a punter on the first round of the draft. Opening-round picks usually are reserved for players in more glamorous positions on either offense or defense, not special-team guys whose only job is to turn the football over to the other team. But Ray was a very special Guy.

An All-American at Southern Mississippi, Guy was the nation's leading college punter in 1972, when he averaged 46.2 yards per kick, including a 93-yarder against Mississippi. His three-season average was 44.7 for 200 punts and he also had kicked a 61-yard field goal against Utah State. Those kicking accomplishments as well as 18 interceptions in three seasons at safety were good enough credentials for the Raiders to invest a No. 1 draft pick on him. They've never regretted the decision.

Guy quickly established himself as one of football's best-ever kickers. He was chosen for the Pro Bowl seven times in his first nine seasons and was named to the All-Pro team for the decade of the 1970s. His career average in nine years as a pro is 43.2 yards per kick for 654 punts.

Because of the specialized nature of their work, punters often must seek different challenges. Guy achieved a kicker's dream when he sent one of his boots into the television screen that hangs over the field inside the

Ray Guy

Louisiana Superdome during the 1977 Pro Bowl game. It was no accident. He was aiming.

Guy was a major factor during the 1980 season in Oakland's march to the Super Bowl in January 1981. In the AFC championship game that season against San Diego, he averaged 56 yards per punt, keeping the Chargers backed up every time Oakland was forced to turn over the ball. That was exactly what the Raiders had in mind when they spent that first-round draft selection on the punter seven years earlier.

Looking for one pure punter on my list, I picked Ray Guy, who supposedly boots the ball higher than any other kicker ever. As I said, I'm not sure Yale Lary didn't kick it higher, but Guy sure does boot it high. Others have kicked it farther, but Guy gets his kicks off under pressure and they seldom are returned. The 1981 season was his ninth in the league and he's been consistently outstanding.

Punters

Tommy Davis was an even greater punter than he was a place-kicker, I think. So was Don Chandler. Frankly, I doubt that anyone boomed the ball higher than Horace Gillom of the Browns in the 1940s and 1950s. Bobby Joe Green was a great one. I had him in Chicago and he saved many a game for us. And he lasted 14 years. One of the great ones of recent years was Jerrell Wilson. And he lasted 15 years and led his league in punting as many times as Yale Lary did. Still active, Dave Jennings of the Giants completed 10 years of super punting in 1981.

But Ray Guy seems to me to have set himself a little apart from the rest. The only punter ever picked in the first round of the college draft, he proved himself as worthy of that singular distinction with pressure punting of the highest order in the Raiders' many big games in the playoffs and Super Bowls. He is cool, quick, and consistently outstanding at his critically important specialty. He has kicked off powerfully and while his team seldom has used him for field goals, he has established himself as a great all-around kicker, a player worthy of completing my list of the 100 greatest professional football players.

AFTERWORD

Yes, picking the 100 greatest pro football players of the past 50 years turned out to be enjoyable. But it was painful at times, too. I hated to leave off my list many really fine players, and I tore up more than a few pieces of paper before making my final selections. In the end, though, I was satisfied that I gave this project all that I had.

Studying my final list, I find that I have 55 players on my offensive unit and 41 on my defensive unit. There also are three place-kickers and three punters. Two among the latter were not counted toward the total of 100 because they already had been chosen for other units.

I think it was inevitable that there would be more offensive players than defensive players because, for many years, most coaches have put their most skilled athletes on offense. I didn't, but others did. I believe defense wins games for you a little more than offense does. Defense gets the ball for you and, hopefully, gives it to you in good field position, where your offense can operate effectively.

I did not try to balance my selections by position, but I find that there is not a great deal of difference in the numbers at different positions. I picked more running backs than I did players for any other position, and I think that was inevitable too, because the greatest all-around athletes have played there, or at tailback, as it used to be known, especially in the early years. Most tailbacks were more runners than passers.

A number of my offensive players from the days of two-way football could have been placed on defense, or vice versa, in my selections, but I put them where I thought they belonged.

I see that a lot of players came from a few teams. I think this, too, is inevitable. Great players make great teams.

There are more players from the Chicago Bears than any other single team, but the Bears dominated professional football for many years.

I think it is hard to argue against Bronko Nagurski, Bill Hewitt, Sid Luckman, Bulldog Turner, Danny Fortmann, Joe Stydahar, George Connor, Joe Fortunato, Mike Ditka, Gale Sayers, Walter Payton, Doug Atkins, and Dick Butkus being listed among the 100 greatest pro football players.

I also picked quite a few players from other outstanding teams, such as Green Bay in the 1930s and, under Vince Lombardi, in the 1960s, and the Pittsburgh Steelers and Dallas Cowboys of the 1970s.

I could have chosen Tony Dorsett from the Cowboys, but I didn't think he had played long enough to qualify. The same goes for another running back, Earl Campbell. Earl had his poorest of four seasons in 1981. He was still a standout, but there's no way of telling how long he will last in the league.

Afterword

I was fortunate to have coached some of the players I picked for the list. I tried very hard not to be prejudiced. I'd have liked to have given recognition to a number of other players who gave me a lot out on the field. But if they didn't belong, in my opinion, they didn't make the list.

I'd like this book to be more of a celebration of the outstanding players I chose to honor rather than a target for criticism because of those who were omitted.

There have been so many great players over the past 50 years of professional football. I hope you enjoyed reading about the 100 I selected and have fun debating the choices.

George Allen
Palos Verdes, California
September 1982

GEORGE ALLEN'S ALL-TIME TEAM

OFFENSE

WR — Don Hutson
WR — Lenny Moore
TE — Pete Pihos
T — Jim Parker
T — Forrest Gregg
G — Danny Fortmann
G — Ron Mix
C — Mel Hein
QB — Sammy Baugh
HB — Jim Brown
HB — O. J. Simpson
FB — Bronko Nagurski
PK — George Blanda

DEFENSE

E — Deacon Jones
E — Gino Marchetti
T — Bob Lilly
T — Leo Nomellini
MG — Bill Willis
LB — Chuck Bednarik
LB — Bill George
LB — Dick Butkus
CB — Herb Adderley
CB — Dick (Night Train) Lane
S — Jack Christiansen
S — Emlen Tunnell
P — Sammy Baugh

GEORGE ALLEN'S COACHING RECORD

Assistant coach, Ann Arbor, Michigan, High School, 1947
Head coach, Morningside College, 1948–50
Head coach, Whittier College, 1951–56
Assistant coach, Los Angeles, NFL, 1957
Assistant coach, Chicago Bears, NFL, 1958–65

Year	Club	Position	W	L	T
Head Coach—NFL					
1966	Los Angeles	Third*	8	6	0
1967	Los Angeles	First†	11	1	2
1968	Los Angeles	Second†	10	3	1
1969	Los Angeles	First*	11	3	0
1970	Los Angeles	Second‡	9	4	1
1971	Washington	Second§	9	4	1
1972	Washington	First§	11	3	0
1973	Washington	First^ǁ	10	4	0
1974	Washington	First^ǁ	10	4	0
1975	Washington	Third§	8	6	0
1976	Washington	Second^ǁ	10	4	0
1977	Washington	Second§	9	5	0
		Pro head-coaching totals	116	47	5
		Post-regular season totals	4	7	0
		Overall totals	120	54	5

*Western Conference
†Coastal Division (Western Conference)
‡Western Division (National Conference)
§Eastern Division (National Conference)
 Eastern Division (National Conference), tied for position

layoff Results

ost conference championship game to Green Bay, 28—7)

von Playoff Bowl from Cleveland, 30—6)

st conference championship game to Minnesota, 23—20)

von Playoff Bowl from Dallas, 31—0)

st conference playoff game to San Francisco, 24—20)

von conference playoff game from Green Bay, 16—3)

von conference championship game from Dallas, 26—3)

st Super Bowl game to Miami, 14—7)

ost conference playoff game to Minnesota, 27—20)

ost conference playoff game to Los Angeles, 19—10)

st conference playoff game to Minnesota, 35—20)

PLAYER STATISTICS

QUARTERBACKS

Player	Ht.	Wt.	Team(s)	Years Played
SAMMY BAUGH	6-2	180	Washington	1937–52
SID LUCKMAN	6-0	195	Chicago	1939–50
JOHNNY UNITAS	6-1	195	Baltimore	1956–72
			San Diego	1973
TERRY BRADSHAW	6-3	215	Pittsburgh	1970–81
BART STARR	6-1	200	Green Bay	1956–71
OTTO GRAHAM	6-1	195	Cleveland (AAC)	1946–49
			Cleveland (NFL)	1950–55
ROGER STAUBACH	6-3	202	Dallas	1969–79
BOBBY LAYNE	6-2	190	Chicago	1948
			N.Y. Bulldogs	1949
			Detroit	1950–58
			Pittsburgh	1958–62
NORM VAN BROCKLIN	6-1	190	Los Angeles	1949–57
			Philadelphia	1958–60
BOB WATERFIELD	6-2	200	Cleveland Rams and Los Angeles Rams	1945–52
ARNIE HERBER	6-1	190	Green Bay	1930–40*
			N.Y. Giants	1944–45
FRAN TARKENTON	6-0	190	Minnesota	1961–66 and 1972–
			N.Y. Giants	1967–71
KEN STABLER	6-3	210	Oakland	1970–79
			Houston	1980–81
JOE NAMATH	6-2	200	N.Y. Jets	1965–76
			Los Angeles	1977

*No statistics kept for 1930–31.

ears eague	Pass Attempts	Completions	Completion Pct.	Total Yards	TDs	Int.
5	2,995	1,693	56.5	21,886	186	203
2	1,744	904	51.8	14,686	139	130
3	5,186	2,830	54.6	40,239	290	253
2	3,653	1,893	51.8	26,144	193	199
5	3,149	1,808	57.4	24,718	152	138
4	1,061	592	56.0	10,085	86	41
5	1,565	872	55.7	13,499	88	94
1	2,958	1,685	57.0	22,700	153	109
5	3,700	1,814	49.0	26,768	196	243
2	2,895	1,553	53.6	23,611	173	178
8	1,618	813	50.3	11,849	98	127
3	1,175	481	40.9	8,041	78	98
3	6,467	3,686	57.0	47,003	342	266
2	3,223	1,944	60.0	24,268	177	189
3	3,762	1,886	50.1	27,663	173	220

RECEIVERS

Player	Ht.	Wt.	Team(s)
DON HUTSON	6-1	180	Green Bay
LENNY MOORE	6-1	198	Baltimore
ELROY HIRSCH	6-2	190	Chicago Rockets (A Los Angeles
CHARLEY TAYLOR	6-3	210	Washington
RAYMOND BERRY	6-2	187	Baltimore
TOM FEARS	6-2	215	Los Angeles
PAUL WARFIELD	6-0	188	Cleveland Miami
LANCE ALWORTH	6-0	184	San Diego Dallas
DON MAYNARD	6-1	185	N.Y. Giants N.Y. Jets St. Louis
BILL HEWITT	5-11	191	Chicago Philadelphia Philadelphia-Pitt.
Tight End			
PETE PIHOS	6-1	210	Philadelphia
MIKE DITKA	6-3	225	Chicago Philadelphia Dallas
JOHN MACKEY	6-2	224	Baltimore San Diego

*Played for Memphis (WFL) in 1975.
†Played for British Columbia (CFL) in 1959.

Years Played	Years in League	Receptions	Yards	Average in Yards	TDs
1935–45	11	488	7,991	16.4	99
1956–67	12	363	6,039	16.6	48
1946–48	3	44	730	16.8	7
1949–57	9	343	6,289	18.3	53
1964–75 and 1977	13	649	9,110	14.0	79
1955–67	13	631	9,275	14.7	68
1948–56	9	400	5,397	13.4	38
1964–69 and 1976–77 1970–74*	13	427	8,565	20.1	82
1962–70 1971–72	11	542	10,266	18.9	85
1958† 1960–72 1973	15	633	11,834	18.7	88
1932–36 1937–39 1943	9	101	1,606	15.9	31
1947–55	9	373	5,619	15.1	61
1961–66 1967–68 1969–72	12	427	5,812	13.6	46
1963–71 1972	10	331	5,238	15.8	39

RUNNING BACKS

Player	Ht.	Wt.	Team(s)
JIM BROWN	6-2	232	Cleveland
O. J. SIMPSON	6-2	212	Buffalo San Francisco
GALE SAYERS	6-0	200	Chicago
BRONKO NAGURSKI	6-2	225	Chicago
JOE PERRY	6-0	200	San Francisco (AAC) San Francisco (NFL) Baltimore
JIM TAYLOR	6-0	216	Green Bay New Orleans
WALTER PAYTON	5-10	202	Chicago
STEVE VAN BUREN	6-1	200	Philadelphia
CLARKE HINKLE	5-11	201	Green Bay
HUGH McELHENNY	6-1	198	San Francisco Minnesota N.Y. Giants Detroit
FRANCO HARRIS	6-2	225	Pittsburgh
MARION MOTLEY	6-1	238	Cleveland (AAC) Cleveland (NFL) Pittsburgh
EARL (DUTCH) CLARK	6-0	185	Portsmouth Detroit
FRANK GIFFORD	6-1	195	N.Y. Giants
BILL DUDLEY	5-10	176	Pittsburgh Detroit Washington
PAUL HORNUNG	6-2	220	Green Bay

*No statistics kept for 1930-31.   †No statistics kept for 1931.

Years Played	Years in League	At-tempts	Yards	Average in Yards	TDs
1957–65	9	2,359	12,312	5.2	106
1969–77 1978–79	11	2,404	11,236	4.7	61
1965–71	7	991	4,956	5.0	39
1930–37* and 1943	9	633	2,778	4.4	18
1948–49	2	192	1,345	7.0	18
1950–60 and 1963 1961–62	14	1,737	8,378	4.8	53
1958–66 1967	10	1,941	8,597	4.4	83
1975–81	7	2,204	9,608	4.4	71
1944–51	8	1,320	5,860	4.4	69
1932–41	10	1,171	3,860	3.3	32
1952–60 1961–62 1963 1964	13	1,124	5,281	4.7	38
1972–81	10	2,462	10,339	4.2	84
1946–49	4	489	3,024	6.2	26
1950–53 1955	5	339	1,696	5.0	5
1931–32† 1934–38	7	606	2,772	4.6	27
1952–60 and 1962–64	12	840	3,609	4.3	34
1942 and 1945–46 1947–49 1950–51 and 1953	9	765	3,057	4.0	15
1957–62 and 1964–66	9	893	3,711	4.2	50

PLACE-KICKERS

Player	Ht.	Wt.	Team(s)
GEORGE BLANDA	6-2	215	Chicago Houston Oakland
LOU GROZA	6-3	250	Cleveland (AAC) Cleveland (NFL)
JAN STENERUD	6-2	190	Kansas City Green Bay

PUNTERS

Player	Ht.	Wt.	Team(s)
SAMMY BAUGH	6-2	180	Washington
YALE LARY	5-11	189	Detroit
RAY GUY	6-3	200	Oakland

*Punted from 1939—52 (14 years).

Years Played	Years in League	XP	XPA	FG	FGA	Total Points
949–58						
960–66						
967–75	26	943	959	335	638	1,948
946–49	4	169	176	30	76	259
950–59						
nd 1961–67	17	641	657	234	405	1,343
967–79						
980–81	15	432	448	304	465	1,344

ars yed	Years in League	No. of Punts	Yards	Average in Yards	Longest Punt in Yards
7–52	16*	338	15,245	45.1	85
2–53					
1956–64	11	503	22,279	44.3	74
3–81	9	654	28,262	43.2	74

OFFENSIVE LINEMEN

Player	Ht.	Wt.	Team(s)	Years Played	Years in League
JIM PARKER	6-3	273	Baltimore	1957–67	11
FORREST GREGG	6-4	250	Green Bay	1956 and 1958–70	
			Dallas	1971	15
MEL HEIN	6-2	225	N.Y. Giants	1931–45	15
CLYDE (BULLDOG) TURNER	6-2	235	Chicago	1940–52	13
DANNY FORTMANN	6-0	207	Chicago	1936–43	8
JIM TYRER	6-6	275	Dallas Texans	1961–62	
			Kansas City	1963–73	
			Washington	1974	14
RON MIX	6-4	250	Los Angeles and San Diego Chargers	1960–69	
			Oakland	1971	11
ROOSEVELT BROWN	6-3	255	N.Y. Giants	1953–65	13
JIM RINGO	6-1	235	Green Bay	1953–63	
			Philadelphia	1964–67	15
JIM OTTO	6-2	255	Oakland	1960–74	15
GENE UPSHAW	6-5	255	Oakland	1967–81	15
RON YARY	6-6	255	Minnesota	1968–81	14

FENSIVE
NEMEN

er	Ht.	Wt.	Team(s)	Years Played	Years in League
ID (DEACON) ES	6-5	250	Los Angeles	1961–71	
			San Diego	1972–73	
			Washington	1974	14
MARCHETTI	6-4	245	Dallas Texans	1952	
			Baltimore	1953–64 and 1966	14
LILLY	6-5	260	Dallas	1961–74	14
JG ATKINS	6-8	275	Cleveland	1953–54	
			Chicago	1955–66	
			New Orleans	1966–69	17
WILLIS	6-2	215	Cleveland (AAC)	1946–49	4
			Cleveland (NFL)	1950–53	4
NOMELLINI	6-3	264	San Francisco	1950–63	14
FORD	6-5	260	L.A. Dons (AAC)	1948–49	
			Cleveland	1950–57	
			Green Bay	1958	11
STYDAHAR	6-4	230	Chicago	1936–42 and 1945–46	9
VISTERT	6-1½	219	Philadelphia-Pitt	1943	
			Philadelphia	1944–51	9
IE DAVIS	6-3	245	Cleveland	1958–59	
			Green Bay	1960–69	12
Y ROBUSTELLI	6-0	230	Los Angeles	1951–55	
			N.Y. Giants	1956–64	14
LIN OLSEN	6-5	270	Los Angeles	1962–76	15
N PAGE	6-4	225	Minnesota	1967–78	
			Chicago	1978–81*	15
GREENE	6-4	260	Pittsburgh	1969–81	13
DY WHITE	6-4	250	Dallas	1975–81	7

978 played six games with Minnesota and 10 games with Chicago.

DEFENSIVE BACKS

Player	Ht.	Wt.	Team(s)
HERB ADDERLEY	6-1	200	Green Bay Dallas
DICK (NIGHT TRAIN) LANE	6-2	210	Los Angeles Chicago Cardinals Detroit
JACK CHRISTIANSEN	6-1	185	Detroit
EMLEN TUNNELL	6-1	200	N.Y. Giants Green Bay
YALE LARY	5-11	189	Detroit
LARRY WILSON	6-0	190	St. Louis
KEN HOUSTON	6-3	198	Houston Washington
WILLIE BROWN	6-1	190	Denver Oakland
ED MEADOR	5-11	190	Los Angeles
PAT FISCHER	5-9	170	St. Louis Washington
BOB BOYD	5-10½	192	Baltimore
JAKE SCOTT	6-0	188	Miami Washington
CLIFF HARRIS	6-1	192	Dallas

*Played for British Columbia (CFC) in 1969.

Years Played	Years in League	Int.	Yards	Average in Yards	TDs
1961–69 1970–72	12	48	1,046	21.8	7
1952–53 1954–59 1960–65	14	68	1,207	17.8	5
1951–58	8	46	717	15.6	3
1948–58 1959–61	14	79	1,282	16.2	4
1952–53 and 1956–64	11	50	787	15.7	2
1960–72	13	52	800	15.4	5
1967–72 1973–80	14	49	898	18.3	9
1963–66 1967–78	16	54	472	8.7	2
1959–70	12	46	547	11.9	5
1961–67 1968–77	17	56	941	16.8	4
1960–68	9	57	994	17.4	4
1970–75* 1976–78	9	49	551	11.2	0
1970–79	10	29	281	9.7	1

LINEBACKERS

Player	Ht.	Wt.	Team(s)	Years Played	Years in League
CHUCK BEDNARIK	6-3	230	Philadelphia	1949–62	14
BILL GEORGE	6-2	230	Chicago Los Angeles	1952–65 1966	15
DICK BUTKUS	6-3	245	Chicago	1965–73	9
GEORGE CONNOR	6-3	240	Chicago	1948–55	8
JOE SCHMIDT	6-0	222	Detroit	1953–65	13
SAM HUFF	6-1	230	N.Y. Giants Washington	1956–63 1964–67 and 1969	13
RAY NITSCHKE	6-3	235	Green Bay	1958–72	15
TED HENDRICKS	6-7	225	Baltimore Green Bay Oakland	1969–73 1974 1975–81	13
JOE FORTUNATO	6-1	225	Chicago	1955–66	12
CHRIS HANBURGER	6-2	218	Washington	1965–78	14
JACK HAM	6-1	225	Pittsburgh	1971–81	11
JACK LAMBERT	6-4	220	Pittsburgh	1974–81	8
MAXIE BAUGHAN	6-1	230	Philadelphia Los Angeles Washington	1960–65 1966–70 1974	11 1